Tourism and Indigenous Heritage in Latin America

Following the surge of regional multiculturalism and indigenous political mobilization, how are indigenous Latin Americans governed today? Addressing the Mexican flagship tourist initiative of 'Magical Villages,' this book shows how government tourism programs do more than craft appealing tourist experiences from ideas of indigeneity, tradition, and heritage. Rather, heritage-centered tourism and multiculturalism are fusing into a strategy of government set to tame and steer indigenous spaces of negotiation by offering alternative multicultural national self-images, which trigger new modes of national belonging and participation, without challenging structural political and social asymmetries.

By examining contemporary Mexican tourism policies and multiculturalist ideals through policy analysis and ethnographic research in a mestizo municipal capital in a majority indigenous Nahua municipality, this book shows how mestizo nationalism is regenerated in tourism as part of a neoliberal governmentality framework. The book demonstrates how tourism initiatives that center on indigenous cultural heritage and recognition do not self-evidently empower indigenous citizens, and may pave the way for extracting indigenous heritage as a national resource to the benefit of local elites and tourist visitors.

This work is of key interest to researchers, advanced students, and critically engaged practitioners in the fields of Latin American studies, indigenous studies, social anthropology, critical heritage studies, and tourism.

Casper Jacobsen holds a PhD in American Indian Languages and Cultures, and is a postdoctoral fellow at the University of Copenhagen and the State University of New York at Albany, USA. His research focuses on the history and heritage of indigenous peoples in pre-Hispanic, colonial, and contemporary Latin America.

Routledge Advances in Tourism and Anthropology

Series editors:
Dr Catherine Palmer (University of Brighton, UK) C.A.Palmer@brighton.ac.uk
Dr Jo-Anne Lester (University of Brighton, UK) J.Lester@brighton.ac.uk

To discuss any ideas for the series, please contact Faye Leerink, Commissioning Editor (faye.leerink@tandf.co.uk) or the series editors.

This series draws inspiration from anthropology's overarching aim to explore and better understand the human condition in all its fascinating diversity. It seeks to expand the intellectual landscape of anthropology and tourism in relation to how we understand the experience of being human, providing critical inquiry into the spaces, places, and lives in which tourism unfolds. Contributions to the series will consider how such spaces are embodied, imagined, constructed, experienced, memorialized, and contested. The series provides a forum for cutting-edge research and innovative thinking from tourism, anthropology, and related disciplines such as philosophy, history, sociology, geography, cultural studies, architecture, the arts, and feminist studies.

The Affective Negotiation of Slum Tourism
City Walks in Delhi
Tore Holst

Tourism and Ethnodevelopment
Inclusion, Empowerment and Self-Determination
Edited by Ismar Borges de Lima and Victor King

Everyday Practices of Tourism Mobilities
Packing a Bag
Kaya Barry

Tourism and Indigenous Heritage in Latin America
As Observed through Mexico's Magical Village Cuetzalan
Casper Jacobsen

For more information about this series, please visit www.routledge.com/Routledge-Advances-in-Tourism-and-Anthropology/book-series/RATA

Tourism and Indigenous Heritage in Latin America

As Observed through Mexico's Magical Village Cuetzalan

Casper Jacobsen

Routledge
Taylor & Francis Group

LONDON AND NEW YORK

First published 2019
by Routledge
2 Park Square, Milton Park, Abingdon, Oxon OX14 4RN

and by Routledge
52 Vanderbilt Avenue, New York, NY 10017

First issued in paperback 2020

Routledge is an imprint of the Taylor & Francis Group, an informa business

British Library Cataloguing-in-Publication Data
A catalogue record for this book is available from the British Library

Library of Congress Cataloging-in-Publication Data
A catalog record has been requested for this book

ISBN 13: 978-0-367-58735-2 (pbk)
ISBN 13: 978-1-138-08825-2 (hbk)

Typeset in Times New Roman
by Swales & Willis Ltd, Exeter, Devon, UK

Contents

Figures

Acknowledgments

A fellowship from the Faculty of Humanities at the University of Copenhagen funded the research behind this book. Thank you for that life-defining opportunity, which opened the door to unforgettable experiences and all the wonderful people I met through the research.

I am also grateful to the editorial team at Routledge, particularly Faye Leerink and Ruth Anderson, whose advice and effort have made the task of writing the book a pleasant experience.

In Mexico City, Antonio Machuca and Federico Zúñiga generously discussed my early research ideas, handing over advice and books that have been helpful to me. So did Gabriela Coronado, whose inspiring work and familiarity with Cuetzalan were crucial in preparing for my first trip to Cuetzalan.

In and around Cuetzalan, I was welcomed by many kindhearted people. I soon saw the hardship that permeates the lives of most people there, and against that backdrop my gratitude is only deepened for the care and hospitality my family and I experienced. To all of you, and in the warmest way: thank you! Esperanza, I wish your story would have played as big a part in this book as it did in shaping my experience of the town. We will never forget you and your family. Thank you for taking Julius to heart and for the overwhelming generosity and help you showed us. Lucinda, thank you for your friendship, for sending me illustrated reports from the field, and for your permission to include them here.

A very special thank you goes to Anna Källén for reading and commenting on my work at a critical stage and helping to piece it all together. An equally special thank you goes to Birgitta Svensson for engaging so enthusiastically with my research ideas throughout the whole process. I have learned a lot from our discussions and your theoretical overview, and I will always be indebted to you for your invaluable guidance. Thank you also to Catharina Raudvere, John Gledhill, and Patricia Lorenzoni for providing constructive comments on the manuscript. Una Canger and Jesper Nielsen, thank you for your support before, during, and after my research in Cuetzalan and for all that you have done for me.

I also want to extend my sincere appreciation to the editor of the travel magazine *Enlázate*, Jorge Cortés Sandoval, for kindly granting me the permission to reprint excerpts from a beautiful special edition on Cuetzalan. I am equally grateful to the SBC Noticias Zacapoaxtla for letting me print part of an interview transmitted on their TV network.

These acknowledgments would not be complete without thanking my parents, Kaj and Lisbeth, in general and specifically for taking such good care of Julius whenever I needed extra time for writing. It was very comforting to know that Julius was having the time of his life during my absences. Thank you also to my parents-in-law, Annie and Jack, for letting me use their weekend cottage as my personal writing retreat. Thank you to my sister, Gitte, and an anonymous editor for help with proofreading of the text.

Finally, I want to express my deepest gratitude to my son Julius and my 'ghost-writer' Louise for your care and company, for filling my life with purpose, and for taking my mind off the book (and the fatigued laptop on which it was written) whenever it was needed.

Prologue

Cuetzalan is a hillside town and municipal capital in the state of Puebla, approximately 300 kilometers northeast of Mexico City in the mountainous *Sierra de Puebla*. Due to its proximity to the Gulf of Mexico, the climate is humid, rainy, and, above all, extremely changeable. Throughout history, these climatic and geographic characteristics have complicated travel to Cuetzalan and, compared to other more passable regions, religious conversion of indigenous groups proceeded more slowly, just as settlers arrived late to the area (Haly 2000:163). When, in 1785, the first settlers established themselves in Xocoyolo, 8 kilometers to the south of Cuetzalan, the area was inhabited by Nahuas and a minority of Totonacs. Population growth and famine in and around Puebla City led to increasing migration into the Sierra, where land could be rented from indigenous towns. The first wave of settlers consisted of penniless peasants looking for land to cultivate, and they came to produce maize for Cuetzalan, where more specialized goods were being produced (Thomson 1991:212). In the first part of the nineteenth century, mestizos began to settle in Cuetzalan and neighboring San Andrés Tzicuilan, which held the most fertile soil. This influx accelerated after Cuetzalan had been established as a municipal capital in 1837. From 1850 to 1880, the central part of town passed from hosting a minority of 30 mestizo families to a majority of 177 families consisting of 871 individuals (Valderrama Rouy and Ramírez 1993:194), comprising a little more than a fifth of the town residents (Thomson 1991:218). This second wave of settlers was interested in land for livestock farming and for cultivating subtropical crops, particularly coffee. The coffee bean appears to have been introduced by settlers in the 1860s and came to be cultivated on a large scale in the region, sometimes implemented by force by local businessmen, displacing the cultivation of other crops.

The Reform War (1857–1861) and the War of the French Intervention (1861–1867) caused increasing numbers of wealthy mestizo families to flee from the district capital Zacapoaxtla, 35 kilometers to the south, and seek refuge in Cuetzalan (Thomson 1991:214–215). Coinciding with internal migration related to the political turmoil of two wars, the government in Puebla passed the *Ley Lerdo* national act in 1867, which exacted the privatization of communal land, thus undermining collective landownership as it was practiced by indigenous towns of the area and facilitating appropriation of it by incoming settlers (Thomson 1991:207 ff.). Subsequently, during the dictatorship of President Porfirio Díaz (1876–1911), the Mexican government employed an aggressive nation-building strategy that sought to attract European migrants and money to the countryside by offering favorable tax subsidies and promising to supply the needed infrastructure. Attracting European settlers was thought of as a way of importing social progress, boosting industrialization, and elevating Mexico to a higher civilizational stage through cultural "whitening," and with modified immigration laws that allowed migrants to own land and subsoil resources, agents in Europe were promoting Mexico as a country with vast and vacant land, but insufficient workforce (Buchenau 2001:31–36). Consequently, thousands of Italian settlers, among others, arrived during the 1880s to the neighboring state of Veracruz, some of whom moved further inland to Cuetzalan and entered the liquor, sugar, and incipient coffee trade. In the ensuing decades, the Nahuas of Cuetzalan were displaced and dispossessed of their lands, and with the arrest in 1894 of the prominent Nahua military leader Francisco Agustín, who organized local Nahua defense of their territory against land-grabbing migrants, political leadership effectively passed to the settler families (Thomson 1991).

Today, Cuetzalan is predominantly a mestizo town and capital of a municipality that covers an area of 135 square kilometers and holds a population of 47,433, of which the majority is Nahua (INEGI 2011:134–135).[1] The municipality is subdivided into dependent administrative units called auxiliary councils, each of which has a main administrative seat and political representatives. Half of the population live in hamlets of fewer than 500 inhabitants, and an additional third live in villages of between 500 and 1,300 inhabitants. The only exceptions are Cuetzalan, 5,957 inhabitants, and nearby San Miguel Tzinacapan, 2,939 inhabitants. Yet since Cuetzalan is the regional commercial hub and administrative center of the municipality, the inhabitants of the surrounding area frequently go there, particularly on Sundays, which is the prime market day.

Before the construction in the 1950s of an unpaved highway from Zacapoaxtla to Cuetzalan, vehicular travel to Cuetzalan was sparse, with most transport done by horse or mule. Nonetheless, when the highway was paved in 1962, travel to Cuetzalan began to increase (Greathouse-Amador 2000:89); today, travelers get there by bus in six hours from Mexico City, and in four from Puebla City – and often leave again within 36 hours. When asked about the origin of tourism, some locals point to the 1970s and policies of the teachers' union, which sent newly educated teachers from large cities to rural areas. Teachers from all over the country thus began to arrive and told their relatives and friends back home of tiny, idyllic Cuetzalan. Most people, however, point to the soap opera *El Padre Gallo*, which was recorded in town and aired nationwide in 1986. As the story goes, people from all over Mexico started to enquire about this charming little town that had preserved so much of its "culture" with its colonial-style buildings, terracotta tile roofing, cobblestone streets, and a vivid indigenous market. This version also figures on a billboard in the small ethnographic museum, establishing Cuetzalan's fame "in the movies and TV."

Nonetheless, a new account on the origin of tourism is making its way into town memory. Now, tourism is increasingly being attributed to Cuetzalan's participation in the national tourism program Magical Villages, which was launched by the federal government in 2001, and in which the town has participated since March 2002. Judging from the number of official lodgings in town, which increased from four in 1988 to 22 in 2000 (Greathouse-Amador 2000:158–160), tourism and its related infrastructure appear to have been well developed before Cuetzalan entered the Magical Villages Program. Indeed, Cuetzalan and other early participant towns were invited to join the program by their respective state governments on behalf of Mexico's Secretariat of Tourism (SECTUR) precisely because they were already important tourist destinations.[2] Yet nowadays, much effort is put into ascribing the merits of tourism in these Magical Villages to the successful policies of SECTUR's Magical Villages Program. Tellingly, in Cuetzalan, successful business owners are most eager to make this connection, while other inhabitants find it less easy to identify positive impacts of the program. The program has largely promoted itself as oriented toward the safeguarding of intangible and tangible cultural heritage, which is the prime attraction around which a community-based social development is to unfold through a strengthening of tourism, thus converting culture into capital in marginalized regions. In Cuetzalan, program resources have mainly financed restoration projects in the central part of town, and the designation as Magical Village has sanctified Cuetzalan as the place to go in the area, while simultaneously consolidating a promotional strategy constructed around an indigenous image. As a consequence, the Magical Villages Program constructs a marginalizing labor system that rewards indigenous inhabitants with cultural recognition and the mestizo elite with a recognition economy. Yet when seen from afar and through the notion of the homogeneous and unitary rural community on which the program bases its operation, the program is perceived as a social program that reduces poverty and indigenous marginalization. However, while the program is successfully convincing people in Cuetzalan that tourism is their destiny, and almost everyone is trying to make some sort of living from tourism, empty hotels, eateries, and restaurants make explicit the economic hardship most people in town are facing. Thus, while the program has contributed to an ethnic identity-based polarization between mestizo Cuetzalan and surrounding indigenous towns, divides in the town itself are also increasing, as a minor elite appears to be the only group profiting from this kind of tourism.

Hope and despair in Cuetzalan

I will never forget Esperanza, a mestiza woman in her fifties and owner of a humble eatery facing the hotel in which we had been staying during our first days in Cuetzalan. We frequented her place daily during our first weeks, but after our move to the other end of town we saw her only a few times. Now, however, my partner Louise and I felt it was time to see her.

We were both worried about how things had been panning out for her the past days and were speculating on what, if anything, we could do to help her.

Because we were traveling with our 8-month-old son, Julius, our mobility was significantly reduced, and during meals we were at the eatery. Esperanza and her two employees had quickly grown fond of Julius and took care of him while we were eating. A special bond between Julius and the three ladies quickly formed, and we spent many hours conversing with them. When we first entered the eatery, little did we know that eight months earlier, Esperanza was a cashier at the bus terminal. Esperanza had been working there for many years, but a new boss had discharged her, as they were not getting along. We wondered how anyone would not like caring, honest, and modest Esperanza. Nonetheless, Esperanza did not entirely abandon the bus terminal. Instead, she opened the eatery just a block from the terminal. It was not exactly because the town was in need of another eatery, but certainly Esperanza had figured out well the strategic location; on the road from the bus terminal to the town center, this eatery would be the first passengers would encounter, and it even faced the first hotel. What Esperanza could not know when she opened the eatery was that the recently restored highway would undergo yet another restoration. As part of the Magical Villages Program, the highway surface would now be changed for a hydraulic concrete surface with an archaic-like cobblestone simile surface, which meant that for three months the brand-new bus terminal and the main entry into Cuetzalan would be closed. All buses would be redirected to the other end of town. This piece of news reached Esperanza as the highway closed. Esperanza went from having a sparse number of customers to suddenly having none other than us. Realizing this, Esperanza made a quick decision and rented a place in the other end of town, where she intended to swiftly set up an eatery. Having two employees assisting her, she decided to place one at each place, and herself to commute between the two. But the new place turned out to be a bad deal. Sure, the place was near the new spot allocated for long-distance buses, but it was not en route to the town center. Instead, it was placed on a street strangely bereft of motion. Moreover, the premises were placed in the basement of a house and could hardly be seen from the street. Inside, the place was dark, damp, and infested with mildew, had no kitchen, nor electricity – just a fireplace in a wrecked patio. Worst perhaps, the place was a nest for cockroaches. Not so oddly, Esperanza's mood turned from carefree and joyous to preoccupied and concerned.

As we approached Esperanza's place to offer some sort of support, we found the eatery to be closed. "Oh, so you *still* haven't heard?" the hotel clerk in front said, with a perplexed look on his face. He then glanced into the ground silently before giving us a stern stare, "Esperanza died on Saturday." The tragic news reached us several days late, and it was only afterward that we fully understood how fragile an economic life Esperanza had been living. She was renting the premises and lived in a tiny back room of the kitchen behind curtain covers. Her brother had lent her the stove, kitchen utensils, kitchenware, and tableware – even the cheap plastic furniture was not her own. Esperanza had no material possessions, no money, two failed eateries, and double rent. This was more than she could take. The temporary closing of the bus terminal, which had pushed

Esperanza into a desperate move to restore her fragile business, had been the deathblow. Esperanza's two employees hoped to continue the eatery in her honor, but to reduce debts the family had to discontinue renting the premises and sell off the stove and other minor assets.

While this book does not directly follow up on this account, the story of Esperanza underlines two key points to be kept in view throughout. First, it stresses the degree to which people are prepared to believe that tourism is a viable way out of poverty, when few other options appear to present themselves, and when political authorities align with academic experts to present tourism as a means of emancipation. When Esperanza lost her job and found no other work, opening an eatery appeared to be the natural decision in a town putting the stakes on tourism. Although renting that second place turned out to be a fatal decision, the call to do so tells an important story of how much people in town actually believe that tourism presents a way out of hardship, even when there are few tourists to show for it.

Second, the story illustrates that the issues presented cannot be boiled down to a question of mestizos from Cuetzalan versus indigenous inhabitants in the outskirts. Most people in Cuetzalan are also losing on the government-instigated venture in small-town tourism. Basically, the Magical Villages Program is benefiting a very limited clientele, and the tourism sector is growing disproportionately compared to the number of visiting tourists. Yet, as will be pointed out, one cost of organizing tourism around indigenous heritage is the aggravation of an ethnic identity-based conflict with a significant time-depth, as indigeneity becomes a translocal identity project for rural and urban mestizos.

Notes

1 Mexico's National Institute of Statistics and Geography (INEGI) has traditionally counted as "indigenous" citizens of 5 years of age and above who speak an indigenous language. The municipality counts 30,738 speakers of indigenous languages, of which the majority speaks Nahuat and a fraction speaks Totonac (INEGI 2011:135). I apply the term Nahuat to refer to the language variant spoken in the area, which has the phoneme /t/, where other more widely known language variants have the phoneme /tl/. However, some sources cited refer to the local language variant as Nahuatl. I employ the term Classical Nahuatl to refer to the language variant spoken in the central Aztec empire at the time of the arrival of the Spaniards. As to orthography, I follow linguist Michel Launey (2011:3–8), though without marking glottal stops and long vowels. This orthography corresponds to that conventionally used in toponyms. However, sources and institutions cited sometimes employ other orthographies.

2 Mexico consists of a federal district and 31 sovereign states that each consist of various municipalities. Within this structure, federal institutions such as SECTUR are replicated at the state level. Sociologist Gabriela Coronado describes this political structure as a fractal pattern of self-similarity that permeates all levels of economic, political, and social organization and ties all Mexican towns into a network balanced by the federal district (Coronado 2000:14–18). If nothing else is noted, reference is made to federal institutions. Reference to state institutions is specified in brackets. States are also bracketed following sites and towns to specify their location.

References

Buchenau, Jürgen. 2001. "Small Numbers, Great Impact: Mexico and Its Immigrants, 1821–1973." *Journal of American Ethnic History* 20(3):23–49.

Coronado, Gabriela. 2000. *Silenced Voices of Mexican Culture: Identity, Resistance and Creativity in the Interethnic Dialogue*. PhD dissertation, University of Western Sydney.

Greathouse-Amador, Louisa. 2000. *Cuetzalan y el Cambio Social: El Turismo ¿Un Agente de Transformación?* PhD dissertation, Benemérita Universidad Autónoma de Puebla.

Haly, Richard. 2000. "Nahuas and National Culture." Pp. 157–192 in *Native American Spirituality: A Critical Reader*, edited by I. Lee. Lincoln, NE: University of Nebraska Press.

INEGI. 2011. *Panorama Sociodemográfico de Puebla*, vol. 1. Aguascalientes: INEGI. Retrieved November 25, 2015 (www.inegi.org.mx/prod_serv/contenidos/espanol/bvinegi/productos/censos/poblacion/2010/panora_socio/Cpv2010_Panorama.pdf).

Launey, Michel. 2011. *An Introduction to Classical Nahuatl*. Translated and adapted by C. Mackay. Cambridge: Cambridge University Press.

Thomson, Guy P. C. 1991. "Agrarian Conflict in the Municipality of Cuetzalan (Sierra de Puebla): The Rise and Fall of 'Pala' Agustin Dieguillo, 1861–1894." *The Hispanic American Historical Review* 71(2):205–258.

Valderrama Rouy, Pablo, and Carolina Ramírez Suárez. 1993. "Resistencia Étnica y Defensa del Territorio en el Totonacapan Serrano: Cuetzalan en el Siglo XIX." Pp. 189–206 in *Indio, Nación y Comunidad en el México del Siglo XIX*, edited by A. E. Ohmstede. Mexico City: Centro de Estudios Mexicanos y Centroamericanos.

1 Introduction

Observations, objectives, and empirical vantage points

Tourism, as it is panning out for indigenous Latin Americans following the multicultural turn of the 1990s, is increasingly being advanced as an empowering and liberating gesture of cultural recognition that brings social development and economic opportunities to rural indigenous communities and undoes ethnic discrimination associated with colonial and national pasts. As indigenous heritage is being cast as a raw material awaiting extraction, the cultural recognition of indigeneity is invested with the potential to spark a parallel economic appreciation of indigenous communities. In this new synergy, which fuses multicultural politics of recognition with tourism through conceptualizations of indigenous heritage, cultural richness converts into monetary riches and drives for preserving, revitalizing, and performing indigenous heritage become self-evident procedures for boosting ethnic self-pride, social well-being, and economic prosperity. In other words, multiculturalism has given way to *multicultourism*.

This conceptual framework, its means of spatial and temporal distribution, and its social consequences are the analytical concerns of the present book. A central theoretical premise is that conceptual frames are sites of government; they govern and thus need to be governed. Accordingly, this book shows how the sketched framework structures contemporary life in Latin America by mobilizing diverse agents and agencies in the implementation of its vision, and it sets out to highlight the paradoxical and divisive effects of this immanent device and social technology.

I find this selective focus warranted due to the tacit assumption that guides such governance, namely that the recognition of indigenous cultural heritage – through tourism or otherwise – will automatically benefit indigenous citizens. Importantly, the discursive means through which the politics of recognition has gained a widespread appeal in Latin America should not be mistaken for its practical and social effects on the ground. Public appreciations of indigeneity do not self-evidently send profits from tourism into the pockets of citizens who would typically be categorized as indigenous. Rather, as a key resource to new modes of national belonging and to the expanding yet omnipresent industry of tourism, indigeneity is up for grabs as a common national good. As Nancy Fraser argues, redistribution cannot be assumed to follow automatically from recognition (Fraser 1995), and since indigenized identities are increasingly coming into vogue, the symbolic (re)source of indigeneity is not the exclusive property of indigenous agents. One effect of the widespread adoption of a multiculturalist framework of recognition in Latin America is its way of facilitating an increasing incursion into the intangible and symbolic territories of indigenous identities. Thus, rather than seeing the emergence of a tourism organized around indigenous heritage as reflective of a radical multiculturalist reorganization of Latin American society in which indigenous citizens stand central and may finally be accommodated, this book invites the reader to consider the ways in which tourism regenerates dispossessive patterns of extraction by framing such processes as benevolent and respectful gestures set to heal troubled pasts and emancipate indigenous citizens.

Within such a framework, indigenous subjects are understood as chiefly concerned about 'their culture,' which must be recognized at all costs, while economic transactions are seen as less relevant to indigenous lives. In practice, this social order means that often it is the recognizer who is financially rewarded by fellow recognizers, while an abstracted indigenous subject is granted a symbolic act of recognition. This counterintuitive mechanism of what I term the *recognition economy* may be clarified by way of an anecdote.

While preparing to write this book, Sandra, a Danish woman, told me she had been living in Mexico and loved the country. She approached me because she was planning to launch a webshop that would sell items "that represent the traditional Mexico, but in a modern version." Having read in a newspaper "how indigenous Mexicans are embarrassed about their original languages, such as Nahuatl," Sandra requested my help in finding a name in Nahuatl for her webshop to show Nahuas in Mexico that she thought "their history and culture are fantastic." In fact, conveying her webshop to her "suppliers" through the use of a Nahuatl name would only make her "proud."

Sandra's request for assistance and the idea of giving her webshop a Nahuatl name were pitched through references to indigenous Mexicans feeling embarrassed about their languages and Sandra's intention of proudly flagging Nahua culture through the enterprise of her webshop. Sandra's private business venture is implicitly framed as countering a disregard in Mexico of indigenous minorities, which indigenous Mexicans have since internalized, and she endows her business with an activist role within a larger project of cultural recognition toward indigenous people, making them value their culture and giving them a sense of belonging. Sandra thus substitutes her own key role within her private business initiative for the generic figure of the indigenous Mexican or Nahua. She thereby draws in indigenous Mexicans as external agents to her business agenda, and as independent sources they are made to bear witness to the importance of her actions. Within this order, the Nahuas become beneficiaries of her personal enterprise, while Sandra presents herself as a benefactor setting up the webshop – at least in part – due to her concern for the well-being of indigenous Mexicans. Importantly, there is no reason to believe that Sandra does not experience a genuine concern over indigenous issues and that her intention of naming the webshop in Nahuatl is not reflective of that. On the contrary, the fascinating thing is that she in all likelihood *is* concerned about these issues and wants to do good by offering cultural recognition to indigenous minorities. Nonetheless, the paradox is that the seemingly altruistic cultural recognition the webshop offers to imaginary indigenous beneficiaries is simultaneously what exactly constitutes its business strategy. Selecting a name in Nahuatl for a shop that sells "traditional" Mexican crafts is an effective way of subliminally communicating to like-minded shoppers that they are purchasing products made by indigenous artisans. Trading with Nahua artisans, however, did not figure in the business plan.

The anecdote illustrates how indigenous citizens come to be discursively centered as symbolic sources in the construction of economic relations within which expressions of indigenous cultural heritage – and *not* necessarily indigenous citizens –take part. In short, nationalized modes of recognizing indigenous heritage assist in dispossessing indigenous agents of the emerging resource of indigeneity,and this disempowering process is assisted by a political framework, which is perceived to emancipate and empower the very same citizens. Such a format is particularly vivid in current constructions of cultural tourism in Latin America.

Setting aside the intuitive inclination to identify expressions of indigenous cultural heritage with indigenous agents and the propensity to think that such agents must therefore be in the best position to mobilize and profit from said heritage in the tourism industry, there is nothing to suggest that indigenous Latin Americans should automatically hold an obvious advantage in the articulation of indigenous identity. That is, as a contested resource, indigeneity should not be seen as the autonomous indigenous terrain it might otherwise appear to be when gazed at panoramically.

Since identities are fluid, mobile, and continuously inflected in relation to the surrounding economic, political, and social settings, expressing and constructing indigeneity is not the exclusive privilege of indigenous citizens. As anthropologists Jacques Galinier and Antoinette Molinié note (Galinier and Molinié 2013) concerning a growing tendency they term "neo-Indianism," urban mestizos increasingly embrace, practice, and reinvent nationalized indigenous identities through New Age spiritualist interpretations of indigenous heritage. Yet indigeneity is not only an emerging resource for middle-class Latin Americans through which to attain new senses of belonging and existential well-being. Indigeneity equally figures as a social device for mobilizing popular protests against transnational capitalism and extractive economies (Norget 2010; McNeish 2013), and, most famously in the plurinational state of Bolivia, claims to indigeneity constitute fundamental parts of contemporary state-political projects (Canessa 2016). With indigeneity increasingly turning into an encompassing translocal identity project across Latin America, codified in national terms, the identity political debate about "who is indigenous" seems to become ever-more complex and ambiguous (Canessa 2007; Forte 2013). It is, however, instructive that this direction in the blurring of boundaries between dichotomously arranged historical characters in Latin America – mestizo versus indigenous – has been codified into national political climates after indigeneity has emerged as an effective means through which to frame political struggles and to stimulate national economies.

Nonetheless, the increasing ambiguity of indigeneity, it would appear, also pertains to the divergent and intersecting scales at which indigenous citizenship and identities are codified. Departing from the international human rights setting, indigeneity has emerged as a global term and hegemonic conceptual framework (Tilley 2002), yet this international process is filtered into specific state practices across Latin America, as national governments look for ways to address ethnic identity-based rights claims, whether in their national constitutions, institutional organizations, or political practices. In other words, rights claims departing from hegemonic notions of indigeneity require some degree of codification in national terms, and the nationalization of indigeneity across Latin America is becoming an identity project that is open, albeit not equally accessible, to all (Canessa 2016). This process attests to the astonishing mobility of *mestizaje*, which, through its characteristic capacity to encompass the totality (Rogers 1998), manages to embrace cosmopolitan ideas about multicultural citizenship and coexistence and adapt them to a national recognition of indigeneity. In an ironic twist of the national project of "Deep Mexico" as envisioned by anthropologist Guillermo Bonfil Batalla (1989), the recognition of indigenous citizens now materializes as a quest for mestizos to recognize and practice the indigeneity within. Through the frame of the nation, contemporary indigeneity figures as the lost past of the mestizo and the heritage and national history of all, as mestizo citizens and diverse indigenous groups are brought into a figurative kinship relation that casts mestizos as the offspring of indigenous contemporaries.

In engaging with these issues, this book adopts a translocal perspective that considers how supranational, national, and local processes fuse in concrete social settings through the device of tourism. A translocal approach has the double advantage of situating the study in particular localities with all their complexities, without assuming that localities can be taken as discrete and self-evident analytical units. Arguably, the paradoxes accompanying the translocalization of indigeneity in Latin America are most clearly discerned when observed through concrete social relations and settings, particularly in locations where groups with historically dichotomous identities share space, maneuver diachronically anchored interethnic power relations, and find themselves engaged in direct competition over indigenous identity through tourism. Hence, the sense of indigeneity that is sweeping across Latin America and increasingly organizes identity and place-making in the region should be inspected in concrete locations where differently scaled economic, political, and social processes intersect and give life to situated claims to indigeneity.

A translocal approach assists in tuning in on the multi-scalar processes through which group identities materialize, and it equally facilitates a critical engagement with the current state of affairs in tourism. In line with the UN Millennium Development Goals, scholars working in Latin America have argued that development through tourism should be of benefit to local communities, and community-based tourism is increasingly being conceived as a means for alleviating poverty (Baud and Ypeij 2009:3). Although such tourism initiatives aspire to empower disadvantaged populations through participatory processes, they tend to depart from the unstated assumption of rural communities as egalitarian and homogeneous units in which people have largely equal social positions, common aims, and views (Blackstock 2005). This urban notion of the unitary rural community with a flat social stratigraphy facilitates the idea that 'the community itself' is in charge of the kind of tourism 'it' wants. Such community-based tourism is thus not likely to inquire critically about which types of citizens are likely to be integrated into, and take control of, participatory processes, and may unwittingly come to enforce asymmetric power hierarchies. Instead, the perceived ability of heritage-based tourism to create jobs for 'the community' as a unitary entity is seen as decisively positive and as a common good that benefits the community as a whole. Yet participation in tourism as an economic activity tends to be a privatized matter, and the prime participants tend to be citizens with sizeable and favorably located property and money to invest.

While the subsequent sections of the introduction will chart pertinent developments in Latin America, the intersecting national and local processes will be inspected throughout the book from two empirical vantage points: Mexico's tourism program Magical Villages, and the Magical Village Cuetzalan (Puebla), a mestizo town and municipal capital in a majority Nahua municipality. When it comes to the political frameworks that surround tourism, heritage, and indigenous peoples in Latin America, Mexico has long played a key influential role as a regional compass. Hence, if one is looking to spot developments and trends in Latin America within said areas, Mexico, which has the largest number of indigenous citizens (ECLAC 2014), receives by far the largest number of tourists (UNWTO 2017), and has the largest number of UNESCO World Heritage Sites (UNESCO 2017), constitutes a promising vantage point.

Multicultural citizenship in Latin America

In the course of the 1990s, an unprecedented arena of political negotiation emerged for indigenous Latin Americans, as many nations within the region reformed their constitutions to accommodate notions of multiculturalism, officially recognizing the plurality of national citizens (Van Cott 2000:11). Such constitutional reprogramming signaled to the national and international communities a marked change in the anatomy of these nation-states, which was fortified by a surge of multiculturalist ideas in national policies. The changes testified to the official commitment of these nation-states to replace assimilatory and exclusionary policies with policies of cultural diversity, social equality, and inclusion, all of which formed part of a broader democratization process. So, Latin American nation-states articulated a divide between past and present, now and then, and the ancient and the modern nation-state. By denouncing past homogenizing national policies, nation-states loosened their contemporary self-images from troubled national pasts.

While each nation has traveled separate and particularized paths toward various kinds of political multiculturalism, the Latin American transition toward multicultural citizenship is typically attributed to the sustained work of indigenous political movements and NGOs, which organized themselves transnationally beginning in the 1970s, successfully effecting changes in international law, most notably by establishing indigenous rights as human rights through ILO Convention 169 (Van Cott 2000:262–263; Sieder 2002:1–4). In Latin America, only Cuba and Uruguay have yet to ratify this key international convention concerning indigenous rights, but outside the region a total of only six countries have ratified it (Lehmann 2016:1). Within this general explanatory framework, indigenous movements are usually articulated as protagonists assisted by NGOs in a protracted bottom-up grassroots struggle to obtain international and national legal rights.

Although the symbolic message of achievement in this broad sketch should not be disparaged – undoubtedly, the path toward indigenous rights and equal citizenship has been and *still is* one of struggle, and chiefly one to be kept alive by indigenous political agents – it carries with it the unfortunate connotation that the field opened by political multiculturalism is primarily indigenous territory. Thus, while attention has been given to ways in which the international recognition of indigenous rights has contributed to establishing ground for an international political subject position based on indigenous identity (substituting that of class) through which the rural poor may define political struggles, less attention has been devoted to examining the impact of government policies on indigenous political subject positions (Jung 2003).

Given the explosion of multiculturalist state policies in Latin America in the past two decades, time should now be ripe for questioning an explanatory framework constructed around reactionary governments clinging to the status quo, faced by progressive indigenous activists instigating social change. In other words, is it still tenable to view the opening of a multiculturalist space of political negotiation as the exclusive merit of nationally and internationally operating indigenous rights movements vis-à-vis reluctant states?

Anthropologist Charles Hale (2002) argued at the start of the previous decade that there has been a tendency to regard neoliberal strategies of governance as diametrically opposed to indigenous struggle, politics of multiculturalism, and cultural diversity as promoted in the international human rights setting. As Hale shows, they are not. Rather than directly confronting the agendas of cultural rights activists, neoliberal governments have sought to sap their force by proactively promoting and implementing a limited package of cultural rights. Through the strategic use of minimal concessions, Latin American governments have been oriented to redirecting the claims and efforts of cultural rights activists. This has been done by disciplining proponents seen to pose too far-reaching cultural rights demands such as claim on territory and economic resources, while rewarding proponents of limited demands, thus establishing a clear divide between acceptable cultural rights and extreme demands. Attention thus needs to be turned to the ways in which national governments, political institutions, and programs manage and shape this internationally crafted space of negotiation to probe "the 'menace' inherent in the political spaces that have been opened" (Hale 2002:487).

While multicultural policies have been increasing in number since the 1990s and signal an increasing attention to the social circumstances of indigenous groups, the space of negotiation for indigenous Latin Americans has diminished significantly. This point protrudes most clearly in a broad analytical perspective that does not inspect policies from the point of view of the policy areas to which they are officially designated. As various scholars have noted in the case of Mexico, the introduction of political multiculturalism has been accompanied by agrarian reforms and economic policies that have had profoundly negative consequences for indigenous groups (Jung 2003:437–441; Speed 2005; Gledhill 2014:511–512).

With fascinating ease, government institutions have become prime innovators and protectors of multiculturalist doctrine and multicultural policies have become the norm in Latin American state planning. Simultaneously, and paradoxically, multiculturalism has transformed into a lever for the governance of indigenous citizens, rather than a rallying cry of indigenous cultural activists with which to confront and influence government policies. The proliferation of multiculturalism thus needs to be acknowledged not as the triumph of indigenous activism, but as a threat to the politics of indigenous groups to glimpse the counterintuitive ways in which this political arena has emerged (cf. Yúdice 2003:160–163). From constituting an external threat to political legitimacy and social asymmetries, multiculturalism has swiftly turned into a core constituent of legitimate government.

Seen from this perspective, there is no reason to assume that the introduction of state multiculturalism necessarily reflects a profoundly shared concern between indigenous rights activists and governments. Convergence of interests must be regarded as secondary to the diverging aims of indigenous groups seeking to thoroughly reorganize unequal political and social structures and governments seeking ways to reconstitute legitimate ground for democratic rule.

Accordingly, this book aims to show that in Mexico in the wake of the multiculturalist surge, rather than a political and societal reorganization, what has taken place by and large is a reconstitution of the political field. This process has involved a governing effort to narrow down and tame the challenge posed by multiculturalism. One significant strategy of redirection is what this book dubs *multicultourism*. The suave feel of this critical term is intended to reflect the equally benign, at times even benevolent, expression of the described phenomenon. As the book unpacks the social detriment involved in the operation of such a kind of tourism, the mild expression will increasingly stand out in contradiction to the discouraging content to which it refers, adding a crucial analytical dimension to the pernicious workings of the phenomenon.

The emergence of multicultourism: culture as resource

One of the outcomes of the transnational indigenous people's movement's involvement in the human rights setting has been an international identity project that has codified and crafted a global notion of indigeneity. As political scientist Virginia Tilley argues (Tilley 2002), a global notion of indigeneity has become an unescapable point of reference in the configuration of local *ethnopolitics*, asserting itself as an internationally approved gauge of authentic indigeneity. For indigenous groups to frame political struggle in ways incompatible with the global configu-ration of indigeneity means to assume "an extra burden of persuasion" (Tilley 2002:531). Occurring simultaneously with this global sense of indigeneity, by contrast, was the key argument of the transnational indigenous people's movement and human rights agencies that indigenous people's political rights are constituted by their cultural uniqueness, from the standpoint of which indigenous groups may make specific rights claims. The special emphasis on cultural uniqueness places indigenous people in a dichotomous political situation that leaves them torn by the demand to display cultural *uniqueness* in a way that conforms to the *hegemonic* notion of indigeneity. Moreover, such ideal vision of indigeneity contradicts the social life of most indigenous people in Latin America, who maneuver the everyday experience of being minorities in nation-states revolving around mestizo majority citizens. With cultural uniqueness being pivotal to indigenous political claims, cultural traditions shared with non-indigenous communities may weaken, even jeopardize, indigenous ethnopolitics (Tilley 2002:546).

In his work on the concept of aboriginality, anthropologist Patrick Wolfe refers to this contradiction as "repressive authenticity" (Wolfe 1999:163–214). Official notions of indigeneity structure evaluations of authenticity, and groups that fail to render themselves authentic – meaning those that are seen to have become too culturally or biologically hybrid – are rendered inauthentic and see their basis for making group claims on resources crumbling.

In a similar fashion, Charles Hale (1999) has compellingly shown how ideas from hybridity theory have become a prime means in a popular majoritarian discourse of equality in postwar Guatemala. Drawing on the universal condition of hybridity, difference is strategically effaced by ladino society with the claim that they are all mestizos, thus eroding the basis of indigenous ethnopolitics and critique of ladino racism. Conversely, indigenous people's attempts to organize politically in a pan-Mayan movement is challenged by majority Guatemalans pointing out the novelty and inauthenticity of such collective identity, render-ing their means of organizing politically as a case of political opportunism (Hale 2002:516–517, 2006:162). Indigenous identity constructions are thus put under pressure by essentializing and hybridizing tactics, which collaborate to challenge indigenous ethnopolitics. Cultural authenticity, as Wolfe argues, con-stitutes a general condition that can be compromised with tremendous speed (Wolfe 1999:184), and it is particularly prone to be so when its strategic relation to contemporary politics challenges majority society.

All the more interesting, in tandem with an increasing scrutiny of indigenous authenticity, the centrality of cultural uniqueness to indigenous identity poli-tics has likewise catalyzed appreciations of and measures to safeguard cultural diversity (Tilley 2002:546). In this process, UNESCO has played a key role by promoting the idea of intangible heritage beginning in the 1970s, culminating with the 2003 *Convention for the Safeguarding of Intangible Cultural Heritage* and the 2005 *Convention for the Protection and Promotion of the Diversity of Cultural Expressions*. The expansion of the concept of cultural heritage to include intangible expressions is largely understood as an attempt to break with

Eurocentric understandings of cultural heritage and to include the living culture of indigenous groups as part of world heritage (Leimgruber 2010:163–167). Nonetheless, preoccupied with the disappearance of cultural traditions in the face of globalization and modernity, the UNESCO approach to intangible heritage is undergirded by a preservationist concern resembling that of bygone salvage ethnography (Alivizatou 2011:37–39).

Concomitantly with the growing appreciation of cultural diversity, strengthened by the sense of accelerated disappearance of cultural traditions, culture is, as anthropologist Philip Scher argues in the case of the Caribbean, increasingly perceived as a national economic resource within a heritage tourism framework and is simultaneously becoming a source of state sovereignty (Scher 2011). For this reason, cultural performance has increasingly become a domain of biopolitical government intervention. Governments take on the task of protecting and preserving cultural forms. In so doing, they come to select and define cultural expressions within a national frame, while citizens are encouraged to engage in nationalized cultural performances, which are seen to contribute directly to the national economy and identity. In this process, citizens become objects of regulation by government institutions, as governments seek to delineate right and wrong ways to engage with and (re)present national culture. Within cultural policy in the Caribbean, Scher argues, one consequence has been that culture has changed from being a universal human right to becoming a national citizen duty; citizens no longer simply enjoy the right to participate in cultural modes of expression – they are required to contribute to the national culture, identity, and economic prosperity (Scher 2014).

Similar tendencies can arguably be found elsewhere, and, in the case of Mexico, multiculturalist policies appear to stand the strongest when they do not interfere with government agendas, do not look to substantially restructure society, and if they are in harmony with national economic incentives. Differing attitudes toward cultural diversity are found in different policy areas, and a positive attitude toward plurality is likely to occur in areas that would not require high-cost government investment or diminished access to resources. Thus, while indigenous claims to autonomy and self-determination based on control of land and resources or the right to receive education in a first language has had little resonance in government policies (Speed 2005; Hamel 2008; Gledhill 2014), multiculturalist politics of recognition figure as a centerpiece in the heritage and tourism industries.

Intriguingly, Scher's point echoes an earlier parallel development in the attitude toward the tangible pre-Hispanic heritage in Mexico. The early era of Spanish colonial rule (1521–1821) was marked by symbolic destruction of tangible expressions of indigenous culture, and the demolition of religious and political monuments was part of a general repression that came to alienate indigenous people from a vital part of their cultural, political, and social history. After independence, around the time of the armed national revolution (*c.*1910–1920), the tangible indigenous heritage was turned to account within the new national self-image by the academic and political elite, while contemporary indigenous culture was disregarded (Brading 2001). The emergence of pre-Hispanic archaeological monuments as national economic resources was a prime incentive in the founda-tion of the National Institute of Anthropology and History (INAH). Thus, when in 1938 – after nationalizing the oil industry – President Cárdenas put INAH on the drawing board, he argued that the exploration and conservation of archaeological ruins would not just produce "scientific results," but also "magnificent economic yields when signifying [an] attraction for foreign tourism," pointing to recent archaeological investigations in Oaxaca, which he noted were already "decisively" influencing regional economy (Lombardo de Ruíz 1993:177). From the outset, INAH thus came to embody a political strategy that sought to supply the national tourism industry with attraction value based on scientific authority, and scientific and economic aims were hierarchically interlinked within a national framework, while investment in "scientific results" was understood to produce "economic yields" for the nation. Arguably, the subsequent attention to intangible indigenous heritage inscribes itself into a conceptual framework similar to the one that sparked an interest in tangible indigenous heritage.

With the growing economic importance of tourism, and the growing impor-tance of cultural heritage and cultural performance to tourism, it is not strange to find that tourism has become one of the prime spaces within which multicultur-alist policies have unfolded. Cultural and ethnic diversity is highly compatible with the kinds of tourism that rest on the dogma of diversifying products to avoid substitutability; cultural heritage has become a resource that helps differentiate destinations (Scher 2011). Tourism, within this context, presents itself as a pol-itics of recognition and belonging invested with an emancipating potential for cultural and ethnic minorities, whose culture will no longer live in the shadows nor face the threat of falling into disuse, since it is promised to be re-centered in tourism activities that are appreciative and rewarding of diversity. Such optimism has been echoed on a global scale. Recontextualizing the words of postcolonial theorist Gayatri Spivak (1993:56), to take an illustrative example, tourism scholar Keith Hollinshead (2005:31–32) envisions a situation in which tourism will "blossom 'into a garden where the marginal can speak.'" In this vision, tourism is the force that assists "subjugated populations" in achieving "what had seemed impossible" and "only 'imaginable.'"

Leaving aside Hollinshead's astonishing reading of Spivak (1993), this per-spective must above all be challenged for the assumption that tourism as a field of political action should somehow diverge from the larger political terrain and con-stitute a space where the marginal becomes central. If this emerging type of tourism *does* hold any emancipatory potential for "subjugated populations" and *could* help them obtain "what had seemed impossible" and "only 'imaginable,'" then analyses of this new space should proceed with extraordinary care. In the case of Mexico (and New Spain) at least, in the past 500 years no such other promising and pros-perous situation comes to mind regarding indigenous minority affairs. In addition, caution appears to be warranted by the limited number of supplementary signs of increasing indigenous control over other types of resources. To the contrary, indigenous communities in Mexico have, in recent decades, faced paramilitary repression, radicalization of claims to autonomy, and extraction of resources from their immediate environments (Gledhill 2014). Therefore, with indigenous culture discovered as a national resource in tourism, there is no reason to assume that the process of extraction will necessarily pan out differently from other social processes, where indigenous people find themselves in the margins of nation-state society. Rather, it should be expected that the new field quickly emerges as an object of government and that it becomes populated by a diverse array of agents in more favorable political and socioeconomic positions from which to extract and refine indigenous cultural heritage.

This is multicultourism; a strategy of government looking to narrow down, tame, and steer the new space of negotiation opening for indigenous groups by offering a new multicultural national self-image that triggers new modes of national belonging and participation without confronting structural political and social asymmetries. As in other compound nouns, the first noun modifies the second, while the second determines the ontology of the construction. This means that the term does not describe a kind of multiculturalism, although both term and phenomenon have the propensity to deceive the cursory eye, but rather a kind of tourism that draws on multiculturalist aspirations, ideas, and symbols. In this sense, the term sketches a hierarchy in which the first nurtures the second, while the second defines the first. Multicultourism is a kind of tourism that feeds off the utopia of multiculturalism, but with a completely different social order on offer, and so it has emerged as a governmental response to the growing prominence of multiculturalism in Latin America and its associated indigenous political subject position. As a strategy of government, it has emancipating, empowering, and philanthropic aspirations, and it attempts to make citizens take possession of its vision by making them visualize a productive synergy between intangible cultural heritage, national tourism, and politics of recognition, and by issuing concrete paths through which such vision may come into existence. Multicultourism thus promulgates a setting within which rural indigenous people may simultaneously become full-fledged citizens, improve their livelihood, preserve their cultural heritage, and emerge as the central agent and national figure of a new multiculturalist Mexico. Nevertheless, as will be shown, multicultourism becomes a state-sponsored national scramble for indigenous heritage that does not evidently place indigenous agents in the empowered and profitable end of socioeconomic relations. What is worse, multicultourism appears to regenerate the project of mestizo nationalism, since through the frame of the nation, mestizos gain renewed claim over the indigenous past and heritage. The stage is thus set for a power-blind politics of recognition that extracts the economy of indigenous heritage out of the hands of indigenous groups. So, indigenous groups are symbolically projected into the center of the nation, while socially pushed further into the margins. Indeed, the very force of the symbolic projection paves the way for further social marginalization. Inevitably, it seems, the discovery of intangible indigenous heritage as a national resource leads to the realization that indigenous people are not inalienable parts of indigenous culture; within this order, indigenous citizens are dispensable. From this analytical stance I suggest that multicultourism is *not* primarily about tourism, but is rather a response to indigenous political mobilization and the threat posed by the increased attention to the rights of indigenous citizens.

Before and after multiculturalism: Mexico as regional pioneer in indigenous state policy

Before the emergence of multiculturalism, Mexico had long been a leading country in terms of developing specialized cultural and social policies for handling indigenous nationals and their integration into majority society. From the early to the late twentieth century, Mexico thus played a significant role in forming state policies toward indigenous citizens in Latin America by promulgating what has been called populist *indigenism* (*indigenismo*) and officializing it through indigenist policies (Knight 1990; Peña 2005; Souza Lima 2005; Sanz Jara 2009). Indigenism became widespread in late nineteenth-century Latin America, when the newly founded nation-states were looking to forge a national consciousness and identity that would distinguish them from Europe and create a national historical counterbalance to increasing industrialization and modernization. In this early post-independence context, indigenism developed as a growing tendency within non-indigenous elite society of nationalizing and romanticizing the pre-Hispanic past. In Mexico, the pre-Hispanic past was archaeologically and historically explored and selectively and symbolically incorporated in nationalist narratives mediated through visual and literary art (Barnet-Sanchez 2001). In these early nationalist narratives, contemporary indigenous people played little to no part, and they were effectively separated from the glorified pre-Hispanic culture, which was instead appropriated by majority elites.

Indigenism gained widespread prominence in connection with the 1910 centennial celebration of independence in Latin America, and in Mexico it was translated into official government policy in the wake of the armed national revolution. Although the social conflict of the revolution was largely a struggle between classes – peasants against landlords – indigenous participation in the revolution was reframed as an ethnic conflict after the revolution – indigenous groups against mestizos and creoles (Knight 1990:76–77). Attributing the revolution to indigenous groups became a founding ideological basis for post-revolutionary government, which sought to finally do away with the colonial legacy by aiding indigenous groups with entering modern society; indigenism became a key part of official government ideology.

Official indigenism was spearheaded by artists and government intellectuals, most notably anthropologist and archaeologist Manuel Gamio.[1] The movement was self-consciously antiracist, and as part of post-revolutionary politics articulated itself as reacting against the social discrimination of indigenous people; however, indigenists largely substituted biological racism for cultural and sociopolitical racism (Knight 1990; Doremus 2001:377; Sanz Jara 2009:261). Whereas indigenous people had earlier been seen as unfit for modern society as a species, indigenists argued that they were "only" culturally unfit. The problem of culture, however, could be remedied, and indigenists therefore proffered integration through state-planned assimilation and acculturation, focusing on including indigenous people into the post-revolutionary national project through education and economic and social development (Knight 1990:80–83).

The indigenist project expressed a perplexing double stance toward indigenous people. Indigenous crafts and customs were appreciated for their contribution to national identity, but other components of indigenous culture, such as language, were seen as impediments to their entry into modern Mexico and, worse, as obstacles to modernization for the Mexican nation as a whole. From the indigenist point of view, national cohesion was threatened by cultural diversity, and national progress was threatened by cultural "backwardness," and indigenists were looking to create a unified national identity that would spur national allegiance among indigenous people and insert them into the national (economic) project. Indigenists set out to investigate indigenous communities to identify and define positive and negative cultural traits. Policies were designed to handle the pivotal balancing task of sustaining positive traits and sifting out negative ones. Positive traits were those that could fit well with a folkloric expression of nationality, and negative ones were those thought to be incompatible with modern society. In the cultural evolutionist eyes of the indigenists, indigenous communities had a choice between directed acculturation or social marginalization leading to extinction (Wright 1988:368–369; Knight 1990:86–87). Since acculturation was carried out with an eye to majority society, official indigenism played a crucial role in sustaining the national project of *mestizaje*, the process of biological and cultural mixing that would produce the quintessential citizen, the mestizo (Knight 1990:84–87; Doremus 2001:381–382; Tarica 2008:1–3).

Indigenist policies migrated to other parts of Latin America, partly due to Mexico's active role in institutionalizing and promulgating official indigenism. Beginning in 1918, government departments appeared successively in the national setting to direct the planned acculturation process (Peña 2006:282).[2] In the 1930s, Vice-Minister of Education Moisés Sáenz visited fellow Latin American countries as official advisor, sometimes elaborating reports on the indigenous situation of those countries. When, in 1940, Mexico hosted the First Inter-American Indigenist Congress, Sáenz was involved in its organization, which presented as one of its results the formation of the Inter-American Indigenist Institute in 1942, which was based in Mexico and headed by Gamio. Participant countries further agreed to create national indigenist government institutions that would develop and apply official integrationist policies. Thus, with Mexico playing a key role in this process, indigenism in a variety of shadings became official policy across Latin America in the subsequent decades (Doremus 2001:375; Peña 2005:726–728).[3] Not surprisingly, then, the first international legislation on indigenous issues, ILO Convention 107 from 1957 – substituted in 1989 by ILO Convention 169 – had a firm imprint of Mexico's indigenist policies, encouraging the creation of national institutions specialized for the handling of indigenous affairs (Plant 1999:26–27).

Backed by the 1968 Mexican student movement, a new generation of Mexican anthropologists began to criticize official indigenism and the national anthropology that put itself at the service of an authoritarian, paternalist government and its national project of *mestizaje* (Warman et al. 1970; Bonfil Batalla 1989; Lomnitz 2005). Concomitantly, during the 1970s, indigenous intellectuals began to organize themselves, offering public critique of indigenist policy, and arranging congresses on indigenous issues, attended by indigenous community representatives. Some of the intellectuals were partly the product of indigenist education policies and worked in their home areas as bilingual teachers under the auspices of the National Indigenist Institute, thereby creating the vital connection between indigenous communities and indigenist policy (Peña 2006:284–286). Critique from this front therefore proved to be particularly damaging, since it came from a double position of exteriority and interiority to official indigenism. The breakdown of indigenism as official policy thus coincided with the political mobilization of indigenous organizations promoting specialized cultural rights and positive recognition and protection of cultural diversity.

Indigenism, then, as state policy specialized for attending to indigenous citizens, has been replaced by a "regional model" of "multicultural constitutionalism" in Latin America within a brief time span (Van Cott 2000:257–280). Nevertheless, despite this transformation of the political terrain, Mexico has remained a regional driving force in the formulation of policies toward indigenous peoples. Being seventh on the list of countries with most sites on the UNESCO World Heritage List (UNESCO 2017), Mexico is equally becoming a regional role model in the handling of intangible cultural heritage. Indeed, the term intangible heritage itself emerged from the 1982 UNESCO World Conference on Cultural Policy held in Mexico City (Leimgruber 2010:163). Further indication was brought about by Mexico's swift ratification of ILO Convention 169 in September 1990 – the first in Latin America and the second in the world – which was followed by a modification of the constitution in 1992, accommodating a view of the Mexican nation as "pluricultural" and "originally based on its indigenous peoples" (Gledhill 2014:511).

With the ratification in 2003 of the UNESCO *Convention for the Safeguarding of Intangible Cultural Heritage*, the Mexican government has increased its focus on intangible expressions of indigenous culture. In addition to INAH, which is officially in charge of protecting, preserving, and promoting that part of indigenous heritage, SECTUR is becoming increasingly influential in matters of intangible heritage, seeing that this is a prime ingredient of contemporary tourism. Following a long research tradition in Mexico of doing national anthropology (Lomnitz 2005), intangible cultural heritage is largely approached by INAH from the perspective of national identity construction, thus inevitably framing indigenous heritage as *national* heritage. SECTUR's involvement with intangible heritage operates within the same conceptual framework, and thus looks to construct a *national* tourism around the *national* heritage.

The book and its queries

Mexico is located in the middle of Donna Lee Van Cott's Latin American Multicultural Policy Index and is regarded to represent a "modest" version of multiculturalism (Van Cott 2006:274–277). Neither categorized as "weak" nor "strong," Mexican political multiculturalism therefore does not predetermine deep pessimism or high optimism. Add to this that Mexico is the second-largest and second-most populated country in Latin America and by far has the greatest number of indigenous citizens. Of the approximately 44.7 million indigenous citizens in Latin America, 16.9 million reside in Mexico, constituting 15.1% of the total Mexican population and 37.8% of the total indigenous population in Latin America (ECLAC 2014:36–39). Combined with its role as a regional compass in government policies toward indigenous groups, Mexico arguably constitutes a promising empirical arena for glimpsing current and future trends in national dealings with indigenous people in Latin America.

Departing from Mexico's tourism program Magical Villages and the Magical Village Cuetzalan as empirical vantage points, the book is organized around three research questions tied to different analytical scales to illuminate how multicultourism operates and distributes itself:

- *Scale 1: political multiculturalism and tourism in Mexico.* Taking the Magical Villages Program as a publicly profiled example of the fusion of multiculturalism and tourism in contemporary Mexico (2001–2014) embedded in a politically expressive emancipating desire to reduce cultural, economic, and social inequality through community empowerment strategies, how does the program contrariwise, as a majority-defined activity and social technology, contribute to maintain, enforce, and/or expand existing divisions, hierarchies, and asymmetrical power relations between mestizo majority society and indigenous minorities?
- *Scale 2: Cuetzalan.* Zooming in on an example of the example, how is the program enacted and negotiated in the Magical Village Cuetzalan by diverse groupings (mestizo and indigenous citizens, tourists, and newcomers) and political and educational institutions? Which kinds of identity and power configurations arise and clash?
- *Scale 3: Nahuas.* How do indigenous Nahuas of the surrounding communities position themselves in relation to Cuetzalan, tourists, and the Magical Villages Program? Which modes of participation does the program facilitate?

The first three chapters contextualize and introduce the work, its empirical material, ethnographic setting, methodologies, theoretical stance, and mode of analysis, while the final five constitute the analytical chapters. The research questions are geared to the analytical chapters in an accumulative sense, since the first research question crosscuts all analytical chapters, the second research question applies from Chapter 5 onwards, and the final research question applies to Chapters 7 and 8.

Chapter 4 analyzes how the generic Magical Villages Program has developed from its inception in 2001 to the point of the conducted fieldwork in 2013 and 2014, and it points to key social technologies within the program. In Chapter 5, some of these technologies are seen at work in a so-called Magical Villages meeting in which one group of locals discuss a consciousness-raising campaign with the aim of convincing other locals of the benefits of the program. Chapter 6 focuses on how the Magical Villages Program has organized the urban setting around particular conceptualizations of indigeneity that feed into a narrative setting, also analyzed through a travel magazine distributed locally and an interview with a newcomer from Mexico City.

Subsequently, Chapter 7 tunes in on a group of Nahua handicraft vendors from nearby San Miguel Tzinacapan and their attempt to turn the tourism into which they are inscribed to their own advantage. Cuetzalan's annual fiesta and its community queen pageant for young Nahua women of the surrounding area are the objects of interest in Chapter 8. That chapter demonstrates how identity configurations within settler versions of local history are reactivated in public by the recurring fiesta, and how these identity configurations are subtended by asymmetrical power relations that took shape when settlers took possession of the municipal capital and regional commercial hub, and which are reinforced by the Magical Villages Program. The book ends with an epilogue that discusses the social consequences of tourism for indigenous citizens as seen through the way it is developing in Cuetzalan presently.

Notes

1 For more on Gamio and anthropology's role in Mexican indigenism, see Brading (1988) and Lomnitz (2005).
2 Department of Anthropology (1918–1934), Autonomous Department for Indigenous Affairs (1935–1947), and National Indigenist Institute (1948–2002).
3 Indigenist state policies emerged differently and with varying intensity and duration across the Americas (Giraudo and Lewis 2012); however, the point is that Mexico played a crucial role in regionally promoting the idea of state policies specialized for managing and integrating the indigenous population.

References

Alivizatou, Marilena. 2011. "Intangible Heritage and Erasure: Rethinking Cultural Preservation and Contemporary Museum Practice." *International Journal of Cultural Property* 18(1):37–60.
Barnet-Sanchez, Holly. 2001. "Indigenismo and Pre-Hispanic Revivals." Pp. 42–44 in *The Oxford Encyclopedia of Mesoamerican Cultures: The Civilizations of Mexico and Central America*, vol. 2, edited by D. Carrasco. New York: Oxford University Press.
Baud, Michiel, and Annelou Ypeij. 2009. "Cultural Tourism in Latin America: An Introduction." Pp. 1–20 in *Cultural Tourism in Latin America: The Politics of Space and Imagery*, edited by M. Baud and A. Ypeij. Leiden: Brill.
Blackstock, Kirsty. 2005. "A Critical Look at Community Based Tourism." *Community Development Journal* 40(1):39–49.
Bonfil Batalla, Guillermo. 1989. *México Profundo: Una Civilización Negada*, 2nd ed. Mexico City: Grijalbo.
Brading, David A. 1988. "Manuel Gamio and Official Indigenismo in Mexico." *Bulletin of Latin American Research* 7(1): 75–89.
Brading, David A. 2001. "Monuments and Nationalism in Mexico." *Nations and Nationalism* 7(4):521–531.

Canessa, Andrew. 2007. "Who Is Indigenous? Self-Identification, Indigeneity and Claims to Justice in Contemporary Bolivia." *Urban Anthropology* 36(3):195–237.

Canessa, Andrew. 2016. "Paradoxes of Multiculturalism in Bolivia." Pp. 75–100 in *The Crisis of Multiculturalism in Latin America*, edited by D. Lehmann. New York: Palgrave Macmillan.

Doremus, Anne. 2001. "Indigenism, Mestizaje, and National Identity in Mexico during the 1940s and the 1950s." *Mexican Studies/Estudios Mexicanos* 17(2):375–402.

ECLAC. 2014. *Guaranteeing Indigenous People's Rights in Latin America: Progress in the Past Decade and Remaining Challenges – Summary*. Santiago: United Nations, ECLAC.

Forte, Maximilian. 2013. *Who Is an Indian? Race, Place, and the Politics of Indigeneity in the Americas*. Toronto: University of Toronto Press.

Fraser, Nancy. 1995. "From Redistribution to Recognition? Dilemmas of Justice in a 'Post-Socialist' Age." *New Left Review* 212:68–93.

Galinier, Jacques, and Antoinette Molinié. 2013. *The Neo-Indians: A Religion for the Third Millennium*. Boulder, CO: University Press of Colorado.

Giraudo, Laura, and Stephen E. Lewis. 2012. "Introduction: Pan-American Indigenismo (1940–1970) – New Approaches to an Ongoing Debate." *Latin American Perspectives* 39(5):3–11.

Gledhill, John. 2014. "Indigenous Autonomy, Delinquent States, and the Limits of Resistance." *History and Anthropology* 25(4):507–529.

Hale, Charles. 1999. "Travel Warning: Elite Appropriations of Hybridity, Mestizaje, Antiracism, Equality, and Other Progressive-Sounding Discourses in Highland Guatemala." *The Journal of American Folklore* 112(445):297–315.

Hale, Charles. 2002. "Does Multiculturalism Menace? Governance, Cultural Rights, and the Politics of Identity in Guatemala." *Journal of Latin American Studies* 34(3):485–524.

Hale, Charles. 2006. *Más Que un Indio (More Than an Indian): Racial Ambivalence and Neoliberal Multiculturalism in Guatemala*. Santa Fe, NM: School of American Research Press.

Hamel, Rainer Enrique. 2008. "Indigenous Language Policy and Education in Mexico." Pp. 301–313 in *Encyclopedia of Language and Education*. Vol. 1, *Language Policy and Political Issues in Education*, edited by S. May and N. H. Hornberger. New York: Springer Science.

Hollinshead, Keith. 2005. "Tourism and New Sense: Worldmaking and the Enunciative Value of Tourism." Pp. 25–42 in M. C. Hall and H. Tucker, *Postcolonialism and Tourism*. London: Routledge.

Jung, Courtney. 2003. "The Politics of Indigenous Identity: Neoliberalism, Cultural Rights, and the Mexican Zapatistas." *Social Research* 70(2):433–462.

Knight, Alan. 1990. "Racism, Revolution, and Indigenismo: Mexico, 1910–1940." Pp. 71–113 in *The Idea of Race in Latin America, 1870–1940*, edited by R. Graham. Austin, TX: University of Texas Press.

Lehmann, David. 2016. "Introduction." Pp. 1–34 in *The Crisis of Multiculturalism in Latin America*, edited by D. Lehmann. New York: Palgrave Macmillan.

Leimgruber, Walter. 2010. "Switzerland and the UNESCO Convention on Intangible Cultural Heritage." *Journal of Folklore Research* 47(1–2):161–196.

Lombardo de Ruíz, Sonia. 1993. "La Vision Actual del Patrimonio Cultural Arquitectónico y Urbano de 1521 a 1900." Pp. 165–217 in *El patrimonio cultural de México*, edited by E. Florescano. Mexico City: CONACULTA.

Lomnitz, Claudio. 2005. "Bordering on Anthropology: Dialectics of a National Tradition in Mexico." Pp. 167–196 in *Empires, Nations, and Natives: Anthropology and State-Making*, edited by B. de L'Estoile, F. Neiburg, and L. Siguad. Durham, NC: Duke University Press.

McNeish, John-Andrew. 2013. "Extraction, Protest and Indigeneity in Bolivia: The TIPNIS Effect." *Latin American and Caribbean Ethnic Studies* 8(2):221–242.

Norget, Kristin. 2010. "A Cacophony of Autochthony: Representing Indigeneity in Oaxacan Popular Mobilization." *Journal of Latin American and Caribbean Anthropology* 15(1):116–143.

Peña, Guillermo de la. 2005. "Social and Cultural Policies toward Indigenous Peoples: Perspectives from Latin America." *Annual Review of Anthropology* 34:717–739.

Peña, Guillermo de la. 2006. "A New Mexican Nationalism? Indigenous Rights, Constitutional Reform and the Conflicting Meanings of Multiculturalism." *Nations and Nationalism* 12(2):279–302.

Plant, Roger. 1999. "Indigenous Rights and Latin American Multiculturalism: Lessons from the Guatemalan Peace Process." Pp. 23–43 in *The Challenge of Diversity: Indigenous Peoples and Reform of the State in Latin America*, edited by W. Assies, G. van der Haar, and A. J. Hoekema. Amsterdam: Thela Thesis.

Rogers, Mark. 1998. "Spectacular Bodies: Folklorization and the Politics of Identity in Ecuadorian Beauty Pageants." *Journal of Latin American Anthropology* 3(2):54–85.

Sanz Jara, Eva. 2009. "La Crisis del Indigenismo Clásico y el Surgimiento de un Nuevo Paradigma sobre la Población Indígena de México." *Revista Complutense de Historia de América* 35:257–281.

Scher, Philip W. 2011. "Heritage Tourism in the Caribbean: The Politics of Culture after Neoliberalism." *Bulletin of Latin American Research* 30(1):7–20.

Scher, Philip W. 2014. "The Right to Remain Cultural: Is Culture a Right in the Neoliberal Caribbean?" Pp. 87–110 in *Cultural Heritage in Transit: Intangible Rights as Human Rights*, edited by D. Kapchan. Philadelphia, PA: University of Pennsylvania Press.

Sieder, Rachel. 2002. "Introduction." Pp. 1–23 in *Multiculturalism in Latin America: Indigenous Rights, Diversity and Democracy*, edited by R. Sieder. New York: Palgrave Macmillan.

Souza Lima, Antonio Carlos de. 2005. "Indigenism in Brazil: The International Migration of State Policies." Pp. 197–222 in *Empires, Nations, and Natives: Anthropology and State-Making*, edited by B. de L'Estoile, F. Neiburg, and L. Sigaud. Durham, NC: Duke University Press.

Speed, Shannon. 2005. "Dangerous Discourses: Human Rights and Multiculturalism in Neoliberal Mexico." *PoLAR: Political and Legal Anthropology Review* 28(1):29–51.

Spivak, Gayatri Chakravorty. 1993. *Outside in the Teaching Machine*. New York: Routledge.

Tarica, Estelle. 2008. *The Inner Life of Mestizo Nationalism*. Minneapolis, MN: University of Minnesota Press.

Tilley, Virginia Q. 2002. "New Help or New Hegemony? The Transnational Indigenous Peoples Movement and 'Being Indian' in El Salvador." *Journal of Latin American Studies* 34(3):525–554.

UNESCO. 2017. *World Heritage List Statistics*. Paris: UNESCO. Retrieved October 19, 2017 (http://whc.unesco.org/en/list/stat).

UNWTO. 2017. *Tourism Highlights: 2017 Edition*. Madrid: UNWTO. Retrieved October 19, 2017 (www.e-unwto.org/doi/pdf/10.18111/9789284419029).

Van Cott, Donna Lee. 2000. *The Friendly Liquidation of the Past: The Politics of Diversity in Latin America*. Pittsburgh, PA: University of Pittsburgh Press.

Van Cott, Donna Lee. 2006. "Multiculturalism versus Neoliberalism in Latin America." Pp. 272–296 in *Multiculturalism and the Welfare State: Recognition and Redistribution in Contemporary Democracies*, edited by K. Banting and W. Kymlicka. Oxford: Oxford University Press.

Warman, Arturo, Margarita Nolasco, Guillermo Bonfil, Mercedes Olivera, and Enrique Valencia. 1970. *De Eso Que Llaman Antropología Mexicana*. Mexico City: Nuestro Tiempo.

Wolfe, Patrick. 1999. *Settler Colonialism and the Transformation of Anthropology: The Politics and Poetics of an Ethnographic Event*. London: Cassell.

Wright, Robin M. 1988. "Anthropological Presuppositions of Indigenous Advocacy." *Annual Review of Anthropology* 17:365–390.

Yúdice, George. 2003. *The Expediency of Culture: Uses of Culture in the Global Era*. Durham, NC: Duke University Press.

2 Governing frames

This chapter discusses the implications of fusing sociologist Erving Goffman's frame analytical approach with post-Foucauldian conceptions of governmentality and power, and it synthesizes the analytical categories *frame, governmentality,* and *translocality* into a unitary mode of analysis captured by the term multicultourism. A fundamental theoretical premise is that frames direct our perception, thought, and action (Goffman 1986:10–11), for which reason control and distribution of frames is a prime concern in the operation and analysis of government. Multicultourism points to a mode of rule that forges cognitive and social relations across social spaces through tacit framings of Mexico as a post-discriminatory, multiculturalist society. What emerges is a highly mobile manner of directing collective conduct, which traverses and correlates social spaces with frame spaces, and this spatial analytical dimension is elaborated in a discussion of translocality. Additionally, the term multicultourism is itself devised as a frame to recast interpretation of such politics and its translocal effects. Finally, the resultant mode of analysis is specified by relating it to the empirical material.

Governmentality literature offers a rich framework for scrutinizing decentered modes of rule, not the least through the concept of self-government. However, the oftentimes uncompromising focus on regimes of practices and social technologies tends to abstract practices and technologies from the concrete settings, interaction arrangements, and animate entities that bring them into being. The identification of practices, rationalities, and social technologies sometimes conflates with their assumed causality and efficacy.

Therefore, this book favors a governmentality-inspired approach that includes social interaction into its empirical and theoretical platform. Goffman's interactionist approach is appealing since it focuses on the reflexive interplay between the liminal conventions that organize activity, experience, and meaning differently across social occasions (frames) and the structural conditions of social interaction (footing). Goffman not only engages with questions pertinent to governmentality studies, but amplifies the theoretical perspectives that underpin that line of research, while enriching the ontology of its empirical material.

Together, these discrete theorizing traditions stimulate an analysis of translocal governance that accords balanced attention to so-called top-down and bottom-up processes. The question of directionality – top-down versus bottom-up – is a long-standing controversy in constructionist research that depends on theoretical perspectives and units of analysis (Miller 2013). This book favors a flexible approach, since, as the ongoing debate and the theorizing traditions applied illustrate, the question of directionality in social processes is always ambiguous, as is the metaphor of vertically arranged hierarchies of power (Ferguson and Gupta 2002).

Governmentality: analytics and philosophy

Departing from his genealogical analyses of exercise of power, Foucault applied the concept of governmentality to designate a growing aspect of and way of thinking about government that gives preeminence to what he described as the "conduct of conduct" (Foucault 1994:237). That is, a mode of governance exercised *for* the population and *on* the population by working *through* it (Cruikshank 1999:3–4). Governmentality studies highlight the productive qualities of power as they materialize through knowledge forms, practices, and social technologies that look to manage and rule groups and individuals by giving shape to particular forms of subjectivity and incentivizing particular modes of action, being, and reasoning (Villadsen 2006:11–14). The primary object of regulation is thus human subjectivity, which is sought shaped in directions that align the aims and actions of citizens with norms and visions that inform governance. Citizens are thereby instrumented in practices and processes of rule, and assist in ruling by exercising self-regulation and by prompting others to perform equal modes of self-regulation. As a philosophy or strategy of liberal government, it presupposes an autonomous subject with a free will and capacity to act rationally for and on itself, as well as the feasibility and necessity of government to demarcate the space of autonomy and direct the free will of that subject. Consequently, governance seeks to construct collaborative citizens that identify with and assume the logics, objectives, and values that inhabit prevailing political rationalities, and citizens simultaneously become the loci, instruments, and outcomes of political intervention (Cruikshank 1999:3–6; Dean 2010:37–44).

Because the governmentality optics regard subjects as constructed with restricted personal autonomy, governmentality-oriented research tends to split into two analytical foci that produce different accounts of agency; one highlights the autonomy of the subject and the other highlights constrictions on the subject (Miller 2013:264). Each focus implies a preferred analytical order; the former employs a bottom-up view that emphasizes human capacity to act self-determinedly regardless of social technologies, and the latter employs a top-down view that emphasizes how social technologies constrict and shape human self-determination. The implications of each analytical order run deeper, as the bottom-up perspective assumes the existence of a primordial or non-regulable domain of the self, from where the subject can glimpse and resist external regulation. Conversely, the top-down perspective reflects a degree of determinism in assuming that regulatory initiatives are by and large effective, holding that a condition of human subjectivity is that the self is always already regulated and regulating.

Diverging conceptualizations of self and government divide the debate and double the complexity of the notion of self-government. Moreover, the existence of top-down and bottom-up analyses stresses that there are, grammatically speaking, no definitive subjects and objects of rule, but rather an ongoing positioning in which all entities are both subjects and objects, and always stand in a reflexive subject–object relation to "self." Thus, in various ways, governmentality studies have pursued Foucault's project of decentering the state in questions of power by inspecting how power emerges through diverse social relations and networks that cut across the dictum of division between the state and civil society and public and private domains (Villadsen 2006:11–12). Here, Foucault's notion of power as productive (Miller 2013) gains relevance, since a focus on how power opens up paths and possibilities for certain groups and subjectivities equally opens a doorway to the repressive flipside.[1] The structuring of possibilities involves composing and demarcating a field of action. These are the crucial theoretical perspectives this book employs. Although several scholars have sought to convert these insights into an analytical apparatus, their analyses rarely demonstrate the flexibility and mobility that characterize the mode of rule they set out to inspect.

The influential governmentality theorist, sociologist Mitchell Dean, offers a materialist analysis of "regimes of practices" that scrutinizes the rationalities, technologies, and visions that inform these practices and their way of constructing subjects (Dean 2010:30–44). Dean thereby consciously devotes more attention to the role of government practices in shaping subjectivities than to practices of the self involved in regulating subjectivity (Dean 2010:20). Yet such restricted analysis evades the locus of government – the subject in action – and offers minimal room for examining how concrete subjects come into being, beyond the image envisioned by social technologies. Rather, the analysis remains at the level of discursive, idealized practice, excluding social practice or the practice of practices. The analysis thereby omits the connective processes that produce, *or not*, the social beings that may be discursively conjured from regimes of practices. In short, the subject of such analysis is identified discursively, not socially.[2]

Yet, as political scientist Barbara Cruikshank argues, self-government is much more encompassing than we tend to think (Cruikshank 1999:89–103). To Cruikshank, democratic government rests on our reflexive capacity to conjure, problematize, and transform our conduct, and therefore governing is constituted by what "we do to our selves" rather than what is "done to us by those in power" (Cruikshank 1999:91). Governance thus relies on technologies that produce active democratic citizens by forging links between social order and individualized aims and aspirations, and these technologies often surge outside of government, within social movements and the social sciences (Cruikshank 1999:91–92, 101–102). Technologies of citizenship thereby produce citizens by making individuals self-regulating and active in particular ways. Cruikshank thus argues that a fundamental condition for "the conduct of conduct" is self-government. Nevertheless, like Dean, she stays on the discursive side of practice by distilling certain kinds of subjects from inspected technologies of citizenship. This way, Cruikshank argues that self-government stands central in democratic practice, while opting out of the empirical domain within which practices of self-regulation are situated.

One side effect of such approaches is an intellectualized take on governmentality that escapes consideration of how desires and emotions enter into the equation. Arguing that governmentality does not necessarily produce coherent rationalities, anthropologist Monique Nuijten shows how the Mexican government apparatus continually re-emerges to invoke state-backed hope of social justice in marginalized groups by presenting ever-new political "openings" to remedy their social situation and past injustice. By working through the aspirations and desires of its citizens, even the most marginalized groups are instrumented in practices of rule that sustain the idea of a just state focused on treating all citizens equally. Political openings invoke desires and images of a brighter future, yet they are bound to prescribed, bureaucratic procedures that obstruct alternative political modes of action. The primary effect produced by government practices on a marginalized community inspected by Nuijten (2004:210) thus appears to be a disempowering negation of total disempowerment, which debilitates political subject positions in total opposition to state institutional policies.

Nuijten's observations emphasize that the work involved in conducting conduct is more diverse and subtle than oftentimes argued. As cognitive and neuroscientific research stresses, decision-making and reasoning is intricately tied to embodied experience and emotions (Lakoff 2008). Conducting conduct, then, involves both head-work and heart-work, yet it does not necessarily require shared rationalities, but rather the co-production of intersecting interests. Nevertheless, the exclusive selection of empirical material disembodied from concrete subjects and social settings appears to be ruling out considerations of how governmentality ties in with and translocalizes local politics and social relations as well as desires and emotions. This has the unfortunate effect of overlooking the many ways in which individuals with different social locations enter into governmental processes.

If power emerges through social relations and networks that cut across societal scales, then analysis of rule should encompass the interface between policies and citizens, where social relations and roles come into being, that is, the concrete institutional, organizational, and social settings into which policies are inscribed and interact with subjects. Moreover, if the governmentality optics tune in on the productive aspects of power to problematize clear-cut notions of directionality in rule and knowable distinctions between subject and object relations – between acting and being acted upon – governmentality studies amplify such ambiguities by empirically remaining on the discursive level of official policy, stopping short of analyzing how governmental technologies operate in action within concrete settings. If government creates particular self-regulating subjectivities, then this process must materialize through some sort of interaction.

An additional analytical gear is arguably required to process the empirical layer within which concrete subjects exercise self-rule. The following section makes a case for combining key insights from the governmentality framework with Goffman's frame analytical approach, stressing how actors are simultaneously constrained and produced by discursive and interactional frameworks, and how these frameworks equally inform each other and prompt different types of narratives and identities.

Frame governmentality

If modern exercise of power is characterized by a sway toward *incentivization* and persuasion rather than coercion, then rule has necessarily become a profoundly didactic activity. Within this vision, rule bases itself on the stipulation of social categories and roles with which subjects are prone to identify and which hold out a desirable place and plan for them within the envisioned social order.

From this perspective, however, self-government is a somewhat deceptive term. Self-government implies a reflexive subject–object relation of self to self, but self-regulation inevitably occurs in response to something or some situation. Acts of self-government derive their sense as such through their link to a causative entity that transposes some degree of causativity to the subject in question; government manifesting itself through self-government. The efficacy of rule rests on the distribution of social technologies, and this distributive process, while dependent on self-regulation, must somehow precede it. Yet the strict focus on subject formation as the basis for self-government carries with it an unstated view of the self as a definite entity that is essentially enduring and stable. Subject formation implies a process of change within the self; the self is to be reworked and then self-regulates accordingly.

Turning to the work of Goffman, self-government emerges as an extensively commonplace practice and basic condition of being. In Goffman's approach, the self is adjustable, always interdependent, and cannot be dissociated from the social situations and interpersonal relations through which it operates. The self is not just formed experientially. At any given moment, selves are structured into social activities, social relations, and settings, and vice versa, and so the individual brings as much to the social situation as the social situation brings to the individual.

In *Frame Analysis*, Goffman (1986) shows that human thoughts and actions are guided by socially organized assumptions and expectations, and that human beings have the basic social capability to quickly identify activities and their implicit rules, roles, and logics. The capability of human beings to interpret, make use of, and externalize the framework within which they operate arises doubly through socialization. First, socialization exposes human beings to a wide variety of conceptual frames that become familiar and naturalized. Second, socialization as a condition of social life also induces human beings with a sensitivity to conceptual frames, which creates the condition for directing socialization through unfamiliar frames (Goffman 1986:33; Lakoff 2008:1–15). The ability to perceive what is going on, what others perceive to be going on, and what others perceive one perceives to be going on, and so forth in social encounters is the basis for adequately estimating how to contribute to and participate in them. Thus, when human beings operate within social frameworks, they are simultaneously structured and socialized into the roles, rules, and logics that inform these frameworks. Activities make individuals active in particular capacities, and while active in those capacities they strengthen familiarity with the activity, its requirements, and its inherent social order. While some frames are ephemeral and have little lasting consequence, other frames congeal and become integral to the organization of particular social institutions.

There are parallels between Goffman's concept of frame and the concept of *paratext* as developed by literary theorist Gérard Genette (1997), which may be understood as a frame attached to a text to mediate it.³ Since the paratext provides instructions on how to read and understand the text it encloses, it holds the potential of (re)shaping the reception of the text by establishing an authoritative reading and representation of it. The concept of paratext thus shares the mediating function frames also assume, and this book occasionally applies the term paratext to frames that have crystallized and obtained an enduring mediating permanence.

Even though human beings act and think through conceptual frames, the frames are never totalizing entities, and may change within and across social occasions and settings (Goffman 1986:40–82). Likewise, frames never correspond to individuals in their entirety; they merely activate individuals in certain roles that delimit modes of inference and participation. Thus, how subjects act in various social situations is not simply a matter of expressing inner states of being, but of identifying the requirements presented by various social arrangements and gearing individual involvement to those requirements.

Nevertheless, familiarity with particular conceptual frames and their integral modes of reasoning is likely to be enhanced in individuals through frequent repetition, routinization, and training, and this is the case even if one is engaged in negating a particular social frame (Lakoff 2008). The conduct of conduct thus involves a sustained effort to install and keep particular frameworks in force across settings, and so frames can be naturalized and come to structure social life across different settings, although their stability rests on institutionalization and repetition. Social scientist Michael Billig demonstrates exactly this in his seminal work on *Banal Nationalism* (Billig 1995). Billig shows how the nation is constantly "flagged" in everyday life and how the national frame structures the way people think about, speak about, and belong in the world, yet the very ubiquity of this frame and the routinized reactivation of it makes it largely invisible to its members as a social framework. Constant reactivation thereby makes social frameworks exist within and around individuals.

Given that individuals are both structured *and* socialized into conceptual frames, a governmentality framework would ideally highlight long-term subject formation and the instantaneous ways in which subjects are structured into varying social arrangements. By showing how individuals interact and navigate socially by intuitively orienting to frames, Goffman's late work (Goffman 1981, 1986) helps to illuminate the loci and processes of regulation and self-regulation. Frames organize interaction and facilitate focused social encounters by producing shared understandings so that attention is effectively directed toward the social situation as it is framed rather than toward the framing of the situation. Frames operate as subtle social technologies, since they engage citizens in particular activities, which incentivize particular modes of conduct invested in interpretational schemata that bring a larger meaning to individual actions. Frames are thus foundational sites of government, and to show these technologies at work social interaction needs to be included into the empirical domain, since this is where frames are negotiated and subjects are regulated. A focus on frames is thus compatible with the governmentality theoretical perspectives on self-government and decentered exercise of power, since rule is highlighted as an immensely dispersed activity that also ricochets among citizens. Frame governmentality can therefore help show *how particular modes of rule disperse themselves to emerge as a decentered activity*.

Translocalization of frames as governmentality: multicultourism in Mexico's Magical Village

The concept of translocality is applied across the humanities and social sciences to consider globalization issues by directing attention to the political and social processes through which spaces are fused, places and identities are shaped, and human beings, things, and ideas travel, and notably how these processes make themselves felt in concrete localities (Greiner and Sakdapolrak 2013). The approach prioritizes analysis at the 'receiving' end of globalization to show how global currents are processed through national and local sieves, and how global hierarchies come to expression in particular social settings. Translocality is a concept well-suited to a constructionist theoretical framework since it highlights the processual and relational aspects of place and identity by situating local dynamics within wider social dynamics that transgress any single locality. In this book, translocality is mobilized to tune into a frame governmentality that forges connections and identifications between places, and on that account gains purchase on local processes and partakes in organizing the political field. In short, the approach focuses on the translocalization of frames as a type of governmentality that organizes local involvement with national and global issues. Translocalized frames are thereby terrains within which notions of the global, the national, and the local conflate.

The introduction charted central aspects of the international human rights development that gave rise to the concept of multicultural citizenship within Latin America. This development was part of a global reorientation from Keynesian economic policies toward neoliberalism, which coincided with a shift in the balance of claims-making by social movements, turning from class-based claims of socioeconomic redistribution to culture-based demands of recognition (Fraser 2008:103–108). Since citizenship issues are fixed to membership of particular nation-states, this broader multicultural turn is one to be handled by individual nation-state governments. Nonetheless, state citizenship does not apply equally across national or urban territories, nor across variegated collective and individual social locations such as ethnicity, gender, and age (Yuval-Davis 2011:48–49). Multicultourism thus departs from a global discussion on social justice, democratic participation, and cultural recognition for minority groups and a global marketization of social relations, yet multicultourism materializes as a nationalized response to these global tendencies, while nevertheless expressing itself across and within concrete social settings with historical, social, and socio-economic complexities of their own. Correspondingly, the Magical Village is a singular national label that looks to cushion a global discussion on multicultural citizenship in national terms and yet couch it in localized terms across disparate social settings and their varying internal social divides.

This intermingling of processes should be taken into account in discussions of citizenship to show how global, national, and local historical and social processes conjoin to produce places and identities, and how the processes studied situate each other (Svensson 2014). Accordingly, this book stresses the asymmetrical yet open-ended process of translocalization between poles differently located within hierarchies of authority. Places and people are inscribed into translocal currents and relations, constituted by interactional flows subtended by unequal processes of filtration and interpretation. Central to these translocal processes are issues of belonging on various scales and their infusion with particular places, subjects, and local politics with a historical and social life of their own. At stake is thus a politics of belonging (Yuval-Davis 2011) that comes across through the governance of translocal identities in which the Mexican nation reinscribes itself into a new global order and channels a new global order into the nation. The issue, then, is not so much the "production of locality" (Appadurai 1995) as the governmental production of translocality by which global and local issues are fused into the frame of the nation.

To analyze the translocalization of frames means to inspect the seamless process of hyphenation that brings the self into a particular self-relation relative to a frame that asserts a particular socio-spatial order. Translocal frames operate decentrally, but they are only partly configured from these localized positions, since the frames do the job of fusing together notions of the local, the national, and the global. Translocal frames thus infuse places into national and global hierarchies and provide cognitive resources for subjects through which to interpret and define for themselves a meaningful role and place in society.

Mode of analysis

Frame, governmentality, and translocality are the three analytical categories that configure the mode of analysis. Since frames guide perception, thought, and action, frames are units of primary interest to a frame governmentality analysis, and the dispersal and reception of frames across social spaces are the central social processes to be analyzed. The mode of analysis is now further specified by introducing key analytical concepts and relating them to the analytical categories and empirical material.

As Goffman has shown, frames are particularly accessible to analysis through instances of interaction, since interactants continuously monitor and transmit cues as to the frames that are in force. This is so because frames define the portion of social reality that is relevant to the given activity and relative to which interactants can be held morally accountable. Consequently, frames are infused with certain "schemata of interpretation" (Goffman 1986:21) through which an activity, and contributions to it, are given meaning, and by which interactants reach a shared understanding that organizes their differentiated involvement. Interaction thus centers on "coordinated task activity" (Goffman 1981:140–143) with a particular worldview and "interaction arrangement" (Goffman 1981:153) that integrates and distributes certain modes of participation – the "participation framework" (Goffman 1981:137) – and preferred manners of contributing to the activity – the "production format" (Goffman 1981:144–152).

An integral part of interaction, then, consists in interactants offering framing cues as to how their actions and words are to be interpreted, and inspecting these practices is an entry point to the analysis of frames. A condition of interaction is that utterances emerge connected to their source, and the task of recipients is not to discern connections, but to correctly identify how acts and sources are connected verbally and otherwise. For this reason, "connectives" – the linking together of source and action – tend to be received with "unguarded security," and constitute an effective means for fabricating experience (Goffman 1986:479–480).

In a reworking of his frame analytical apparatus, dubbed *footing*, Goffman (1981:124–159) pulls out the structural means by which individuals craft strategies of representation and discursive positions in the interactional negotiation of truth and authority. Frames codify the interaction arrangement, and thus structure the range and applicability of interactional positions – the *footing* – that interacting individuals can successfully adopt. In reverse order, analysis of footing leads to the analysis of the frame space that defines social encounters.

Arguing that the terms *speaker* and *listener* are far too rudimentary to yield an understanding of participant roles in interaction, Goffman segmented both terms into further analytical types to identify the positions, alignments, or "footings" interactants adopt in relation to their own and others' utterances. Departing from any utterance, the participation status of each interactant may be determined by their individual relation to the utterance, while the relation of all members to the utterance, and, in extension, to the entire collective activity being undertaken, can be understood as the participation framework. Zooming in on the speaker, Goffman sets forth three analytical types that constitute the production format of an utterance: *animator, author*, and *principal*, which identify the varied positions speakers may attach to their own and others' utterances. The animator is the one uttering the words, the author is the one who has selected the words that are being uttered, and the principal is the one whose position is being established through the utterance. The category animator stresses that a speaker is not necessarily to be taken as composer of the words uttered (author) or as representative of the point of view expressed (principal), but sometimes assumes a capacity as mere "sounding box" (Goffman 1981:144–145). All three functions may of course merge in a single entity, but often they do not, since even when they may appear to do so, the speaker may be sketching a divide between a previous version of self, who is made principal (and responsible) of the rendered viewpoint against which a new self emerges to express another current, more viable viewpoint that distances the former self. The concepts thus distinguish between three types of sources in interaction by their degree of commitment to the communicated message. As sociologists Steven Clayman (1992) and Nick Hartland (1994) have demonstrated, Goffman's analytical categories are highly useful in showing how people make claims to authority, neutrality, and truth by drawing external agents into their talk as sources that appear to operate independently of the speaker. Any piece of material, whether activity, object, talk, text, and so forth, can be analyzed through the applied approach when articulating a particular "participation framework" and "production format" (Goffman 1981:124–159), and when a concrete subject's engagement with and within these can be drawn forth analytically.

Since government is increasingly spatially dispersed (Fraser 2008:124–130), and since interaction arrangements integral to government may saturate social life and relations in multifarious ways, the more diverse the empirical material, the richer the analysis of governance. To this end, this book adopts a bricoleurist stance to the selection of empirical material, holding that it is in their combination that the different types of source material gain substantial analytical currency, since frames may cut through any aspect of social life.[4]

The analysis includes as empirical material government documents and press releases, Magical Villages Program documents, newspaper articles, institutional interaction, public space, public texts, travel magazine texts, field notes, interviews, and public ritual. Asking about the modes of participation in and production of social interaction brings to the front the "interaction arrangement" (Goffman 1981:153) as a mode of rule, complete with capacities, roles, responsibilities, and rights granted to diverse citizens within the envisioned social order.

Frames thus embed activities and interaction arrangements, and the analysis focuses on identifying how multicultourism cuts across diverse media and settings to emerge as a translocal frame that defines activities and organizes involvement in and across social settings. This approach requires granting a broad meaning to the concept of interaction, and incorporating diverse kinds of empirical material that constitute and are constituted by transversal interaction arrangements.

To trace the temporal dispersal of frames, the analysis alternates between diachronic perspectives and synchronic perspectives. The diachronic moves (see Chapters 4, 6, and 8) are intended to destabilize synchronically anchored frames, and subsequent synchronic moves (see Chapters 5, 7, and 8) are intended to bring the frames to view in action. The diachronic move constitutes one type of deconstruction, facilitating another type of deconstruction, the synchronic move. These moves bring the frames to view as social technologies.

Since multicultourism comes alive in concrete localities, where global, national, and local hierarchies blend, the question of spatial dispersal refers primarily to the means through which multicultourism inserts itself into localized social relations and settings. Nevertheless, for such analysis to materialize, it also has to identify the extralocal properties of the phenomenon, which can be done only by incorporating empirical material from additional domains.

A focus on the translocalization of frames and interaction arrangements points to the distribution of ideas, participatory roles, and social values, and how such orders enter into and create social settings; it draws forth a translocal frame governmentality. Frames are the point of encounter between causativity and self-regulation, and analyzing these frames in motion offers insights into situations in which concrete subjectivities are being negotiated in particular ways and within concrete settings. Tuning in on instances of interaction helps to situate rule by providing spatial and temporal loci to the processes through which social technologies are activated and dispersed. Thereby, some of the limitations on governmentality as mode of rule are also brought to view. Governmentality can only ever be partly successful, since it requires that subjects identify and engage with the roles envisioned for them by government, and such roles are received differently depending on social locations. With this in mind, some sort of politics of belonging (Yuval-Davis 2011:10–21) appears to be at work, and this can be inspected by focusing on frames and interaction arrangements.

Notes

1 As Foucault showed in his *historicization* of government, productive and repressive aspects are constitutive of all power relations (Dean 2010:28–30). Nancy Fraser (2008:127–128) argues that a global governmentality has recently emerged to segment groups according to their degree of individualized participation in market competition. While successful participants rely on self-regulation, less successful participants are met with "brute repression."
2 The question arises as to whether one could arrive at anything else than a discursively situated subject. However, since discursive formations are socially situated, subjects that make use of these discursive formations could be said to be so located too.
3 The paratext may consist of diverse media such as cover illustration, title, introduction, afterword, author interviews, and literary prizes (Genette 1997:7–8).
4 The assumption is not that such an approach will produce an 'exhaustive' analysis, only that such approach allows the analysis to emulate the mode of rule it traces by directing attention to the capacity of frames to disperse into and organize almost any aspect of social life. This approach gives the analysis a performative twist that facilitates a better understanding of how multicultourism works than what could be addressed in purely verbal terms.

References

Appadurai, Arjun. 1995. "The Production of Locality." Pp. 204–225 in *Counterworks: Managing the Diversity of Knowledge*, edited by R. Fardon. London: Routledge.
Billig, Michael. 1995. *Banal Nationalism*. London: Sage.
Clayman, Steven E. 1992. "Footing in the Achievement of Neutrality: The Case of News-Interview Discourse." Pp. 163–198 in *Talk at Work: Interaction in Institutional Settings*, edited by P. Drew and J. Heritage. Cambridge: Cambridge University Press.
Cruikshank, Barbara. 1999. *The Will to Empower: Democratic Citizens and Other Subjects*. Ithaca, NY: Cornell University Press.
Dean, Mitchell. 2010. *Governmentality: Power and Rule in Modern Society*, 2nd ed. London: Sage.

Ferguson, James, and Akhil Gupta. 2002. "Spatializing States: Toward an Ethnography of Neoliberal Governmentality." *American Ethnologist*, 29(4):981–1002.

Foucault, Michel. 1994. *Dits et Écrits: 1954–1988, vol. IV, 1980–1988*. Paris: Gallimard.

Fraser, Nancy. 2008. *Scales of Justice: Reimagining Political Space in a Globalizing World*. Cambridge: Polity Press.

Genette, Gérard. 1997. *Paratexts: Thresholds of Interpretation*. Cambridge: Cambridge University Press.

Goffman, Erving. 1981. *Forms of Talk*. Philadelphia, PA: University of Pennsylvania Press.

Goffman, Erving. [1974] 1986. *Frame Analysis: An Essay on the Organization of Experience*. Boston, MA: Northeastern University Press.

Greiner, Clemens, and Patrick Sakdapolrak. 2013. "Translocality: Concepts, Applications and Emerging Research Perspectives." *Geography Compass* 7(5):373–384.

Hartland, Nick G. 1994. "Goffman's Attitude and Social Analysis." *Human Studies* 17(2):251–266.

Lakoff, George. 2008. *The Political Mind: Why You Can't Understand 21st-Century Politics with an 18th-Century Brain*. New York: Viking.

Miller, Leslie. 2013. "Foucauldian Constructionism." Pp. 251–274 in *Handbook of Constructionist Research*, edited by J. A. Holstein and J. F. Gubrium. New York: Guilford Publications.

Nuijten, Monique. 2004. "Between Fear and Fantasy: Governmentality and the Working of Power in Mexico." *Critique of Anthropology* 24(2):209–230.

Svensson, Birgitta. 2014. "Fördjupning 12: Globaliseringens många ansikten." Pp. 1023–1036 in *En Samtidig Världshistoria*, edited by M. Sjöberg. Lund: Studentlitteratur.

Villadsen, Kaspar. 2006. "Forord til den Danske Udgave." Pp. 9–25 in *Governmentality: Magt og styring i det moderne samfund*, by M. Dean. Forlaget Sociologi: Frederiksberg.

Yuval-Davis, Nira. 2011. *The Politics of Belonging: Intersectional Contestations*. London: Sage.

3   Working the translocal field

To be able to analyze a mode of government, which seeks to efface itself as such by populating social relations, and which in its most potent form atomizes into self-government, a set of methodological moves are required that tune in on the social, spatial, and temporal axes by which government is distributed. The book thus brings processes of government into view by organizing analysis around diachronic axes and synchronic snapshots and along the discursive and interactional continuums that tie together space and social groups, and by searching out the changing boundaries and constraints on modes of government. To do so, the analysis has to trace the translocal movement of government and how it is situated in concrete settings and through concrete practices (Gupta 1995:375–378). The implication is that the local is always translocal, and, to highlight such aspect analytically, research methodologies need to be designed for identifying connections between localities with an eye to the historical contingency of such connections. The major methodological challenges in this regard are thus the intertwined questions of how to transcend the seemingly local and the seemingly stable.

The chapter provides an overview of the conducted fieldwork, the field, and methodological considerations involved in identifying and processing the empirical material. The chapter increasingly turns to a processual view to show how a translocal field and a diachronic dimension emerged during the research, and how in response empirical material was resignified and methodologies reshaped. To put it in simple terms, findings in one domain often had implications on findings in another.

Fieldwork in the Magical Village

Linguist Una Canger first brought my attention to Cuetzalan, which matched my initial research criterion of being a tourist town in a majority indigenous area where I could apply my knowledge of Classical Nahuatl. Canger knows Cuetzalan well and could already brief me on several citizens who would be likely to contribute to my research. A search on the Internet instantly found that Cuetzalan had been part of the large-scale national tourism program Magical Villages since 2002, and it was clear that the program suited the research theme. I was no less intrigued to find that Cuetzalan has been figuring on Mexico's tentative list of

UNESCO World Heritage since 2006, knowing already from Canger that the *voladores* ritual, which figures on the UNESCO Intangible Cultural Heritage list, was performed there during weekends and festivities (UNESCO 2017a, 2017b).[1]

From the outset, then, the research was anchored in a translocal web of connections, rather than in the locality Cuetzalan, and already while planning the fieldwork I was "composing the translocal field" (Hannerz 2003:25–28). This realization enhanced the viability of doing short-term problem-oriented ethnography in Cuetzalan, and stressed that fieldwork would need to trace the direct and indirect making of connections between Cuetzalan and various other settings.

One obvious way to prepare for the on-site field experience was to mine SECTUR's official website of documents to learn about Mexican tourism policies and the Magical Villages Program. The scope of that task was much more encompassing than initially envisioned. At that time, I reflected little on the ephemeral character of the empirical material retrieved, and the task seemed to consist of simply finding 'the' official program document, and so I did, without paying attention to the curious detail that 'the' document offered on SECTUR's website was digitally datable to 2009, eight years after the launch of the program.

Another way of preparing for fieldwork consisted of reading existing academic literature on Cuetzalan. Notably, two PhD theses by sociologists Gabriela Coronado (2000) and Louisa Greathouse-Amador (2000) deal with tourism and interethnic relations in Cuetzalan just prior to its inclusion into the Magical Villages Program, which created ground for drawing in a historical perspective and gave an impression of the ethnographic setting.

The on-site fieldwork took place in January and February 2013 and in September and October 2014. While the first round of fieldwork fell into the low season of tourism, the second round was planned according to the annual peak of community life and regional tourism, the town fiesta held in the beginning of October (see Chapter 8). This division of the fieldwork into low and high season produced contrasting experiences, both of which form part of social life in town.

The early fieldwork was guided by two main aims. The first was to identify signs of presence of the Magical Villages Program within public space, and the second was to outline how different groups participated in the program and tourism. These aims composed a provisional strategy for identifying central ways in which Cuetzalan and the Magical Villages Program were being tied together.

The attention to signs of presence was inspired by urban architect Anja Nelle's study of strategic interventions into public space in World Heritage Towns in Cuba, Mexico, and the Philippines. Nelle devises an approach that examines urban environments according to two kinds of features: the ones that assist in producing a historic image and facilitate "time-travel," and the ones that are tied to "contemporary life" (Nelle 2011:77–79). By examining the distribution of these features, Nelle demonstrates one way to inspect the management and production of public space within a UNESCO heritage framework.

Upon arrival, it was readily apparent that the Magical Villages Program had a more direct presence than the one envisioned in Nelle's methodology, and "signs" of presence took on a literal meaning. Attention was directed at obvious program objects such as display boards, street signs, and shop signs, which carried the official program logo. I also visited the Municipal Office of Tourism to see which, if any, promotion materials were circulating. To my surprise, I received a lavish 32-page promotional travel magazine, sponsored in part by SECTUR and the Mexico Tourism Board, Visit Mexico. Printed in color on coated paper and richly illustrated with photos from Cuetzalan's fiesta, the magazine showed indigenous people in ritual vestments performing ritual activities. The magazine had been issued in 2012 in celebration of Cuetzalan's decennial anniversary as a Magical Village. Such direct references to Cuetzalan's participation in the program pervaded public space. In the ethnographic museum, which displayed mestizo versions of local history side by side with indigenous material culture, the narrative culminated with a display board pointing to "the millenary cultures" and "World Heritage" that constitute "a living past" and for which "Cuetzalan has been designated as a Magic Town."

Tellingly, even the logo of the municipal government had incorporated the program logo and title into its design (see Figures 3.1 and 3.2). The Magical Villages Program thus inhabited public space quite explicitly, manifesting Cuetzalan's being a Magical Village as an overarching community identity. This trivial observation was significant for how subsequent fieldwork was organized, since it became apparent that all citizens, regardless of their degree of involvement with the program and tourism, could be expected to adopt some kind of position relative to the program.

Figure 3.1 The logo of the municipal government (2011–2014) – the capital C represents the headdress used for the *cuezali* dance into which the Magical Villages logo has been inserted; the logo condenses the strategic efforts to link Cuetzalan's designation as Magical Village to the indigenous heritage

Source: Municipal government, Cuetzalan

Figure 3.2 Cuezali headdress

Source: Casper Jacobsen, October 2014

Following what Cruikshank argues about social movements, the question became one of finding out how the program was shaping "the terrain of political action" (Cruikshank 1999:6). Although there is an inside and outside to the Magical Village, there is, from the perspective of such an approach, no inside or outside to the program, and on-site fieldwork would need to identify how different groups participated and how the program organized the field.

Four key groups to the research

By following Canger's lead, I struck upon two individuals belonging to two influential groups in town. One was O, a shop owner, event-maker, and freelance IT specialist for the municipal government when I arrived in 2013. At that point, he was working on getting into the tourism business and had just been admitted to the Municipal Council of Tourism, a civil advisory board with the task of coordinating private and public efforts to strengthen tourism. In 2014, he was part of the municipal government staff concerned with administrating tourism. Knowing O opened many doors, and he became my pass to a Magical Villages meeting, and he also secured me an interview with the Municipal Director of Tourism.

O was part of a group of citizens who were eager to volunteer their professional assistance to the municipal government through public committees dealing with tourism. Their prime concern with tourism was to make it grow in a way that would increase demand for their professional skills and services. As illustrated by O's road to the municipal administration, it was a question of cultivating and filling out a need for their professional expertise within the public system. For this purpose alone, the Magical Villages Program was considered pivotal to their careers, since it has been generating an increasing workload on the municipal government, which needs to document, evaluate, manage, and promote tourism in ways that increase demand for their services. If nothing else, the program has the long-term effect of generating public employment for tourism professionals. For others, their assistance was a potential platform for influencing municipal tourism policies in a direction of benefit to their individual businesses – hotels, restaurants, travel agencies. For yet others, the Magical Villages Program was seen as the sure path to a profitable tourism, and time invested would return as dividends from tourist wallets.

Benito was the other local contact associated with another influential group in town. I still recall entering his always busy shop and how he ejected from his seat with the phrase, "Let me tell you about the Magical Villages!" when I inquired about the program. Before I could blink, Benito escorted me through a series of dark back rooms leading to his café next door, where I was seated and served a cappuccino while he passionately told me all about the problems with the Magical Villages Program, instructing me to "report *that* to your university!" Of particular concern to him was the dramatic increase in the number of street vendors, who disturbed not only tourists by begging them to buy something, but also the magic scenery. As Benito rightly stressed, the Magical Villages Program forbids ambulant vending, and Benito wanted ambulant vendors off the streets and relocated to a building outside the town center where they would have all the facilities they would need. I had already met many of these vendors and knew that the overwhelming majority were Nahua women and children from nearby San Miguel Tzinacapan and San Andrés Tzicuilan, who struggle with extreme poverty. After our talk, I found myself in yet another uncomfortable scene. Exiting the café, I first noticed a sign prohibiting ambulant vendors from entering (see Figure 3.3), and then, as I looked to the street, found myself being greeted by a group of vendors from Tzinacapan with whom I was trying to get acquainted.

Benito single-handedly arranged interview sessions with municipal chronicler Hernando and shop owner Virgilio, both of whom Benito stressed were knowledgeable about town history. The insistence Benito showed in effectuating these meetings was duly honored by Hernando's insistence that we could not talk before I knew town history, about which he then lectured me. Disquieting as it was to be force-fed a version of local history that began with the arrival of settlers in the 1850s and narratively obliterated the Nahuas, the experience made me glimpse connections between practices of settler history-making, the performance of identities in the annual town fiesta, and the multicultourism, which is at the base of the Magical Villages Program. It turned out Benito, Hernando, and Virgilio were all

Figure 3.3 Sign prohibiting ambulant vendors from entering Benito's café

Source: Casper Jacobsen, January 2013

descendants of early settlers, which explained their fascination with town history and Hernando's privileged position as sage. For this group, the heritage dimension to the Magical Villages Program was a prime concern, since it not only tied in with family history, but was also seen as the engine of tourism.

Then there was the cosmopolitan crowd, newcomers from large Mexican cities, particularly Mexico City and Puebla, and a few from abroad. Being myself identifiably an outsider, newcomers was a group of people to which I was rapidly introduced. Already, in Mexico City, I heard of Lucas from Europe who had moved to Cuetzalan six months earlier. Lucas introduced me to other newcomers, one of whom was Ernesto, a cultural activist who had been active in the Other Campaign of the Zapatista Movement in 2006.[2] The campaign had brought Ernesto to San Miguel Tzinacapan and he decided to move to Cuetzalan to focus his political work on this part of the Sierra. Another newcomer was Lucinda from Mexico City, who had been living in town from 1988 to 1992, before spending years abroad in the United States and Europe. She had returned to Cuetzalan in 2012 with the hope of starting up private English teaching, perhaps also a café, and finding a more peaceful life. Nevertheless, in 2013, Lucinda left town, disillusioned by the combination of poor business opportunities and the irony of finding small-town life obsessed with making it big. Common to the cosmopolitans was their fascination with indigenous cultural heritage and their antipathy toward the Magical Villages Program.

Of final consideration are the Nahua ambulant vendors from Tzicuilan and Tzinacapan. With the exception of a few boys, this group is composed of women and girls from some of the poorest families in those towns. As was the case for Maria in 2013, the vending of handicrafts was the sole source of personal income, yielding so little that most days a 14-peso round trip by bus was simply unafford-able and on other days a luxury that would erode the day's income. I was puzzled to see that many of the handicraft vendors came to town most days of the week during low season, and not just during weekends when some degree of tourism was to be expected. At first, I suspected that sales were perhaps better than they tended to indicate, but from what I could observe next to nothing was sold. Their presence in Cuetzalan appeared to be something of a conundrum during most of the week, since their efforts appeared hardly to be economically worthwhile. Part of the answer is, of course, that however slim the income of vending would turn out to be, going to Cuetzalan constituted a slightly better alternative to staying in Tzinacapan, where there was no opportunity of vending their goods. In 2014, Maria had found part-time work and went to Cuetzalan only on weekends and holidays. Nevertheless, even during the annual fiesta, the high point of regional tourism, she and her 6-year-old daughter Yolani were selling frighteningly little. As argued in Chapter 7, it appears that the vendors were engaging in something of potentially much more significance to their lives than the casual vending of low-cost items; they were aiming to establish meaningful translocal relations with visitors. For the vendors to conduct this activity successfully, being on the spot in Cuetzalan when tourists arrived was pivotal.

Probing the field through interviews

One of the effects of interviewing people on the topic of tourism and the Magical Villages Program was that it prompted interviewees to make sense of and reflect on their position vis-à-vis the program. In preparing interviewees for interviews, I therefore stressed that I was looking for their personal views, qualifying any type of reaction or account they might have for the topics we would discuss. During the introduction, I would present myself and explain that I was doing a study on life in Cuetzalan and was interested to know more about tourism and the Magical Villages Program. Such an introduction allowed me to set the topic of discus-sion, yet the emphasis on personal experiences and opinions was equally meant to encourage interviewees to take some degree of control of the conversation.

The interviewees by no means constituted a homogenous group, and they responded differently to my way of interacting with them. While some inter-viewees reacted nervously due to their apparent uncertainty of what I wanted to know from them, other interviewees hijacked the interview and dismantled my preconceived notion of coming with authority. Those interviewees were male, significantly older than me, had locally notable educational backgrounds, and held prestigious positions as municipal chroniclers. As mentioned, munici-pal chronicler Hernando maintained that we could not discuss my topics before I knew about local history (see Chapter 8).[3] Consequently, 57 minutes passed before we reached present-day Cuetzalan and what I conceived as the topics of interest. Another interview with municipal chronicler Cecilio lasted a measly 26 minutes, before I was told to return when I had more questions.[4] Despite such problems, the interview technique worked well in most cases. In my interview with newcomer Ernesto (see Chapter 6), I suppressed a growing desire to interrupt him, as he launched our talk – for no apparent reason, as I experienced it in the situation – by outlining the life and whereabouts of the *mythistorical* pre-Hispanic figure Topiltzin Quetzalcoatl.[5] I desperately wanted to bring him to the 'real' topic and let him know that I knew all about Topiltzin Quetzalcoatl so we could cut to the chase. Luckily, I retained that pressing desire and finally realized that Ernesto was explaining his own life and whereabouts through reference to the pre-Hispanic mythistorical past. Had I interrupted him, I would not only have missed a fascinating account; I would also have displayed a notable insensitivity by dismissing an autobiographical account that contextualized his life and ensuing accounts. As in other cases, the interview flowed nicely and touched on issues pertinent to the research without a need to be in strict control of the interview.

Regardless of the question of effecting direct control, the interview situation demanded some kind of active positioning from the interviewees in relation to the Magical Villages Program. Indeed, without such active positioning there would have been no (meaningful) interaction within the frames of the concrete interview situation. A fundamental assumption structuring the interview situation, then, was that the Magical Villages Program mattered *somehow* for the interviewee and that basic assumption was only strengthened by my coming all the way from Europe to learn about the program and its workings in Cuetzalan.[6]

While this interactional premise carries with it the obvious danger of overestimating the role of the program in local life, this mode of interaction was useful since it requested interviewees to construct social positions for self and others in relation to the program. To that end, the interviews conducted during fieldwork may be regarded as sources to the ways in which people made sense of the Magical Villages Program and their engagement with it, when directly requested to do so.[7]

Since meaning-making is never an individual effort, but must take into account and respond to conflicting views (Gubrium and Holstein 2009), interviews also became sources to common sourcing practices related to the program. Intriguingly, as Goffman has shown, sourcing has the finality of constructing a web of exterior agents that appear to be independent of the agent doing the talking (Goffman 1981:124–159). By engaging in interaction structured around the Magical Villages Program, I became familiar with how the program was employed as a source to and resource in local political discussions, and how various social groups invested their own positions with authority and delegitimized conflicting positions. Dedicating time for undisturbed talk in confidential settings allowed for such positions to be elaborated in ways that were less feasible in the bustle of everyday business or among fellow citizens with opposing views. On a practical level, interviewing also simply helped me to keep track of whether I was engaging with different groups in terms of age, ethnicity, gender, profession, and social position.

In total, 23 formal interviews were conducted with the participation of 24 individuals. People referred to from the ethnographic record have been anonymized by name, and personal information that would serve to identify them has been omitted almost invariably. Nonetheless, individuals who were selected for interview due to their professional capacity have not been anonymized (completely) as to profession, since this capacity gives extra weight to the positions established through the interview situation. However, since several individuals often hold the same titles, and since institutional positions are transitory and several individuals have entered and exited the positions referred to, the individuals in question are not readily identifiable.

Fifteen of the interviewees are male and nine female. The unequal distribution in terms of gender probably reflects the varying importance gender groups ascribed to their own words. Men in all ages were very willing to share their opinions with me, while women, except for newcomers and those holding prominent positions, tended to doubt the utility of their opinions, sometimes referring me to their husbands.

Distribution in terms of ethnicity was unequal too. Seventeen interviewees were mestizos (six of whom were newcomers), three were Nahuas, three were Totonacs, and one came from Europe. One reason for the unequal distribution is that mestizo Cuetzalan was the primary field site and that incoming Nahua vendors were predominantly women. Interviewing them appeared to be out of reach due to their marginalized position in terms of ethnicity, gender, and socioeconomic status. It was my conviction that arranging formal interviews would only enhance the asymmetries of our relation, and spontaneous conversation when hanging out with them and tagging along was instead my preferred mode of interaction.

Concluding each interview, I would ask if the interviewee knew of additional topics of potential interest to me. Interviewees rarely provided extra information, although in one case Maria used the opportunity to flip the script and ask me a question departing from our discussion of travelers becoming co-parents to Nahua children. How did *I* experience and feel about the way people from San Miguel Tzinacapan had received me and my family? Maria thereby clearsightedly opened the door to a self-exploration that was central to the questions I had been posing. The self-reflection Maria requested from me inspired me to make myself my own informant concerning these interpersonal relations between Nahuas and travelers (see Chapter 7), and her comment equally stressed the translocal underpinnings of our relation.[8]

While arranging interviews with the incoming Nahua vendors seemed largely out of reach, getting into conversation with them was easy, since both parties had an interest in creating some kind of relationship. In general, getting into conversation posed no problem, and least of all when I was moving about with my family. The following section highlights connections between the now-defunct notion of the isolated field and the ongoing tendency to exclude accompanying family from ethnographic accounts, and the subsequent section reflects on how the presence of my family accentuated the translocal underpinnings of the research situation.

Transcending isolation: the family and the translocal field

In his *Argonauts of the Western Pacific*, anthropologist Bronisław Malinowski sets forth three principles of ethnographic method, of which the most basic is that the ethnographer should "live without other white men, right among the natives" (Malinowski 1966:6). For a long time, this principle figured in ethnographic writings as the spoken or unspoken ideal of proper fieldwork, often conceptualized as the lone male ethnographer's individual rite of passage in a distant community, disconnected from the home community and "the company of other white men" (Malinowski 1966:6; Okely 1996:33, 41). To safeguard fieldwork from contaminating influence, ethnographic studies have favored rural villages as field sites, which were perceived to have limited contact to a broader political and societal sphere, and hence to be "more pure" (Pelto and Pelto 1978:179; Berger 1993:179–180). The presence of other non-Others in the field not only threatened to pollute the object of inquiry, but also posed a threat to the ethnographer's ability to become immersed in the studied community. Such was the assumption, even though the field situation of Malinowski himself diverged from the ideal presented in his work (Okely 1996:38).

The isolated community with a bounded culture therefore appears to be an object "made rather than found" (Gupta and Ferguson 1997:2–3). The same can be said about the lone ethnographer given that this ideal is fundamentally tied to the conceptualization of bounded community culture and how to do fieldwork in such a place. The prevailing ideal of solitary fieldwork indicates why accompanying families rarely figure in ethnographic accounts, even though their mere presence significantly molds the fieldwork (Flinn 1998; Poveda 2009). Although it is well acknowledged that ethnographers and their personal and cultural baggage enter into the research, self-reflection has rarely been extended to include accompanying family, even though family members form part of the ethnographer's perceived and perceiving self.

Anthropologist Barbara McGrath argues that unstated assumptions about ethnography underlie the tendency to omit the family from fieldwork accounts. To do proper ethnography, the ethnographer needs to be immersed in the studied community, a process thought to occur more easily when the ethnographer brings "few personally identifying characteristics" into the field. Downplaying the role of family in fieldwork thus works to minimize the perceived threat of family to immersion, and consequently to protect the validity of the research (McGrath 1998:61–62).

Nonetheless, ideas about site purity and the lone ethnographer belong to the days when the ethnographic project was conceived as a holistically descriptive enterprise that organized itself around standard themes such as kinship relations and economic, religious, and social organization. Perhaps because research categories in community studies were largely invariable, ethnography has been understood to study certain localities or people rather than certain cultural or social phenomena *in* certain locations or *among* certain people (Geertz 1973:22). Beginning in the 1950s, however, ethnographic studies in Latin America have turned toward a problem-directed approach (Mulhare 2000:12–13), sparked by increasing attention to processes of modernization, nationalization, and globalization, which has generated a perspective on rural communities as neither internally homogeneous nor isolated from broader economic, political, and social currents and networks.

Given this theoretical reconfiguration of what constitutes the field, and consequently how fieldwork may be organized, Cuetzalan is not the archetypical field site of early ethnography it might seem to be. Though it is a Mexican mountain village in a majority indigenous area far from larger cities, Cuetzalan hardly exists in isolation from the surrounding world, having experienced growing tourism since the 1970s. Moreover, Cuetzalan's entry into the national tourism program Magical Villages in 2002 has tied the federal and state governments into a prime economic activity in town. That these political and social circumstances could be glimpsed from the other side of the planet and were the crucial factors that brought me to Cuetzalan only emphasizes the significance of translocal connections to social life.

It therefore appears that my and my family's presence in Cuetzalan together with that of (other) tourists and newcomers could be taken as situated embodiments of this translocality, which would entail a view of Cuetzalan as a connecting point. This would imply that translocal connections were as important to the way we were positioned in the field as they were to the way we positioned the field. For instance, while the concierge in our Mexico City hotel was perplexed to hear about our plan of an extended stay in Cuetzalan ("*Nobody* goes to Cuetzalan!"), no one in town wondered about our being there. After all, Cuetzalan is a Magical Village. Methodologically, this opens for considering how the ethnographic research itself entered the translocal meaning-making it had set out to find.

Accompanying family or participating family?

How our being in Cuetzalan tied in with translocal meaning-making was the last thing on my mind before our departure.[9] As a first-time father, most of my concerns prior to the fieldwork revolved around Julius: Could we get the stuff we needed for him? Would we be able to find an accommodation that could meet our different needs? A place in the town center would be most suitable for the fieldwork, but would such a place be compatible with Julius' strong sensitivity to noise and his need for three daily naps? How would we traverse a hillside town with a baby? Then, realizing that the logistical challenges were infinite, I began to imagine us never managing to leave our accommodation. Many of these concerns disappeared as we got to know the village and our daily life became routinized, although we did face some serious logistical challenges. Simultaneously, I came to understand that I had been misguided in thinking that *I* would be doing *my* fieldwork; much of the time, *we* were doing fieldwork *together*. My family was not merely accompanying me; it was participating in and influencing the fieldwork through emotions, practicalities, symbolic values, and mere presence.

The biggest challenge was to locate a suitable home. Tellingly, we ended up staying at six different places, never managing to find, as we had hoped, two quiet rooms with access to a kitchen, but instead switching from one noisy single-room accommodation to the next with sleep-deprived Julius. Although the many moves were exhausting, they provided a brutally explicit view of local sufferings during low season; each and every hotel we stayed in and inspected was empty or, usually during weekends, near-empty. The single exception to this happened during a long weekend, when the town center suddenly filled up with tourists for two days. Most of the time, then, hotels were excellent conversational settings, since desk clerks and managers had plenty of time to talk and were unlikely to be interrupted.

Another advantage brought about by the many moves was that we came to know most parts of the village very well. Contrary to my initial fear, we did find time to walk the village. Indeed, because we lacked access to a kitchen, we came to rely on eateries, which kept us on the move during the day. In several places with little customer activity, the staff took care of Julius during the meals. This not just spurred spontaneous conversation, but also secured our return, and for each return ties were strengthened.

Luckily, we had brought a backpack-like child carrier that eased transport of Julius. The carrier caused much attention from locals, who were smiling, laughing, pointing, or complimenting Julius when we moved about. With Julius on my back, getting to talk to people was easy. We rarely approached people to talk because people approached us instead. The encounter almost always started with them inquiring about us (i.e. Julius) than the opposite, and it became apparent that, first and foremost, many locals saw Louise and me as a parenting couple, and the lot of us as some variety of a tourist family, which caused the field situation to be turned upside down. Within the first week, we had become familiar faces in town and were transformed into local versions of ourselves. Now we were *Julio, Louisa*, and *Gaspar*, and *Julio* was the most famous baby in town – a local celebrity sometimes affectionately referred to as *Niño Dios*, meaning *Baby Jesus*. Incidentally, we had arrived just in time for the Catholic celebrations of *Baby Jesus*, and, apart from reflecting Julius' well-timed arrival, the appellation conveyed his perceived likeness with the emblematic version of *Baby Jesus*: a white baby with fair, wavy hair, and *Advertisement Baby, Calendar Baby*, and *Gerber Baby* covered related themes.[10] Corresponding with what anthropologist Joan Cassell argues about her own children's celebrity roles during fieldwork in Jamaica (Cassell 1987:19–23), Julius not just represented our locally perceived status and wealth, but embodied an access point to our family unit and its locally ascribed values, and, perhaps because of this, he became a platform for verbalizing straightforward perceptions of class and race.

Julius also became the entry point of conversation with the Nahua handicraft vendors. In the beginning of our stay, child vendors would often approach us by catching Julius' attention with toys they handed to him for inspection, while adults would establish eye contact by making a hiss that attracted Julius' attention. Conversation would first center on Julius and then move to other topics. Later, as we got to know people, conversation flowed more freely, but Julius neverthe-less played an important intermediate role. As an integral part of engaging with the locals, they came to carry him around, which spurred informal conversation and created mutual trust, while the care involved induced a sense of intimacy. In short, thanks to Julius, our circle of acquaintances accelerated beyond anticipation to the point that (due to tragic circumstances) we became honorary participants at the nine-day vigil of Esperanza after having spent only three weeks in Cuetzalan. The devastating news reached us several days late, and in the meantime a group of mourning relatives and friends had been scanning town to locate us. During the daily vigils, we were placed next to the mourning mother, whom we had not previously met, and family members discreetly asked us to comfort her, implicitly stressing that our participation was important. It remains uncertain whether we became honorary guests merely due to our friendship with Esperanza and her affection for Julius, and to which degree our ascribed class and race status mattered. What can be asserted, however, is that Esperanza ran an eatery that we had frequented habitually exactly because we were traveling with a baby. Our limited mobility and tendency toward repetitive routines actively shaped our relations. We stayed longer in fewer loca-tions than had we traveled without a baby.

Some locals, however, initially faced us with skepticism. Isabel, a Nahua handicraft vendor from Tzinacapan, appeared noticeably dismissive toward Louise and me. We also felt that when Isabel carried Julius in her arms, she was testing us by moving slightly out of sight. This feeling was justified when one time, Lila, a young girl of the group, with whom we had a close relation, spon-taneously got up from a bench and said she would follow Isabel and keep an eye on Julius. When, at a stroke, Isabel's attitude toward us changed, Julius was the source of this change. I was trying to get a better grasp of local co-parenthood practices because I had a hunch that the handicraft vendors were attempting to establish co-parenthood relationships with incoming tourists. Inquiring about this topic was a delicate matter, and I eventually thought of asking with reference to Julius, explaining that it would be useful for me to know how co-parenthood relationships come into existence in Cuetzalan. Inadvertently, and without real-izing it, I had encouraged the group to find a co-parent for Julius. Four days later, we met Isabel, who was suddenly smiling and laughing, joyously notifying us that her mother "had accepted" to become co-mother of Julius.

Doing fieldwork with my family naturalized my presence in the field doubly; traveling as a family not just corresponded well with local ideas of family, but also kept me largely in the areas where one could expect to find tourists. My family role, which was played out in public, became perhaps the prime optics through which I was seen. I saw the contrast situation only on solitary excursions to nearby villages, where people did not know me and approaching people for conversation seemed less natural.

Alternating between solitary and family excursions made me think about the degree to which we are positioned and how such relations shape our field experi-ences. Generally, when I was with my family, informal conversations centered on family and daily village life, but conversations departed from the way we were positioned by the field. When I was out on my own, conversations departed from my notions of the field, and my research topics thus came to create the premise of the dialogues.

Exiting the Magical Village

Shortly into the fieldwork, I was becoming unsure of how the Nahua communities fitted into the Magical Villages Program. I was beginning to see that tourism in Cuetzalan and Cuetzalan's participation in the program are tied to the symbolic inclusion of Nahua communities and cultural heritage, yet apart from this symbolic role, the Nahua communities were not involved in running the program. Therefore, a strict focus on the people 'in charge' of the program and the representation of Nahua culture would risk reproducing the asymmetries I was beginning to note. The ethical aspect of this concern, combined with my academic interests, prompted me to devote much of my time to being around the Nahua street vendors. I also found it necessary to exit the Magical Village and do fieldwork in neighboring Tzinacapan, where most of the incoming vendors lived. This was an important move, since community identity in Tzinacapan is decisively defined in opposition to community identity in Cuetzalan. This stood out more clearly in Tzinacapan than in Cuetzalan, but, more importantly, my being there provided testimony to our shared understanding that Tzinacapan had something important to offer that could not be found in Cuetzalan. My presence in Tzinacapan was thus ascribed significant weight because it embodied a translocal connection that is otherwise channeled into Cuetzalan. Tourists go to Cuetzalan, not to Tzicuilan or Tzinacapan, and so residents from Tzicuilan and Tzinacapan must go to Cuetzalan to meet tourists. To see myself as an embodiment of translocal structures, I had to transcend the Magical Village and experience the paradox of living 'outside' the Magical Village, yet 'within' the program, and methodologically I had to embrace how my own presence entered into a translocal meaning-making fixed to the program.

This dawned on me irrevocably when I read my early field notes as a coherent text before the follow-up fieldwork. At that point, the notes had changed their status as a source within the research. They no longer comprised a mere inventory of conversations, observations, and "salient" experiences, but emerged instead as entry points into the "tacit" interaction orders that had structured encounters and interpretation during fieldwork (Wolfinger 2002:89–92). Within the field notes, the textualized fieldworker thus emerged as a figure on par with additional figures, and the textualizer who had been selecting what to report and how emerged as an informant. The field notes thus became a source to the tacit cooperation between fieldworker and textualizer, but also to the tacit, often unclear cooperation between fieldworker and interlocutors. To be sure, the textualizer holds the final authority to include and omit observations and occurrences and imbue them with salient significance; however, upon reading the notes, it also became clear that interlocutors had effective means of imbuing activities, encounters, and topics with pertinence. As anthropologist Barak Kalir (2006) argues, reflections on fieldwork methodology often endow the fieldworker with maximized agency by portraying how the ethnographer has purposefully acted in and on the field, and less attention is granted to show how the field has acted on the ethnographer. One reason, of course, may be that our own strategizing is less hazy than the strategizing occurring around us, especially in unfamiliar social environments. Furthermore, as anthropologists Bruce Jackson and Edward Ives note, fieldwork methodology is intricately tied to accounts on fieldwork, which are inherently retrospective and lead to purposive reports structured by conclusions and outcomes (Jackson and Ives 1996).

What makes early field notes a fascinating and vital source is that they are not purposive in quite the same way as later field notes, because they are written before discursive and social positions within the field are worked out to any reasonable degree. This fragmentary understanding of the field is a significant social handicap that gives interlocutors with a better understanding of the social setting an upper hand in social encounters. When positions are unclear, it is extremely difficult to interpret activities, gestures, and words, and often one has little clue as to what the received information is a source. This task has to be worked at through daily interaction with various groups and through retrospective reflection that incorporates fresh insights, and since field notes are filled with reports on interaction and provisional modes of grappling with their significance, returning to early field notes may provide significant insights into interlocutors' strategic engagement with the researcher. Early field notes are written in a state of *plotlessness* and are replete with unresolved inklings and queries. But in going back over these notes, many reported experiences can be reframed through now familiar plots. One can therefore redo 'participant observation' with increased attention to the ways in which one's own agency has been structured into social relations, and, in so doing, sources are reconfigured. Reported encounters with vendors from Tzinacapan, for instance, provided an opportunity to observe how they interact strategically with tourists to rapidly establish relationships that may stretch beyond their brief stays. Moreover, attempts by mestizo elites to introduce the practicing of intangible indigenous heritage into school curricula in Cuetzalan, which were presented as an altruistic gesture of recognition toward indigenous communities, suddenly appeared to represent a repressive politics seeking to dispossess indigenous communities of an effective resource for maneuvering in local politics. Nevertheless, to overcome the caring attitude of mestizo preservationists, one needs to know about the growing difficulty they face in recruiting traditional dancing troupes for Cuetzalan's annual festivity, and that reluctance of surrounding Nahua towns to participate is not about rejecting traditions, but fixed to local politics. Then, in turn, one may see how the Magical Villages Program contributes to a further identity political polarization, as Cuetzalan is designated Magical Village due to its indigenous heritage. And finally, the researcher, in returning to early field notes, may find that from the very beginning he emerged in the field as a translocal resource to local power struggles.

Revisiting the armchair

With limited time for on-site fieldwork, Internet research proved to be a productive way of retrieving empirical material on the Magical Villages Program from across the Atlantic. Mexico has been prioritizing government transparency through online access to public information since its Good Government Agenda from 2002 (OECD 2005:35–42), and since government documents were just a few clicks away, retrieving this kind of empirical material appeared to be a walk in the park. An afternoon's work trawling the websites of SECTUR and the Magical Villages Program yielded exactly the kinds of documents I was looking for: the official program document, policy statements about cultural tourism, and plenty more. During this initial phase, the analytical task materialized as a purely hermeneutical one. There was enough to do with getting hold of technical jargon, organizational structures, and modes of cooperation between government agencies and civil society. Nonetheless, for reasons unknown to me at the time, the analyses seemed always to be condemned to reproduce the terms of the program texts. The analysis was caught within the frames of reference the program had produced in advance and always came to match the descriptions the program made of itself. Obviously, the problem was a methodological one, but this realization did not bring me closer to breaking the conceptual frame of the textualized program.

The contours of the methodological problem presented itself when I struck upon a former program document, which had been labeled as the "final version." Finding this document pointed out a central part of the problem: the program resisted its own historicization. This made sense, since admitting to the existence of different program texts throughout its rather brief history would counter the central assumption guiding the program policies, namely that tourism can be cultivated through well-planned governance. While the obsession with planning is pervasive in modern management practices and politics, convincing people of the feasibility of planning tourism to develop in a progressive manner would be hampered by presenting a program biography that failed to sustain the program itself as an expression of thoughtful planning. At any given moment of its operation, the program's doings need to demonstrate the same adherence to and feasibility of planning as the program expects of its participants.

Now the problem consisted in retrieving previous program documents that had been replaced online by more recent documents. Apart from posing a threat to aspirations of democratic transparency through the right to information, the transition to e-government also constitutes a serious methodological challenge to research on political processes and governmentality-style analysis. What I initially assumed to be *the* program document and *the* official description were merely the most recent public projections of the program; I had been facing a synchronic snapshot that denied a diachronic dimension to the program.

The Internet Archive (www.archive.org) was an invaluable research tool in that respect. The archive had from March 2002 to September 2012 recorded

SECTUR's main web page 590 times, and from June 2004 to September 2012 it had recorded the Magical Villages subpage 149 times. Since documents linked to tend to be recorded too, the archive opened a diachronic dimension to an otherwise synchronic program matter, as earlier program documents re-emerged, and the revision history of the websites could be inspected.

By extracting empirical material from the Internet Archive, it thus became possible to sketch the program's diachronic movements and to inspect the program's operation and self-image at different moments throughout its course. This made me see that all research up to that point analyzed synchronic and ephemeral snapshots produced by *the* program document and *the* description on the webpage, thus strengthening the view of self, which is integral to the program, namely the notion that since 2001, it has proceeded in an orderly fashion by making use of such-and-such procedures. Moreover, the diachronic inspection facilitated a view of how the program at given moments has been positioning itself within the public realm and how it has been tying itself to the participant localities.

With this extended empirical horizon, it was possible to work against the program simply by tracing and juxtaposing the disparate program narratives and manuals that have emerged throughout its course. While each narrative operates within a conceptual frame established by the program, the emergence of a series of alternative frames assisted in their mutual deconstruction.

Returning

If the Magical Villages Program is in a continuous state of becoming, Cuetzalan too must be involved in a process of becoming a Magical Village rather than having been one since entering the program in 2002. From this perspective, the field emerges as an ongoing translocal identity project that constructs the nation, its citizens, and a social order complete with different modes of participation. Translocality, then, is a social process with a historical trajectory of its own, and inspecting the historical contingencies of translocality is a means of unraveling the dispersal of government. A diachronic view on translocal connections therefore serves to transcend the seemingly local.

The second round of fieldwork therefore increased attention to the diachronic constitution of the program in town. But even before returning, the diachronic perspective had transformed the previously collected material as sources. Now all types of material could be approached as different moments in a translocal interaction and pointed to how translocal relations were continually being recast and intensified.

The program objects in public space were no longer mere sources to a situated practice of representation vis-à-vis tourists. Interestingly, their moment of installation turned out to coincide with the wider attempts of the program to gain public prominence. Equally, a travel magazine that circulated in Cuetzalan during 2012 and 2013 could no longer be regarded merely as a source to how local authorities represented the town and indigenous heritage textually and visually for visiting tourists. It also became a source to a translocal interaction order within which

Cuetzalan continually needs to justify its place in the Magical Villages Program, and within which the program itself and the social order it envisions have become objects of veneration. As several analytical chapters show, modes of translocalization intersect with modes of temporalization, and these crosscutting processes protruded more clearly as social technologies in the follow-up fieldwork, as I experienced a changing urban setting with a changing cast and new ways of tying together Cuetzalan and the Magical Villages Program.

Notes

1 Five *voladores* (flying men/women) climb a pole of about 30 meters, at the top of which four of them tie themselves to a frame, while the fifth dances, drums, and plays the flute in all cardinal directions on top of the pole. Subsequently, the four *voladores* fall backwards into the air and spin around the pole before landing on the ground, while the fifth slides and climbs down one of the ropes.
2 The campaign ran during the 2006 presidential elections and sought to tie together communities and social movements across Mexico in an alternative political project to circumvent conventional party politics (Magaña 2014:70–71).
3 This narrative militancy indicates the importance of the perspective represented by the narrator – here, settler history and identity, the narrator himself descending from a locally distinguished early settler.
4 Apparently my questions were too probing, signaling to the interviewee that I knew too little to justify taking up his time. The interviewee was simply frustrated and wondered which *facts* I wanted to know about.
5 The term mythistory, coined by anthropologist Dennis Tedlock (1996:52), is used within Mesoamericanist research to convey a view on the past in pre-Hispanic Mesoamerica, which fused mythical events and figures with historical ones (Restall 2004:xvi–xvii).
6 Since the program inhabited town space explicitly, it could be argued that this framing of public space entered into the framing of the research and interaction.
7 And by noticing how interviewees constructed the positions of fellow citizens and to whom they would refer me, a rudimentary glimpse of social networks emerged.
8 My working language during fieldwork was predominantly Spanish, which is spoken by mestizos and the majority of the indigenous population. In engaging with the Nahua street vendors, I applied my Classical Nahuatl skills strategically, adapting them to what I knew about the Nahuat spoken in the area, to demonstrate my knowledge of the language. Some of the vendors picked up on this immediately and actively assisted me in expressing my interest in their first language.
9 An earlier version of this section appears in *University Post* (Jacobsen 2014).
10 These names further highlight dimensions of class and race in Mexican society. Gerber is a company known for producing baby foods, and the name refers to Julius' perceived likeness to the white baby model in the company logo.

References

Berger, Roger A. 1993. "From Text to (Field)Work and Back Again: Theorizing a Post(Modern)-Ethnography." *Anthropological Quarterly* 66(4):174–186.
Cassell, Joan. 1987. "'Oh No, They're Not My Shoes!' Fieldwork in the Blue Mountains of Jamaica." Pp. 1–26 in *Children in the Field: Anthropological Experiences*, edited by J. Cassell. Philadelphia, PA: Temple University Press.
Coronado, Gabriela. 2000. *Silenced Voices of Mexican Culture: Identity, Resistance and Creativity in the Interethnic Dialogue*. PhD dissertation, University of Western Sydney.

Cruikshank, Barbara. 1999. *The Will to Empower: Democratic Citizens and Other Subjects.* Ithaca, NY: Cornell University Press.

Flinn, Juliana. 1998. "Introduction: The Family Dimension in Anthropological Fieldwork." Pp. 1–21 in *Fieldwork and Families*, edited by J. Flinn, L. Marshall, and J. Armstrong. Honolulu, HI: University of Hawai'i Press.

Geertz, Clifford. 1973. *The Interpretation of Cultures: Selected Essays.* New York: Basic Books.

Goffman, Erving. 1981. *Forms of Talk.* Philadelphia, PA: University of Pennsylvania Press.

Greathouse-Amador, Louisa. 2000. *Cuetzalan y el Cambio Social: El Turismo ¿Un Agente de Transformación?* PhD dissertation, Benemérita Universidad Autónoma de Puebla.

Gubrium, Jaber F., and James A. Holstein. 2009. *Analyzing Narrative Reality.* Thousand Oaks, CA: Sage.

Gupta, Akhil. 1995. "Blurred Boundaries: The Discourse of Corruption, the Culture of Politics, and the Imagined State." *American Ethnologist* 22(2):375–402.

Gupta, Akhil, and James Ferguson. 1997. "Culture, Power, Place: Ethnography at the End of an Era." Pp. 1–29 in *Culture, Power, Place: Explorations in Critical Anthropology*, edited by A. Gupta and J. Ferguson. Durham, NC: Duke University Press.

Hannerz, Ulf. 2003. "Several Sites in One." Pp. 18–38 in *Globalisation: Studies in Anthropology*, edited by T. H. Eriksen. London: Pluto Press.

Jackson, Bruce, and Edward D. Ives. 1996. "Introduction: Ideas of Order." Pp. ix–xvi in *Reflections on the Fieldwork Process*, edited by B. Jackson and E. D. Ives. Urbana and Chicago, IL: University of Illinois Press.

Jacobsen, Casper. 2014. "Fieldwork with Baby Jesus on Your Back." *University Post*, May 13. Retrieved May 13, 2014 (http://universitypost.dk/article/fieldwork-baby-jesus-your-back).

Kalir, Barak. 2006. "The Field of Work and the Work of the Field: Conceptualising an Anthropological Research Engagement." *Social Anthropology* 14(2):235–246.

Magaña, Maurice Rafael. 2014. "Mexico: Political Cultures, Youth Activism, and the Legacy of the Oaxacan Social Movement of 2006." Pp. 67–84 in *Rethinking Latin American Social Movements: Radical Action from Below*, edited by R. Stahler-Sholk, H. E. Vanden, and M. Becker. Lanham, MD: Rowman & Littlefield.

Malinowski, Bronislaw K. [1922] 1966. *Argonauts of the Western Pacific: An Account of Native Enterprise and Adventure in the Archipelagoes of Melanesian New Guinea.* Prospect Heights, NY: Waveland Press.

McGrath, Barbara Burns. 1998. "Through the Eyes of a Child: A Gaze More Pure?" Pp. 60–70 in *Fieldwork and Families*, edited by J. Flinn, L. Marshall, and J. Armstrong. Honolulu, HI: University of Hawai'i Press.

Mulhare, Eileen M. 2000. "Mesoamerican Social Organization and Community after 1960." Pp. 9–23 in *Supplement to the Handbook of Middle American Indians*, vol. 6, edited by J. D. Monaghan. Austin, TX: University of Texas Press.

Nelle, Anja B. 2011. "Urban Intervention and the Globalisation of Signs: Marketing World Heritage Towns." Pp. 73–91 in *The Heritage Theatre: Globalisation and Cultural Heritage*, edited by M. Halbertsma, A. van Stipriaan, and P. van Ulzen. Newcastle: Cambridge Scholars Publishing.

OECD. 2005. *OECD E-Government Studies: Mexico.* Paris: OECD.

Okely, Judith. 1996. *Own or Other Culture.* London: Routledge.

Pelto, Pertti J., and Gretel H. Pelto. 1978. *Anthropological Research: The Structure of Inquiry.* Cambridge: Cambridge University Press.

Poveda, David. 2009. "Parent and Ethnographer of Other Children." *Anthropology Matters* 11(1):1–10.

Restall, Matthew. 2004. *Seven Myths of the Spanish Conquest*. Oxford: Oxford University Press.

Tedlock, Dennis. 1996. *Popol Vuh: The Definitive Edition of the Mayan Book of the Dawn of Life and the Glories of Gods and Kings*. New York: Touchstone.

UNESCO. 2017a. *Tentative Lists*. Paris: UNESCO. Retrieved October 19, 2017 (http://whc.unesco.org/en/tentativelists/state=mx).

UNESCO. 2017b. *Ritual Ceremony of the Voladores*. Paris: UNESCO. Retrieved October 19, 2017 (https://ich.unesco.org/en/RL/ritual-ceremony-of-the-voladores-00175).

Wolfinger, Nicholas H. 2002. "On Writing Fieldnotes: Collection Strategies and Background Expectancies." *Qualitative Research* 2(1):85–95.

4 The diachronic Magical Villages Program

Frames and technologies in motion

This chapter draws a diachronic sketch of the generic Magical Villages Program through analysis of publicly available material: government and program documents, newspaper articles, and press releases. The historicizing approach applied is indispensable for critically engaging with a program that has transformed greatly since its inception in 2001, yet which has consistently displayed itself through the static frame of multicultourism.

The strict use of publicly available texts has two purposes. First, a focus on the program's front-stage activities highlights how the program constructs and displays itself in front of the general public through different types of media. Second, by assuming no privileged access to undisclosed material and backstage processes, the chapter puts to test the aspirations of recent governments to political transparency; textual analysis and deconstruction of front-stage material will illustrate to which extent the general public is likely to glimpse the program's subtle workings.

A diachronic perspective facilitates deconstruction by highlighting the processual aspect of how the program has been constructed and displayed, which the chapter shows to stand in contradiction to the individual crystallizations that have emerged at various stages. To accentuate such contradictions, strips of front-stage activity are treated as signifiers in an evolving storyline that disrupts individual front-stage doings and calls for a reflection on the program's backstage processes.

As sociolinguist Charlotte Linde demonstrates, it takes serious amounts of narrative work to sustain continuity in institutional identity and memory under changing conditions (Linde 2009:9–10). By highlighting the contradictory interplay between an ongoing modification of program matter and a narrative display of continuity, the chapter renders visible a subtle social technology by which the program accumulates and exercises authority while consistently refuting such accumulation and exercise of authority. This does not mean that the program is only narratively wrapped in continuity, because certainly over time the program has announced structural changes. However, changes are always posited as necessary adjustments to preserve programmatic continuity or to release the original intentions within the program. Hence, change is fueled by ideas of continuity, and continuity rests in the frame of multicultourism.

Opening statements

On September 14, 2001, following the first State of the Union Address by President Vicente Fox (2000–2006), Secretary of Tourism Leticia Navarro (2000–2003) appeared in the Chamber of Deputies to elaborate on the government's tourism policies. Before concluding her speech, she took the opportunity to inform the deputies of a forthcoming national tourism program, Magical Villages, which was to stimulate social development in places with tourism potential. As announced, three towns were already included in the program, and it thus followed that the program was not just forthcoming, but already operating (Cámara de Diputados 2001).

In November, SECTUR published a National Program of Tourism 2001–2006 (SECTUR 2001) under the slogan "Tourism: the force that unites us," declaring that the National Development Plan 2001–2006 had made tourism a "national priority for its extraordinary capacity to generate economic and social development."

The document opens with an introductory endorsement by President Fox (SECTUR 2001:6–7). As a paratextual commentary, the introduction expresses the president's authoritative reading of his own policies, and thus preempts public reception of the policies by expounding on what they can be taken to mean and achieve. In short, Fox crafts and selects the frame within which interpretation of his policies may legitimately unfold.

In the first phrase, Fox presents a forceful critique of official Mexico by pointing to "a country that over many years attempted to categorize itself as culturally homogeneous, only at last to assume and admit its multicultural and multiethnic character" (SECTUR 2001:6). Apart from being an introspective critique of majority mestizo society, the phrase is directed at the Institutional Revolutionary Party (PRI) and its preceding 72-year hold of the presidency. The initial phrase therefore also serves the purpose of marking a clear temporal and ideological divide between PRI's policies, seen as homogenizing, exclusive, and of the past, and the policies of Fox's National Action Party (PAN), seen as heterogeneous, inclusive, and pointing toward an imagined multiculturalist future. By doing so, Fox equates PAN's rise to power with a widespread desire to break with the homogenizing of Mexico. He thereby disavows the old policies and appropriates a new political climate, presenting it as a logical consequence of PAN's inclusionary political ideology. A vision of inclusionary policies thus constitutes a vital part of PAN's claim to political legitimacy, and Fox provides testimony to this legitimacy by siding with the marginalized groups that have been negatively affected by earlier unjust policies, thereby firmly categorizing his text and the policies it introduces as acting on behalf of the marginalized. In other words, while Fox animates a critique of Mexico's traditional political elite, he does so by embedding two sources that invest his position with legitimacy and for which he makes himself an advocate: the Mexican people who elected him and an unspecified multicultural and multiethnic mass symbolizing PRI's inability to create equal democratic opportunities for all Mexican citizens. The announced political course is configured as coming 'bottom-down,' that is, from the people and to the people, President Fox being a mere intermediary between the 'two.'

The policies thus discursively devise a generalized citizenry and marginalized minorities as embedded agents, whose perspectives become founding justifications of Fox's tourism policies and his grip on the presidency.

Having established his position by rejecting earlier homogenizing national policies in which cultural and ethnic diversity figured as a national problem, Fox flips the coin, arguing that diversity could prove to be a solution to economic depression. To this end, Fox presents tourism as the space of recontextualization that will establish cultural and ethnic heterogeneity as a national resource: "Within tourism the diversity is precisely our grand capital" (SECTUR 2001:6).

While this first part of Fox's introduction criticizes past oppression of the diversity of the Mexican population, it also passes on a foundational idea inherent in the oppression, namely that multicultural and multiethnic dimensions are in their very essence national issues that the state needs to address politically (cf. Kernerman 2005). As Fox highlights diversity, he picks out for exaltation only expressions of a diversity that has the potential to be converted into "capital." Hence, only multicultural features that may generate an economic surplus may be defended, and not diversity per se. Fox thus conveys a hierarchical sorting of cultural elements according to their probability of generating economy, and this politically proclaimed hierarchy has repercussions beyond the mere application of tourism policies; it promulgates an affirmative multicultural recognition structured by market logic.

Contrasting a national North of "progress" with a national South of "nostalgia," "immense heritage," and "a glorious past," Fox stresses how a lack of opportunity has left "enormous capacities" unreleased in the South (SECTUR 2001:6). Fox then returns to tourism, characterizing it as one of the largest and fastest-growing industries in the world and emphasizing its positive economic impact in Mexico, while simultaneously stating that such impact has not translated itself into "social development." It thus follows that the "enormous capacities" residing in said inhabitants are of a cultural kind and to be triggered by inserting them into the national economy.

Having identified problems of social and economic development, hitherto unexploited resources among Mexican citizens, and a surging and "generous" tourism industry, all that remains is to combine these factors. The overarching presidential message is that the tourism industry will create the long-awaited opportunity for marginalized populations to release their otherwise dormant capacities, which will morph into social and economic development. Concluding his exposé of past, contemporary, and future Mexico, Fox addresses the program's slogan to mobilize Mexicans in the tourism industry: "[W]e cannot delay even one day further the important task of building the bridges that permit Mexican men and women to look upon themselves as one sole nation [. . .] and in this work tourism is also a powerful ally" (SECTUR 2001:7).[1] Although Fox's vision of tourism moves diversity and heterogeneity to the forefront, the surrounding frames of the nation and tourism industry are heralded for their ability to create homogeneity and unity.

The vision of cultural diversity as a resource to national economy and tourism resonates beyond Mexico. As anthropologist Philip Scher (2011) intriguingly argues, the growing appreciation of cultural heritage and increasing national measures to safeguard it coincide with radical shifts in the global economy, which have attenuated the sovereignty of nation-states. According to Scher, these developments have fostered a "neoliberal nationalism" in which government institutions incentivize the privatization of public culture (Scher 2010:199–201) and renew national sovereignty through practices of authentication, promotion, and surveillance (Scher 2011). Public culture has thereby become a domain of "biopolitical governmentality" (Scher 2010), as citizens are morally compelled to perform a national culture that can be branded in the global market in differentiation from other national cultures (Scher 2011). Neoliberal nationalism thus prompts its citizens to participate in an identity politics immersed in socioeconomic competition, since participation in the national economy depends on the ability to take hold of and profit from specialized identities that contribute to authenticated national culture.

Evidently, the National Program of Tourism encompassed much else than what Fox delimited; casinos, golf courses, marinas, and state-planned resorts were all part of the policies (SECTUR 2001:48 ff.). Nonetheless, its vision was firmly anchored in Fox's introductory framework, emphasizing tourism for its ability to create "cohesion," "national pride," and "a more equitable distribution of wealth" (SECTUR 2001:65). In more powerful terms:

> The present vision of tourism situates itself at the intersection of the two grand challenges that confront humanity [. . .]: the fight against poverty, and the conservation of the environment and the cultural heritage. Tourism is capable of contributing in the struggle against marginalization and poverty [. . .] through the creation of wealth, [. . . and] by utilizing the natural and cultural resources in a rational manner, [tourism] is an efficient ally in the protection of said heritage.
>
> (SECTUR 2001:68)

Hence, this vision of tourism embeds as principal sources the poor and marginalized, whose positions SECTUR assumes by announcing a "*struggle* against marginalization and poverty" and "the protection of [cultural and natural] heritage" [emphasis added]. Within this frame, SECTUR emerges as the protector of the poor and marginalized by showing them how to employ their "natural and cultural resources" in tourism to generate wealth.

Fox's introduction and SECTUR's vision are of relevance precisely because their overarching message came to be addressed by the Magical Villages Program; it carried into effect Fox's *speaking on behalf of the marginalized*.

The launch of a support program

Yet within the 175-page National Program of Tourism, merely half a page was dedicated specifically to the Magical Villages Program. Notwithstanding its brevity, this public starting point expresses a political commitment that justifies regarding it as representative of the emblematic intentions and foundational work-ings of the early Magical Villages Program.

In the National Program of Tourism, the Magical Villages Program was launched as part of an effort to strengthen domestic tourism (SECTUR 2001: 116–117). A two-line description categorizes the program, defines its target group, and identifies a demand: "Support program for typical villages with cultural-historical attractions of grand singularity, which are in need of conservation and improvement of their identity and urban image." Equally, the text states that recip-ient villages must have "tourism potential" *and* require "improvement of tourist services." An accompanying fact sheet lists the design of funding resources, the tourist segments addressed, the types of federal institutional support offered, and four prerequisite characteristics towns need to present to obtain the offered support. First, the village should be located close to tourist sites, and second be accessible by highway. Third, the village should present a historical or religious theme, and fourth there would have to exist "will" within society and government to participate (SECTUR 2001:168).

Despite its brevity, the description contains several inherent discrepancies. Participant towns should be both "typical" *and* display "singularity," and their "identity" and "urban image" are to be conserved *and* improved. These con-tradictions between the generic and the unique and between conservation and transformation also surface in the types of support offered. The program text offers assistance in designing regulations of public space to protect the urban image, but it equally signals which features the urban image should preferably present. The urban image up for protection, then, is not a present one, but one that is visualized through the types of support offered. Installation of street furniture, tourist signage, particular forms of pavement, and painting of facades according to a "chromatic palette" are both generically asserted improvements of the urban image *and* intentions to conserve existing unique, albeit typical, rural urbanities (SECTUR 2001:168).

The National Program of Tourism is, however, clear about the Magical Villages Program not being fully developed from the outset, and it explicitly rejects a "static" view of SECTUR's policies, proffering instead an ongoing adaptation to the changing field of tourism (SECTUR 2001:20, 60).

The rise of a brand

In August 2005, SECTUR, now headed by Secretary Rodolfo Elizondo Torres (2003–2010), introduced the biennial National Magical Villages Meeting. The first meeting took place over three days in San Miguel de Allende (Guanajuato), one of the 21 participant towns at the time. The meeting gathered mayors and committees from all participant localities and representatives from state and federal institutions to monitor participants' fulfillment of program obligations (SECTUR 2005a, 2005b). SECTUR thereby organized an event in which town representatives would have their work revised by teams of government officials with the aim of "strengthening" local efforts in tourism. Through their superior and specialized expertise, officials could thus mold local efforts with the pro-claimed purpose of maximizing profits for the receiving community, advising on how to modernize tourism businesses, and develop handicrafts, gastronomy, and commerce (SECTUR 2005a). Plenary presentation by local representatives was instituted to "share experiences" (Cámara de Diputados 2006), and Elizondo Torres highlighted the five most important Magical Villages as instructive tem-plates for success. These seemingly coordinating activities became founding practices of subsequent meetings. Yet the meeting additionally works as a cali-brating device of institutional memory and identity, providing an occasion for authoritative mediation of results, current status, and prospects for the future, sewn together under the headline of institutional continuity and strategic inten-tionality. This comes across in the inauguration speech by the secretary, who declared the program a success before iterating the origin and purpose of the pro-gram and reminding participants of the four criteria that had brought them into the program. After reeling off the first three criteria in conjunction, the secre-tary emphasized the final criterion concerning "will" to participate. In his speech, "will" figures as a mutual "commitment" to the program by the "community" and local "authorities." Stressing such will as determinant of incorporation into the program, the secretary redefines the criterion from being a prerequisite for admission to the program to being a requirement for *continued* participation. In this manner, the secretary stressed that the designation as Magical Village is not granted once and for all. Rather, participant villages and municipal governments need to continually demonstrate that they merit inclusion by activating program policies in coordination with state and federal institutions. Showing will to par-ticipate in the program thus means to implement the program's subject matter, which is defined (and redefined) by SECTUR. As will be shown later, the stress on this criterion reflected another modification underway; the initial top-down selection procedure to recruit participants for the program was soon substituted for a bottom-up application process.

During the meeting, Elizondo Torres announced an equally significant new direction:

> Magical Villages is also conceived as a brand, and to be able to support that, it has been necessary to develop and comply with a series of standards that guarantee the expectations of our visitors, who certainly will look for a dif-ferent experience, with a taste of Mexico.
>
> (SECTUR 2005b)

By presenting the "brand" function as a conception that originated with the program, the secretary naturalizes the otherwise sudden occurrence of a new marketing effort and he facilitates the creation of centrally regulated universal "standards" through which individual participant towns may be directed and cri-tiqued. The secretary thus crafts a new centralized subject matter to be imple-mented in the participant towns, and he ranks the central aims of the program above individual town interests. An inversion of the interaction arrangement and the participatory roles allocated to individual Magical Villages and SECTUR is implied. Now the "visitor" emerges to substitute a marginalized population as the principal of the program, requiring a fulfillment of expectations only SECTUR can pretend to know about. The "visitor" equally becomes principal of changes in policy, and SECTUR emerges as mere author of "standards" required by an external, abstracted agent. Hence, on behalf of visitors, government intervention is necessary.

To invest the brand function with authority, the secretary emphasized the total provisional program funding, MXN 294,000,000, pointing to the increase in funding throughout 2005, totaling MXN 93,000,000, before declaring: "To date, this program includes 21 populations backed by a brand that is positioning itself more and more on a national and international level" (SECTUR 2005b). Even as the brand function is launched and measures are introduced for its protection, it follows that the brand is already in effect and benefiting the participant towns. Furthermore, the brand function is legitimized by explaining national and international visits to the Magical Villages as direct consequences of brand potency. Hence, SECTUR's place-branding strategy becomes the connective between tourists and destinations, and the program harvests credit for attracting tourists rather than the villages per se.

The "final version": centering the community

When, in December 2005, the first full, public version of the Magical Villages Program was disclosed, the document had grown to 22 pages in nine sections (SECTUR 2005c). The document defined the juridical basis of the program, set forth its aims, strategies and subject matter, informed of the program's possibilities, workings, and results, and instructed (aspiring) participants and municipal and state governments of participatory obligations.

The turnabout reflected in the secretary's inauguration speech is solidified as "types of support" in the initial program document have been transformed into "lines of strategic action" to be implemented in participant towns to safeguard program standards (SECTUR 2005c:6–8). "Strategy" appears centerpiece and the program now presents itself as, above all, strategic, while "support" occurs either subordinate to "strategy," detached from the program itself, or directed at local tourism, infrastructure, educational programs, and so forth. Whereas "types of support" indicate a palette of support from which individual participants may choose according to local needs, "lines of strategic action" connote a centrally defined nonnegotiable mandatory package.

Equally pointing to SECTUR's growing control over participant towns is the multiplication of "criteria for incorporation" from the original four to 20 (SECTUR 2005c:3–5). A "final version" further expanded the criteria (SECTUR 2006a), some of which stipulate tasks that materialize as ongoing processes, most notably the submission of quarterly reports that document accomplished projects and demonstrate the impact of the program on local economy and tourism (SECTUR 2006b:8).

Paradoxically, in outright contradiction to these measures, which diminish local definability of tourism, the program simultaneously emphasizes the importance of local democratic participation, indicating a desired bottom-up process. A section stresses that "determined participation is unavoidable," since each participant town is required to install a civil association, whose members must be included in program projects (SECTUR 2005c:18). Local participation is also highlighted by placing it first in the body of criteria and in the chronology of the incorporation procedure; the process of inclusion starts on the ground with "local society" soliciting the municipal and state governments to apply for the locality to be included into the program (SECTUR 2005c:3). However, civil society never reappears in the criteria and the political process is elevated to another level beyond the reach of local society.[2]

Increasing the stress on the importance of participation by civil society, the "final" text now frames on-the-ground participation and "commitment" as the foundational principle of the program: "The Magical Villages Program bases its strategy on the communal participation, its inclusion and permanence; its advances and achievements will be the result of the level of work that the community itself carries out" (SECTUR 2006a:1). The excerpt places the fate of the program in the hands of the involved localities, giving the impression that they, rather than the political authorities, have the decisive power to define its implementation. This connects to the application procedure, which is equally presented to rely on whether or not "local community" desires to participate. Local community is made to select the program, rather than vice versa, and local community thereby becomes principal of ensuing processes. However, initiating the process comes with a "commitment," and "advancements" and "achievements" are stressed to depend on individual communities' determined effort. From the outset, the program places the entire responsibility on the shoulders of locals in case of failure; success depends on how well the program is implemented locally. Hence, the program looks not merely to secure local participation; it also attempts to ensure that community participation shall not counter program policies, but rather assist in smoothing policy implementation. The process begins by having local society affirm its adherence to the program aims, ideals, and methods, as reflected by the "indispensable commitment" of constituting a "Magical Village Touristic Committee," "civil association," or "Pro Magical Villages Group." Since local society has affirmed adherence to the program, the civil association to be included in program processes is destined to be "pro" and work according to program ideals. Framing public participation so, the program attracts citizens enthusiastic about inserting the program into local processes, precluding participation by less enthusiastic locals. In the program document, the committee has the coordinating role of "voicing ideas, projects, and priorities" between municipal, state, and federal authorities and local society to ensure cooperation and communication, giving the impression that the committee commands a dialogue between equal partners. However, accompanying the increased prioritization of local participation, mediated by the totalized abstraction of "community" or "local society," is the surge of policies that constrain local ability to counter program objectives.

This is expressed not just by policies securing local "pro" groups as representatives of communities in their totality, but also by the simultaneous introduction of program courses in participant towns to develop "local capacities" and prevent that program "objectives be distorted" (SECTUR 2006a:6).

While such courses may be regarded as measures to secure that localities enter the program on an informed basis, they equally work as training sessions that provide authorities with the opportunity to instill program objectives in the minds of participants. Moreover, the transformation described earlier is solidified; the program no longer offers a palette of support from which localities may pick selectively according to felt needs; it rather assumes the strategic task of carrying into effect its utopian subject matter in participant towns. The program no longer suggests; it governs.

SECTUR's on-site workshops, then, both inform about program objectives and communicate that these centrally fixed objectives are obligatory. This procedure points to an asymmetrical decision-making process, since all significant decisions are premeditated in the program's subject matter; the criteria for incorporation, the lines of strategic action, the objectives, the types of technical assistance from government institutions – all are predefined. Local participation is therefore an add-on restricted to operate within a predetermined plan. The first step in securing this order is to initiate the inclusion process with a public declaration of interest in the program. Thereby, local society is excluded from the political process by their very inclusion, since the only way to become engaged is by working in accordance with program objectives.

SECTUR equally minimized local decision ability by specifying five mandatory categories of tourist attractions participant towns should present (SECTUR 2006a:3–4):

- architectural harmony and conservation;
- emblematic buildings and their history;
- fiestas and traditions;
- artisan production; and
- traditional gastronomy.

These generic categories, in turn, instruct participant towns on how to present their "singular value," the "magic" quality that sustains their candidacy: "The locality must base its argumentation on the rescue or preservation of its tangible and intangible cultural heritage, emphasizing those expressions that stand out in a particular way as attractions and motives for a visit to the locality" (SECTUR 2006a:5). After finalizing the criteria, they slid into the program document without further notice, and the Magical Villages web page stated that the document presented the "methodological instruments" that had been utilized in selecting the first 23 Magical Villages (SECTUR 2006b). However, when the first program document emerged online in December 2005, the web page also asserted that the "methodological instruments" in *that* document had determined the selection of the first 23 participants (SECTUR 2005d). And prior to that, the web page referred only to the original four criteria (SECTUR 2005e). Crucially, the web page presented these new policies as having always been in play within the program, and this assertion came to be taken for granted by all parties. Newspapers reported of towns in danger of losing their denomination as Magical Villages because they did not fulfill the basic criteria for participation. Off the record, scholars remarked that SECTUR had knowingly included many towns into the program, which upon entry did not fulfill the program criteria. Yet many of these towns were included *before* the expansion of criteria.

Additionally, prior to the disclosure of the first full version (SECTUR 2005c), SECTUR's Magical Villages web page did not inform about an application or selection procedure. The new bottom-up application procedure was detailed online when the final criteria slid into the program document, superimposing itself on a previous, less clear selection procedure. As noted earlier, even before the program was officially launched, three towns were included, which indicates a top-down selection directed by SECTUR. Thus, an unspecified number of towns have not applied for inclusion. Rather, as in the case of Cuetzalan, SECTUR prompted state governments to invite towns to join the program, and most of these towns were already regionally or nationally well-reputed tourist towns. Their early inclusion appears to have worked to create a network of successful tourist towns, and subsequently to ignite public interest. Simultaneously, a paratext was crafted for the program to attract positive attention and make the program well known, as shown next. Hence, as the application procedure was launched, other towns would be eager to enter the program and become associated with the prestigious group of tourist towns. Opening for applications would thus be viable and the application procedure gave weight to the introduction of elements of participatory democracy.

Politics of recognition: a return to the paratext

If the program was to be made publicly known and rise as a brand that would appeal to tourists, it would be pivotal to have a clear profile that could be used in promotional campaigns. Moreover, the intention of having towns apply for inclusion, rather than handpicking them for the program, equally demanded a program narrative that would appeal to citizens in rural areas. Prior to the launch of the program text, SECTUR's Magical Villages web page had stressed the federal institutions involved in the program and the policies set to boost tourism. Now, however, the program text split into two states of talk with discrete interaction arrangements adjusted to different audiences. While one was oriented toward practices, purposes, and program policy to enhance local tourism, another mediated the program as a symbolic act of recognition.

Three interrelated texts emerged around the same time to define the program and the Magical Village. One appeared in the program document below the heading "What is a Magical Village?" (SECTUR 2005c:9), another constituted the descriptive text on SECTUR's Magical Villages web page, replacing the former policy-oriented description, and the third adorned the Visit Mexico website.

The texts form a symbolical paratext that appears whenever the program seeks to appeal to and justify its existence in front of a broad audience.

Because this paratext has been distributed widely in diverse media such as government and program documents, the public web page, promotional material, travel magazines, television broadcasts, and newspaper articles, and because it bears little relation to the technical side of the program, it may be understood to mobilize interest, support, and sympathy from the general public, including citizens of (aspiring) participant towns and potential visitors. The paratext appeals also to municipal and state politicians and businesses because it facilitates the technical and political process by steering public attention away from it. The incongruity between the two states of talk is illustrated by the web page, which immediately substituted the symbolical paratext for the former technical (para)text. The new paratext may thus be seen as brand mediation aimed at the by-standing public, while the technical program content is directed toward an interior group of policy actors. Significantly, the interaction arrangement integral to the paratext works to preclude criticism of the program, since it locates citizens of rural villages as the principal sources of the program. The program is framed as *acting on behalf of the marginalized*; government intervention through program policy is presented as something desired by rural citizens and which consequently occurs on their initiative. By the same token, critique of the program is easily reframed as a disparagement of the people for whom the program acts.

As seen on the program web page, the paratext centers the Magical Village within an act of recognition. The program aspires to:

> revalue a group of populations of the country, which has always been part of the collective imaginary of the nation as a whole, and which represents fresh and different alternatives for the national and international visitors. More than a rescue, it is a recognition of those who inhabit such wonderful places in the Mexican landscape and for the good of everyone have cared for the cultural and historical richness that they embrace.
>
> (SECTUR 2005d)[3]

The statement evokes both multiculturalist and nationalist ideas by referring to the collective Mexican imaginary and the wish to revalue certain populations with "cultural and historical richness." Such revaluation is accentuated as an act of recognition, consisting in displaying the said towns and their populations to the surrounding world as central constituents of national identity. An implicit hierarchy informs the text; nationalism is the frame that defines how multiculturalism may materialize, rather than the opposite. Insofar as the program wishes to bestow recognition on certain populations, the recognition consists of urban, majority mestizo society accepting rural (ethnic) minorities as valid nationals by acknowledging their significance to the nation. The recognition itself, then, relies on a concept of nation defined by the metropolitan majority, and recognition cannot occur outside the national reference machine. Such hierarchy reflects the tendency for nation-states to exist as unquestioned frameworks of social and political thinking

(Wimmer and Glick-Schiller 2002). The Mexican nation becomes the prerequisite for how citizens in the Magical Villages can be ascribed and may ascribe to themselves value and meaning.

Compared to the website, the program document aligns more closely with Fox's *speaking on behalf of the marginalized*. Through an implicit critique of majority Mexico, the text sides with long-oppressed minorities:

> A Magical Village is the reflection of our Mexico, of what has made us, of what we are and should feel proud of. It is its people, a village which through time and in face of modernity has known to conserve, value, and defend its cultural-historical heredity, manifesting it in diverse expressions through its tangible and intangible heritage.
>
> (SECTUR 2005c:9)

By stressing that a Magical Village *should* evoke a sense of pride in Mexicans, the text indicates that this has not always been so and is still not given. Hence, such villages have had to single-handedly "defend" their "cultural-historical heredity" from pressures of "modernity." The word "defend" implies that local heritage has been under attack or jeopardized by external forces. This perspective is thus anchored in the 'defenders' of the Magical Villages with whom the program rhetorically sides. However, the program equally appropriates local traditions on behalf of majority society; the Magical Village represents "*our Mexico*," meaning the *Mexico* of the recognizers. The program thus assumes a majoritarian perspective by holding that the main threat has been a failure to recognize said villages as Mexican villages, which represent ancient characteristics that are part and legacy of all Mexicans:

> In effect, the Magical Villages of Mexico have been there for a long time, waiting for the recognition of their values and cultural-historical riches. Their authenticity, their Mexicanness, their ancestral enchantment, their colors and scents, their villagers, their singularities taken together demand today their revaluation, to elevate them to a level of distinction, as an icon of the tourism of Mexico.
>
> (SECTUR 2005c:9)

While the inhabitants of the Magical Villages have 'defended' their heritage, kept modernity off the doorstep, and longed for recognition, the Magical Villages Program becomes the instrument to facilitate the long-awaited recognition from majority society, taking charge of defending the heritage by creating a scene for its display. The program thus sides with the marginalized to speak out against majority society; the villagers are the real and authentic Mexicans, pure representatives of ancestral ways of life, and they may now return to how things once were. This alleviating promise is supported by the use of the prefix "re-" in the words recognition and revaluation, which indicates an act of repetition that brings back an original, rightful order. Such argument spills over into other parts of the program text, linking the paratext with policy texts. Almost all interventions in the urban space are described with the prefix "re-." Facades, buildings, streets, parks, plazas, commercial life – in total, the "urban image" – have been *re*habilitated, *re*novated, *re*cuperated, *re*generated, *re*created, *re*converted, and *re*organized. The transformations of the urban setting are therefore not transformations, but constitute a return to the origin, which draws places out of obscurity and oblivion, makes them more comfortable and friendly, makes them places of *re*union, *re*novates locals' sense of belonging. This return to original village life is what brings more visitors, business life, employment, opportunities that release local capacities and allow inhabitants to step out of "socioeconomic lethargy" (SECTUR 2005c:19–21).

In promoting the Magical Villages to potential visitors, Visit Mexico also contributed to the circulating paratext:

> The grand cultural and historical richness of Mexico holds – and has always held – a large secret. Next to its large constructions, its millennial cities converted into an icon of the force of the past; together with the big modern cities, which multiply across its geography and concentrate a large part of the wealth and the productive thrust, there are delicate triumphs of the tradition and the ancestral enchantment: the Magical Villages, small towns, and small cities that avidly treasure the other wealth [. . .] that of the tradition.
>
> (Visit Mexico 2006)

The paratext never refers directly to indigenous people, but nonetheless constructs the idea of the Magical Village around implicit reference to indigenous inhabitants. As this excerpt from the Visit Mexico web page illustrates, the Magical Villages are presented as counterpoints to "big modern cities," "wealth and the productive thrust," which stand against "millennial cities," that is, pre-Hispanic archaeological sites. The Magical Villages are thereby chained together with the pre-Hispanic cities, which have been subdued and now reflect "the force of the past," and relative to which the Magical Villages emerge as "delicate triumphs of the tradition and ancestral enchantment." Thus, the paratext employs indigenous imagery, but it makes no explicit claims about inhabitants in the Magical Villages being indigenous. Nonetheless, the connective is there, directing public perception of the program as being "heavily indigenous" (cf. Wilson 2008:49).

Permanent participation, periodic permits

By the time of the second National Magical Villages Meeting, held in San Cristóbal (Chiapas) in October 2007, there were 32 participant towns. SECTUR announced that the final number of participant towns would be 50 and had invited for the meeting representatives of aspirant towns. The presence of not-yet-included towns underlines the novelty of a bottom-up application procedure and indicates the central function of the meeting. Arranged as a conference with discussion panels and workshops, the meeting constitutes a setting in which government officials may direct participant expectations toward program objectives, opportunities, and policies.

During the meeting, SECTUR informed of the recently founded Interinstitutional Evaluation and Selection Committee (CIES), composed of representatives from eight federal institutions. Participants were instructed on how to submit applications or dossiers to the committee, how to present their strategies and objectives, and which objectives counted as legitimate. SECTUR thereby introduced mandatory tasks and provided the possible range of actions through which to solve them satisfactorily, all of which required federal institutional knowledge, expertise and "technical assistance."

Following the surge of criteria for participation, an evaluation apparatus is set into motion to ensure that all towns operate according to a growing policy package. This procedure came with a sanctioning resource, since the evaluation would determine whether participants would have their Magical Villages certificate renewed. Although these periodic permits were clearly another novel feature, the renewal procedure was presented as a way to ensure the permanence of participants within the program (SECTUR 2007). Again, new policies are presented as measures to maintain the status quo. In effect, participant towns are made principal of an evaluation procedure, which is to ensure the correct implementation of program policies that will generate economic progress and safeguard continued participation in the program.

In defense of the brand

At the third National Magical Villages Meeting in March 2009 in Tapalpa (Jalisco), SECTUR announced the introduction of a biennial evaluation procedure and a tightened control over participant towns. CIES would conduct the evaluation and the Magical Villages themselves would assist in collecting data. This evaluation procedure was to play a decisive role in the periodic renewals of the Magical Villages' participatory licenses. Prior to the meeting, SECTUR had prepared a 61-page *Manual of Indicators* with a detailed evaluation procedure (SECTUR 2008). Ironically, the document was presented as a commitment to transparency in public expenditure and its impact, yet it was saturated by an insurmountable topography of intertextual references to comprehensive national plans and programs, federal institutional practices, and methodology primarily derived from economics. Of further irony to the proclamation of public transparency, the evaluation procedures produce floods of information that conceal the more direct effect of such measures, namely that the program, in the name of transparency, subtly installed yet another device securing centralized control of local policymaking. While the secretary outspokenly presented the evaluation as a new feature, he justified the novelty by stating that the new measures were implemented to secure the "ordered growth" of the program, to avoid that the brand "be discredited," and to assure that participant towns offer services of quality (SECTUR 2009a). Hence, he presented the program itself as unaltered, since the new monitoring measures were intended to safeguard brand values by ensuring that the original program objectives are realized in participant towns. Moreover, as the manual states, an increased control over local spending of program funding is simply a firm commitment to political transparency and efficiency in public spending (SECTUR 2008:3). Multiple principals may be identified. On behalf of taxpaying citizens who have the right to know about public spending, on behalf of visitors risking low-quality services, and on behalf of exemplary Magical Villages that may worry about decreasing brand potency, SECTUR takes on the task of securing that participant towns implement program policies the correct way. The already established hierarchy between program brand and program participants is thereby solidified. Towns are posited as potential threats to the brand, which must be protected from the incompetence and unwillingness of individual participant towns to follow program objectives. Enhancing the hierarchy between brand and participants, an asymmetrical reciprocity is underlined by implying that while the program may provide the town with unlimited benefits, the towns may aspire only to implement the ideal version of the program. Moreover, with the taxpaying citizen and dissatisfied visitor lurking in the background, incomplete policy implementations in participant towns may threaten the political legitimacy of the program itself. The program is thus compelled to supervise participants strictly.

While the evaluation procedure is in itself a disciplining mechanism that facilitates government intervention into local policies, the outcome of a failed evaluation would, even more so, work as a disciplinary measure; villages that did not rectify an identified problem within 90 days would face expulsion from the program (SECTUR 2009b). Indeed, in August 2009, following failed evaluations, SECTUR removed Mexcaltitán (Nayarit), Papantla (Veracruz), and Tepoztlán (Morelos) from the program. The installation of CIES and the capacity to expel participant towns were the main effects of an expanded version of the program (SECTUR 2009c:15), which signaled that none of the participant towns ranked above the brand, especially because the expelled towns were among the most prominent tourist destinations. Tepoztlán and Papantla eventually re-entered the program and no participant town has since been excluded, yet the disciplining mechanism continues to play out the desired social effect. Typing *pueblo mágico* (Magical Village), *peligro* (danger), *riesgo* (risk), or *perder* (lose) into a web search engine produces numerous news stories about how given Magical Villages are in "danger" of expulsion from the program, or how municipal authorities are refuting that their town "risks" expulsion. Many of these articles revolve around the (in)ability of local authorities to fulfill program criteria, indicating that "losing" the denomination as Magical Village is equal to local political incapacity or incompetence, and is regarded as a catastrophe for local tourism.

At the meeting in 2009, the practice of exalting exemplary participant towns reached new heights when the secretary announced that SECTUR would withdraw San Miguel de Allende (Guanajuato) from the program:

> [. . .] not because it has not complied with the criteria – on the contrary, it has surpassed them – but because its declaration as UNESCO World Heritage Site has brought them to climb to a status different from that of a Magical

development, the literature on the Magical Villages Program often materializes as a policy science that evaluates the program on its own terms. Nonetheless, the basic term is that the terms are never fixed, but change gradually. The continuous and centrally conceived reconfiguration of the program is a forceful governmental maneuver, because it gradually reworks premises for participation according to existing political aims, while simultaneously making villages dependent on participation in the program. Towns thereby enter the program on the basis of certain premises, but step by step they come to participate on the basis of another set of premises. The transformative mechanism cooperates with another unspoken mechanism, namely that the program is configured as infinite. Combined with the transformative character, the temporal infinity turns the program into a social technology through which government institutions may install and test infinite criteria, objectives, and policies. Paradoxically, as the program facilitates centrally coordinated steering of the participant towns, antithetic narratives surge to reject such centralized management. Furthermore, new elements are presented in a manner that denies their novelty by referring them to the original intentions of the program or presenting them as consolidations or clarifications of already established practices. The program thus continuously superimposes its current form upon its former practice and accumulates merits and authority in concert.

Crucially, what has remained static throughout is the paratextual frame projected to the general public, which invests the Magical Villages Program with emancipatory potential for marginalized ethnic minorities, who are to experience social development by inserting their intangible and tangible cultural heritage into a labor system centered on tourism. While the paratext initially applied to President Fox's entire National Program of Tourism, the Magical Villages Program came to be the key policy to fulfill this vision, starting when SECTUR launched the program as a brand. Multicultourism is the term the book applies to designate this frame, which has been guiding public perception of the program and contemporary Mexico as revolving around social equality through market-based national recognition of cultural diversity.

Notes

1 Unless otherwise noted, quotes from this point on are translated from Spanish by the author.
2 This is illustrated by criteria demanding that villages create an "Urban Touristic Development Plan," a set of "Regulations of the Urban Image," a "Magical Villages Program Management Plan," and a "Program for the Reorganization of Semifixed and/or Ambulant Commerce," tasks that require state and federal institutional expertise (SECTUR 2006a:1–2).
3 This text since entered the program document (SECTUR 2009c:1).
4 The town had recently suffered severe flooding. During his reconnaissance of the damages, President Felipe Calderón (2006–2012) stated that he would prioritize making Angangueo a Magical Village (Notimex 2010).
5 This most recent version of the program was not in operation at the time of fieldwork and is not considered here.

References

Cámara de Diputados. 2001. "Comparecencia de la Secretaria de Turismo, Leticia Navarro Ochoa, correspondiente al Primer Informe de Gobierno del Presidente Vicente Fox Quesada." *Crónica Parlamentaria*, September 14. Retrieved January 10, 2014 (http://cronica.diputados.gob.mx/Comparecencias/58/2001/2001Turismo.html).

Cámara de Diputados. 2006. "Año IX, número 2074, jueves 17 de Agosto de 2006." *Gaceta Parlamentaria*, August 17. Retrieved March 5, 2014 (http://gaceta.diputados.gob.mx/Gaceta/59/2006/ago/20060817.html).

Espinosa, Héctor Hugo. 2010. "Gobernador Pide a Turismo Promueva a Angangueo Como Pueblo Mágico." *El Sol de Morelia*, June 17. Retrieved March 14, 2014 (www.oem.com.mx/elsoldemorelia/notas/n1675267.htm).

Ferguson, James. 1994. *The Anti-Politics Machine: "Development," Depoliticization, and Bureaucratic Power in Lesotho.* Minneapolis, MN: University of Minnesota Press.

Kernerman, Gerald. 2005. *Multicultural Nationalism: Civilizing Difference, Constituting Community.* Vancouver: UBC Press.

Linde, Charlotte. 2009. *Working the Past: Narrative and Institutional Memory.* New York: Oxford University Press.

Notimex. 2010. "Presidente quiere que pueblo afectado por las lluvias sea 'mágico.'" *CNN*, February 15. Retrieved July 7, 2014 (http://mexico.cnn.com/nacional/2010/02/15/presidente-quiere-que-pueblo-afectado-por-las-lluvias-sea-magico).

Notimex. 2013. "Revalúan program de Pueblos Mágicos: Ruíz Massieu." *Excélsior*, August 17. Retrieved September 23, 2013 (www.excelsior.com.mx/nacional/2013/08/17/914115).

Notimex. 2015. "Sectur incorpora 28 nuevos Pueblos Mágicos." *El Universal*, September 25. Retrieved December 9, 2015 (www.eluniversal.com.mx/articulo/cartera/economia/2015/09/25/sectur-incorpora-28-nuevos-pueblos-magicos).

Scher, Philip W. 2010. "UNESCO Conventions and Culture as a Resource." *Journal of Folklore Research* 47(1–2):197–202.

Scher, Philip W. 2011. "Heritage Tourism in the Caribbean: The Politics of Culture after Neoliberalism." *Bulletin of Latin American Research* 30(1):7–20.

SECTUR. 2001. *Programa Nacional de Turismo 2001–2006.* Mexico City: SECTUR. Retrieved December 5, 2012 (www.sectur.gob.mx/work/models/sectur/Resource/9795/PNT20012006_PDF.zip).

SECTUR. 2005a. *Boletín 089: Inicia Primera Reunión Nacional de Pueblos Mágicos.* Mexico City: SECTUR. Retrieved January 20, 2014 (www.sectur.gob.mx/wb/sectur/sect_Boletin_089_Inicia_Primera_Reunion_Nacional_).

SECTUR. 2005b. *Discurso del Secretario de Turismo durante la Primera Reunión Nacional de Pueblos Mágicos.* Mexico City: SECTUR. Retrieved January 15, 2014 (www.sectur.gob.mx/es/sectur/sect_1808_Discurso_del_Secretario_de_Turismo_duran).

SECTUR. 2005c. *Programa Pueblos Mágicos.* Mexico City: SECTUR. Retrieved February 27, 2014 (http://web.archive.org/web/20060213212910/http://www.sectur.gob.mx/wb2/sectur/sect_Pueblos_Magicos).

SECTUR. 2005d. *Pueblos Mágicos.* Mexico City: SECTUR. Retrieved February 27, 2014 (http://web.archive.org/web/20060213212910/http://www.sectur.gob.mx/wb2/sectur/sect_Pueblos_Magicos).

SECTUR. 2005e. *Pueblos Mágicos.* Mexico City: SECTUR. Retrieved February 27, 2014 (http://web.archive.org/web/20051120005732/http://www.sectur.gob.mx/wb2/sectur/sect_Pueblos_Magicos).

SECTUR. 2006a. *Criterios de Incorporación al Programa "Pueblos Mágicos": Versión Final 31 de Julio 2006*. Mexico City: SECTUR. Retrieved September 6, 2012 (www.sectur.gob.mx/work/models/securing/Resource/14192/CRITERIOSDEIN CORPORACIONALPROGRAMAPUEBLOSMAGICOS.pdf).

SECTUR. 2006b. *Programa Pueblos Mágicos*. Mexico City: SECTUR. Retrieved February 27, 2014 (http://web.archive.org/web/20060901025551/http://www.sectur. gob.mx/wb2/sectur/sect_Pueblos_Magicos).

SECTUR. 2007. *Boletín 116: Se Consolida Programa Pueblos Mágicos como Alternativa de Desarrollo de las Comunidades*. Mexico City: SECTUR. Retrieved January 21, 2014 (www.sectur.gob.mx/es/sectur/sect_Boletin_116_Se_consolida_Programa_Pueblos_ Mag).

SECTUR. 2008. *Manual de Indicadores: Programa Pueblos Mágicos*. Mexico City: SECTUR. Retrieved September 23, 2013 (www.sectur.gob.mx/sub/conacyt/temas/ documentos/pdf/respuestas/11/1-Manual-de-Indicadores-Programa-Pueblos-Magicos. pdf).

SECTUR. 2009a. *05/03: Palabras del Secretario de Turismo, Rodolfo Elizondo Torres, en la Ceremonia de Inauguración de la Tercera Reunión Nacional de Pueblos Mágicos, en Tapalpa, Jalisco*. Mexico City: SECTUR. Retrieved January 15, 2014 (www.sectur. gob.mx/es/sectur/sect_0503_Palabras_del_Secretario_de_Turismo_Rodol).

SECTUR. 2009b. *Boletín 024: Anuncia Elizondo Nuevos Criterios de Evaluación para Pueblos Mágicos*. Mexico City: SECTUR. Retrieved January 15, 2014 (www.sectur. gob.mx/wb/sectur/sect_Boletin_024_Anuncia_Elizondo_Nuevos_Criterios).

SECTUR. 2009c. *Reglas de Operación*. Mexico City: SECTUR. Retrieved September 6, 2012 (www.sectur.gob.mx/work/models/sectur/Resource/99fbd793-a344-4b98-9633-78607f33c b8f/Reglas_de_operacion.pdf).

SECTUR. 2010. *Boletín 060: Inversiones por Mil 900 Millones de Pesos se Destinaron al Programa Pueblos Mágicos*. Mexico City: SECTUR. Retrieved January 20, 2014 (www. sectur.gob.mx/en/sectur/sect_Boletin_060_Inversiones_por_Mil_900_Millones_).

UNESCO. 2017. *Tentative Lists*. Paris: UNESCO. Retrieved October 19, 2017 (http://whc. unesco.org/en/tentativelists/state=mx).

Velarde Valdez, Mónica, Ana Virginia del Carmen Maldonado Alcudia, and Minerva Candelaria Maldonado Alcudia. 2009. "Pueblos Mágicos: Estrategia para el Desarrollo Turístico Sustentable – Caso Sinaloa." *Teoría y Praxis* 6:79–93.

Velázquez García, Mario Alberto. 2013. "La Formulación de las Políticas Públicas de Turismo en México. El Caso del Programa Federal 'Pueblos Mágicos' 2001–2012." *Diálogos Latinoamericanos* 21:89–110.

Visit Mexico. 2006. *¿Que son los Pueblos Mágicos?* Mexico City: Visit Mexico. Retrieved February 27, 2014 (http://web.archive.org/web/20060318045105/http:// www.visitmexico.com/wb/Visitmexico/Visi_pueblos_magicos).

Wilson, Tamar Diana. 2008. "Economic and Social Impacts of Tourism in Mexico." *Latin American Perspectives* 35(3):37–52.

Wimmer, Andreas, and Nina Glick-Schiller. 2002. "Methodological Nationalism and Beyond: Nation-State Building, Migration and the Social Sciences." *Global Networks* 2(4):301–334.

5　When pros turn pro

Community ambassadors and social order

Goodbye interview, hello meeting

For weeks, I had attempted to get an interview scheduled with the Municipal Director of Tourism, Marcelina, a vibrant middle-aged woman with a degree in English teaching. When we arrived to Cuetzalan, Marcelina was more than busy. Not only was she preparing a dossier for SECTUR as part of the annual evaluation of the town as a Magical Village, she was also planning Cuetzalan's contribution to the approaching national tourism fair *Tianguis Turístico*. Our initial contact was therefore mediated by O, a new member of the Municipal Council of Tourism, who scheduled and rescheduled our interview appointment as Marcelina's calendar clogged with urgent meetings and tasks. When, finally, I decided to pay Marcelina a spontaneous visit at the Municipal Office of Tourism, a brief moment of friendly introductions reassured me the interview was still on. I then agreed with O to schedule the meeting for 6 p.m. two days later.

When I reached O's shop as planned, 15 minutes before the interview, it came as no surprise when he announced that the interview was off. He and Marcelina were going to attend a Magical Villages meeting. Nonetheless, O proposed I could join the meeting. That way, I could greet Marcelina and meet some of the people locally involved in the Magical Villages Program. When I inquired about the purpose of the event, O declared that some university students had called for the meeting, but beyond being a Magical Villages meeting he was not sure what was to be discussed.

I found it notable that no further explanation was needed to summon the relevant parties, since by implication expectancies were appropriately addressed merely by categorizing the meeting as pertaining to the Magical Villages Program. Moreover, it appeared to reflect a municipal task hierarchy, which assigned high priority to such meetings. Prior to this occasion, I had heard of other Magical Villages meetings, but always *after* they had taken place. From the accounts I had received, such meetings appeared to vary in form, but nevertheless shared a particular frame of reference captured by the descriptive label and the location; the issue of concern would be the Magical Villages Program and Cuetzalan's participation within it.

I accepted the invitation straight away and perceived it as an offer of consolation for the cancelled interview. Only later, it struck me that perhaps I was also invited along because the meeting was thought to serve as a fitting illustration of how the citizenry and the local government cooperated on conducting the program – a key criterion in the annual program evaluations. It would thus serve municipal interests well if, as a scientifically sanctioned firsthand witness, I were to transmit in my academic work the experience of a well-functioning dialogue between civil society and municipal authorities, concertedly engaged in operationalizing the program.[1]

The meeting, it turned out, was organized by a teacher and five students of tourism administration at a local branch of a large university. Participating in the meeting were also a hotel owner and member of the Municipal Council of Tourism, and two invitees from Puebla City, who were creating an online platform for cultural tourism and ecotourism. The declared purposes of the meeting were for the students to present a study they had carried out to examine to which degree locals felt included into the Magical Villages Program, and most pertinently to discuss a consciousness-raising campaign, which they were designing to inform locals of the benefits of the program, and consequently to make them embrace the program. The late cancellation of the interview gave me the impression that the meeting was a spontaneous event. The noisy setting confirmed that impression; a café with small talking guests and a manager meticulously microwaving one cup of coffee after the other, while also blending ice for smoothies, was not exactly the ideal acoustic arena for an academic presentation and the exchange of opinions. As the meeting evolved, it became apparent that it depended on the participation of Marcelina, which helped explain why the meeting had to be semi-spontaneous, perhaps also waiting on standby for a vacancy in Marcelina's calendar.

Analytical approach

Taking the meeting as a window to the local interaction on and enactment of the Magical Villages Program in Cuetzalan, this chapter analyzes how locals come to engage in and negotiate the program. The analysis highlights the foundational feature of all such meetings, namely that they come into existence as specialized forms of interaction in which participants orient to and operationalize concepts and understandings within the Magical Villages Program in their discussions of local social life. The institutional character of the interaction being a structuring principle in such Magical Villages meetings, they serve as narrative occasions and environments that give precedence to institutional identities and modes of meaning-making (Gubrium and Holstein 2009:173–183), and the chapter examines how the participants enact the institution and negotiate their social and institutional roles (Asmuß and Svennevig 2009:7).

Doing so, the chapter charts a mode of government that Cruikshank terms "technologies of citizenship" (Cruikshank 1999:3–5). Within the program, such technologies aim at forming, mobilizing, and empowering a particular class of citizens who identify with the program's vision of and paths to creating a certain tourism economy. Through their involvement in a program based on notions of community development, these citizens come to recognize, reframe, and promote group interests as community interest, while disregarding the particularity of their politics, the privileges of their classed positions within local power hierarchies, and the potentiality of a heterogeneous citizenry with diverging interests and social positions. In short, participants come to acquire and embody the program's totalizing aspirations.

As Goffman emphasizes, the production of utterances is an interactional phenomenon that is socially situated, meaning that the interaction in a given encounter does not take place in a neatly delimited social, spatial, and temporal locus (Goffman 1981:3, 131). Meeting interaction takes place in a broad intertextual field consisting of written documents (Asmuß and Svennevig 2009:11) as well as oral narratives and utterances produced by or ascribed to people or entities not present at the meeting. In this sense, participants interact not merely with each other, but also interact with and manage an endless number of additional sources. For the meeting in question, participants mobilize the Magical Villages Program and other citizens as sources in the discussion through various kinds of intertextual references. They may employ specialized terminology or refer to themselves with the pronoun "we," both of which function to signal an institutional identity and a dis-identification with people who are not well versed in the program vocabulary. Through such maneuvers, a team of experts emerges in contrast to the laypeople (Drew and Heritage 1992:29–32). In other instances, "we" is used to bridge the gaps and comes to signify "the community."

According to Goffman, *coordinated task activity* is the center around which utterances are given meaning (Goffman 1981:143). Similarly, linguist Stephen Levinson (1992) has coined the term *activity type* to capture the way language usage is socially context-dependent in being attached to activities. As he shows, activities have a commanding voice in interaction, since the structure of an activity constrains the range of relevant or allowable verbal contributions and, equally, activity types are tied to certain inferential frameworks that direct the interpretation and reception of an utterance. Sending out an invitation for a Magical Villages meeting marks the opening of an institutional activity type and is the first instance of narrative activation (Gubrium and Holstein 2009:41–53) because the invitation prepares participants for the topical content, the interactional format, and inferential schemata through which participants may engage in the subject matter.

The chapter first analyzes the opening and closing of the meeting to show how narrative consensus comes to be established. The chapter thereby tunes in on the emergence of inferential schemata, meaning-making structures, and aims that construct links between the meeting participants and the program, and create didactic templates for problematizing the conduct of other citizen groups. The emerging consciousness-raising campaign is subsequently inspected to bring to view the social order and technologies of citizenship that the campaign visualizes to achieve its ends. Finally, attention is turned to the recursive aspect of social technologies, showing how the meeting itself works as a technology of citizenship, as problematizations and discussions of others' conduct equally becomes an occasion for problematizing and regulating the conduct of meeting participants.

Opening and closing: establishing narrative consensus and ratifying participants

Departing from the pregiven categorization of the event, the teacher launched the meeting by specifying how it addressed the Magical Villages Program. She and her students had observed a lack of involvement in the program on the part of local society, which had occasioned them to examine "how well the concept [of Magical Villages] has penetrated the citizenry." A survey had been carried out the preceding month, January 2013, and encompassed 46 interviews with people not directly involved in the tourist sector, but who reside in the part of town that has been subject to "improvement of the urban image," the so-called "Magical Villages polygon."[2] Because that area was chosen, all respondents were both homeowners and shopkeepers. The interviews inquired about how well the respondents felt they were integrated into the program, how much they felt like or part of a Magical Village, and how much information they had received about the program:[3]

> **Teacher:** We noted that there is a lack of more . . . [We need to] integrate us more as citizenry in *this thing about* "involvement with society" concerning Magical Villages. [. . .] And we noted that people were interested in *that*; in feeling as a Magical Village, but they do not have much information. In other words, it is *as if* they view it *as if* merely the authorities are the ones using the concept, and that the citizenry is not being taken into account. Now, in the coming course, which is called Seminar of Investigation, this project is started, which is the program of consciousness-raising concerning the concept of Magical Village [. . .] They [the students] already did a study concerning what it is people need. They know a lot about the outlines [of the program] and how the concept of Magical Village has developed here. They have already done an interview in the television, where they announced that from that moment the consciousness-raising project set forth. [. . .] So, as I am their teacher, as I am on the Magical Villages Committee, and taking advantage, right, that they are interested in the same thing . . . And now they will convey to you something they are working on.[4]

According to this account, the survey was launched because they had noted a lack of involvement in the program from local society. In asserting this observation as a problem, the teacher refers to an established notion within the existing Magical Villages Program document: "involvement with society" (SECTUR 2009:3–4, 10). A technical term from the Magical Villages Program thus serves as a cognitive cue (Louwerse and van Peer 2002) to justify how they came to assert their observation as a problem. In this first key phrase, the teacher embeds and introduces herself and the students as collective author unit ("we noted"), by which she signals her professional endorsement of and alignment with the students' activities. However, she further authorizes the perspective by drawing in the program as an external source to the study and making it principal of the asserted problem. This change in footing is flagged by the modification "this thing about" preceding the program term "involvement with society," which indicates that the teacher presents a compressed representation of a notion that is known to and uncontroversial among the participants.

The study proceeded to show that people were interested in *feeling* like a Magical Village, but that they felt "as if" the citizenry were not included in program processes and "as if" only the authorities run the program. Reporting the experience of the citizenry through a distancing "as if," the teacher adopts a mere animating posture to mark her disaffiliation with the utterance, immediately assigning such experience to a hypothetical realm superimposed by her own informed experience of how the program *really* works. She thus defines local experience and segregates it from *actual* program practice. This categorization of experience removes from the discussion an exploration of citizens' experiences of program practice, clearing the ground for interpreting local experience as an expression of respondents' lack of information about program workings. Personal experience is deemed irrelevant in advance by concluding that it is based on a failed understanding of program practice. Nevertheless, by emphasizing that people are *interested in feeling* like a Magical Village, the teacher makes the same people principal of the consciousness-raising campaign because the campaign intends to help them achieve the aspiration of feeling included. As the aims of the citizenry and the program merge, wrongheaded experience becomes the obstacle to a full realization of the program and the self-realization desired by the citizens. This casts meeting participants as active and progressive citizens, who attempt to mold reactionary fellow citizens in their exemplary self-image by making them capable of understanding the workings of the program. They thus assume altruistic community roles as program ambassadors and professionals who educate citizens to convert the community into a successful tourist destination. Integral to this role-casting is a discursive asymmetry that feeds into the ensuing interaction format, since consciousness-raising implies that an entity believed to have a superior comprehension acts on someone believed to have an inadequate comprehension.

This maneuver demonstrates, as Cruikshank argues, how a target group for empowerment is identified through their "lack of something" and how the application of social scientific knowledge may structure problematization and remediation of their conduct (Cruikshank 1999:3). The authority of teacher and students is constituted through the classic distinction between and hierarchic ordering of objective and subjective knowledge and their command of the former. While their university affiliation and scientific enterprise facilitate such objective position, the teacher secures objective authority by accentuating their knowledge of "the outlines" of the program. The comprehensive role of social scientific knowledge in technologies of citizenship thus shows itself through the teacher's ability to recognize such knowledge forms in the program. The teacher thereby transforms the program into a manual of tourism rather than a mode of government.

Identifying a mismatch between what is perceived as subjective experience of program practice and actual, objective program practice constitutes an immediate categorization of experience that prescribes a particular interpretation: locals misapprehend program practice due to their lack of objective information about the program. Through this interpretation, the teacher moves with ease to the self-evident solution to the problem: designing and implementing a consciousness-raising campaign to inform citizens of the benefits of the program, which will make the citizenry embrace the program and which, in turn, will be of benefit to the whole community.

Making the citizenry principal of the consciousness-raising campaign serves a double legitimizing purpose. The teacher sketches a social order that distinguishes a general citizenry from the specialized group of citizens to which she and the students belong. Within this hierarchy, the students are granted authority to produce knowledge about "what it is *the people* need." Thus, teacher and students construct for themselves an ambivalent position of superiority and subordination; a target group is to be reworked, but this process springs from an ostensible desire identified in the very target group. From this perspective, the teacher and the students are working *on* the community only to work *for* the community. The campaign, which they command, is requested by the target group, and by taking command of the situation they put themselves at the service of that same group.

In her introduction, the teacher navigates her two institutional roles as teacher at the university and as president of the Magical Villages Committee. By way of scientific inquiry, she identifies a problem in the way the Magical Villages Program is running in Cuetzalan compared to how it should be running according to program documents. The main problem identified is that the citizenry is not adequately involved in the program, yet the conditions for scientifically measuring adequate involvement are drawn beforehand from the program itself. The teacher thus maneuvers a position of objectivity by identifying a problem scientifically, which nonetheless has another principal, namely the program. By making the program principal of the research, the teacher avoids assuming such a principal position herself, and she and the students merely undertake to evaluate the program scientifically and assist it in fulfilling its aims of community development. Significantly, the survey shows the citizenry to be principal in that they desire to be included and in charting "what it is the people need." Hence, the scientific inquiry creates the basis for instrumenting their objective program knowledge to raise the consciousness of the target group. The teacher thereby separates, yet combines, her two institutional roles and position as fellow citizen by narratively matching her endeavor with the interests of the program, objective research practice, and the community.

Having introduced the problem, the solution, and the guiding inferential schemata, the teacher exits the collective author unit ("we") to singularly author the institutional credibility of the students ("they"/"them"). These differing uses of footing render different modes of ratifying the students as capable participants in the meeting. The initial use of "we" signals complete alignment between teacher and students in the formulation of problem and solution, and the subsequent use of "they" highlights the students' expertise regardless of their relation to the teacher. Correspondingly, by emphasizing their scientific skills ("They already did a study . . .") and their professional, objective knowledge of the program ("They know a lot about the outlines . . ."), the teacher constructs two institutional roles for the students that converge with her own.

This introductory presentation of the students may be understood as the opening ritual bracket to the anticipated encounter. According to Goffman, every talk is enclosed within ritual brackets that establish and dissolve joint commitment and "ratified participation" (Goffman 1981:130). The introduction constitutes the opening bracket through which the teacher ratifies the students for the planned institutional interaction and encourages the additional participants to ratify the students in their institutionally pertinent roles. The introduction equally serves as a paratext that situates their preceding efforts and the subsequent presentation and discussion. That is, the teacher establishes the *inferential framework* intended to guide the meeting; she lays forth the conditions of the coordinated task activity to be undertaken, and thereby delineates narrative consensus. Outlining her own institutional roles and demonstrating the accordance between the two, duplicating and offering such roles for her students, figuratively embedding a general citizenry unaware of but interested in the program, defining a problem and corresponding solution – all these moves delimit interpretive space and delineate the ensuing activity. In her portrayal of the survey and its results, the teacher validates particular inferential schemata that facilitate a mode of meaning-making in which not program practice, but citizen conduct, is to be problematized. As the main authority of the presenting group – teacher and president of the Magical Villages Committee – she prepares a narrative path for the students and the external participants to follow, and, by introducing the event with a paratextual summary of the key findings, she ensures that the institutionally viable line of interpretation she represents will become the point of reference for the meeting and ensuing actions. Since the solution will be to inform citizens of the outlines of the program to alter their experience of it, the teacher leaves limited room for criticism of local program practice, and during the meeting the program itself is never questioned. In sum, the critical perspective on program practice the teacher sketches at the outset coincides with the perspective of the program itself.

Following the teacher, Carla, a student and owner of a large, locally prestigious hotel, assists in situating the discussion, explaining that the meeting would be one out of several in which the students would listen to different opinions as to how to structure the "real message" that would "reach the people":

> **Carla:** So, what we want is, to fit well, above all, this message, because we have some [messages], but perhaps they do not serve very well, right? And it is for that reason we want meetings with the service providers as well – with prominent people – so that [the campaign] can have a clear idea and so that the people will accept it, in some way. [. . .] Because that would be the end purpose, namely, that they come to accept it.

since they both "offer jobs with salaries" and buy their supplies locally, as do their employees. With this storyline, the hotels and restaurants occupy key positions in the community economy and become the *raison d'être* of income from tourists. Yet simultaneously they emerge as mere monetary entry points and assume an altruistic position as mere intermediaries in a larger economic transaction between tourists and the total community. A social order is thus sketched in which the hotel and restaurant owners are local benefactors who create an economy for a beneficiary community. In effect, the narrative brings about the message that obstructing their efforts would be to obstruct the efforts of the community.[6]

Rendering visible such an economic cycle was thought to make people capable of recognizing the same pattern in their everyday experiences, which would make them more appreciative of tourism, the program, and the determined efforts of hotel and restaurant owners. Making citizens "conscious" that tourism is a community activity pertinent to their individual lives would thus prompt them to regulate conduct conceived as counterproductive to tourism.

To this end, the short film would be backed by statistical data that would invest the storyline with "objective" authority by providing quantitative testimony of the increase of local tourism and its positive economic effects. Collecting statistical data of the effects of tourism within the locality is one of the obligations of being in the Magical Villages Program and is needed for the annual evaluation (SECTUR 2009:13). Within the evaluation, the statistical data constitute measurable indicators of the degree to which the village has implemented the program successfully. The statistical data therefore come to serve legitimizing purposes, because it is from these figures that SECTUR may demonstrate growth in participant localities, and hence claim the program successful, in the same way that the villages themselves may legitimize their participation in the program by demonstrating increasing figures. Crucially, the consciousness-raising campaign would need to attribute local tourism economy to Cuetzalan's participation in the Magical Villages Program.

Negotiating proper representation of local experiences

The decision to resolve local dissatisfaction with the Magical Villages Program through a campaign set to raise the consciousness of local critics signals the existence of the indisputable premise that the program is beneficial. Critique of the program is thereby reframed as the inability among certain citizens to fathom the workings of the program. Those citizens are seen to constitute a threat to the program because their stubborn conviction hinders the full implementation of its aims. The consciousness-raising campaign thus creates a unidirectional interaction order founded on a hierarchy of binary opposition between the informed, rational proponents and the uninformed, irrational objects of the campaign. The assumed benevolence of the campaign is constitutive of this unidirectional relation, since it derives its legitimacy from the assertion that a change within the subjectivity of the citizen will lead to a positive change in the life of the citizen and the total community.

These pre-settings came to inform the interpretation of local perception of the program. While the students had identified discomfort with the program, they never intended to explore the dimensions of the discomfort experienced because the critique inherent in it had been pre-categorized as invalid. The teacher had embarked on this task by placing local experience of the program within a subjective realm nurtured by a vacuum of information about objective program practice. This way, she had invested program documents with authority and drew her own authority from her professionally informed reading of program conceptualizations and terminology. The task, it seemed, consisted in portraying discomfort from the angle that best allowed for its rhetorical and practical nullification because any acknowledgement of discontent would lend support to critical attitudes. The topic of discomfort surfaced whenever the participants negotiated a coherent representation of local attitudes toward the program, which could be converted by the campaign.

In delineating the target group, the student Sergio was first to touch upon the topic. Sergio portrayed a citizenry disinterested in the program, finding it of little relevance to people outside the tourist sector. He therefore diagnosed discontent as a sign of resignation toward the tourism sector, spurred by the deceptive experience of not benefiting from the program. Following the teacher, Sergio interprets such local experience as a lack of information about how the program actually works:

Sergio: The initial investigation was focused on the non-tourist sector, because we consider it to be easier, let's say, to convince the persons that are already integrated in the tourist sector. After all, they know, well, that "the benefits we have are these," since, let's say, they see more directly the benefits they have. But, um, the persons that are not integrated, let's say, directly in the [tourist] sector, they see themselves as more ummm . . .

Hotel owner: Relegated!

Sergio: Ahaaa! In other words, they say: "And how does it benefit *me*," right? And partly because of the lack of information they have. "I am not a service provider; I am not interested in [knowing] where the cascades or Las Brisas, are located; I am not interested in [knowing] when the church was constructed." [. . .] We already count on sufficient information, which gives us the basis to be able to, um, realize now, as such, in this second phase, the campaign, which is to raise consciousness of the benefits that this Magical Village has.[7]

Sergio sketches a divide in the citizenry between people within and people outside the tourist sector. While citizens within the tourist sector point to experienced program benefits, citizens outside the tourist sector do not readily see themselves benefited by the program, due to which they find the program irrelevant. During his account, Sergio hesitates long enough for the hotel owner to come to his assistance. According to her, people outside the tourism sector feel "relegated," indicating that people are aware of and feel excluded from the benefits that the program brings to the tourist sector. The hotel owner thus portrays a citizenry disappointed by being excluded from the program benefits, which they understand to be channeled to a privileged recipient group. In consequence, people would have appreciated inclusion, but feel that they have not been given an opportunity to participate. While Sergio initially affirms her interpretation, his elaboration casts the interpretation into doubt. To illustrate how the program is being misconceived by the target group, Sergio animates the said group of citizens through an embedded statement that renders absurd their claims as to why the program does not apply to them. By including into his interpretation another voice, ascribed to an original source, he invests his interpretation with a sense of empirical truthfulness. Thereby, he illustrates that disinterest rests on a lack of knowledge of the real program benefits. Hence, people themselves close their eyes on opportunities within the program by wrongfully holding that the program is not of their concern. Conversely, making people aware of program benefits and how to access them will secure their involvement with the program.

Sergio and the hotel owner thus present two different versions of local discontent, which nonetheless render critique invalid through the shared understanding that local discontent is based on a lack of information about the program. From both perspectives, then, the objective is to show people the indisputable fact that the program *is* beneficial. Such generalized and mendable discontent with the program entails no valid critique of the program, as it can be traced to an erroneous assessment that makes people feel *as if* they are excluded from the program, or *as if* the program has no relevance to them.

Departing from a clarifying question concerning the objectives of the campaign posed by an invitee from Puebla, Carla took the opportunity to rephrase local discontent, undermining Sergio's interpretation that people feel they have no firsthand experience of program benefits:

> **Carla:** The basis of this investigation is that many . . . people *do know*, right, of the Magical Villages, but they say that they are not taken into account to participate in this. That is: "To be frank with you, they did not take into consideration my opinion." "There are meetings, which only invite the tourist sector, but they do not involve us." And they are very conscious that it *does* benefit the tourist sector: "Yes, we are conscious, because we continue to sell products in the small shops, in the pharmacies," right? [. . .] And all, um, concurred that it *does* benefit them, because more tourists arrive. Well, they buy a bottle of water from you, they buy a brush from you [etc.]. So, they are all very conscious that it *is* of benefit to them that tourists arrive and that this continues to be conserved. Well, they would like to be taken into account, and oftentimes they damage the urban image because of ignorance. Oftentimes we do things, and we do not know the damage that we are causing, and so we do it. But as one becomes more conscious, or, when you have the information, you say: "Oh no!"

According to this interpretation, people do readily experience firsthand one of the benefits of the program, revenues from selling grocery products to tourists, and therefore they are not disinterested in the program. On the contrary, viewing already one program benefit, they desire to be more involved in program processes to increase benefits. This interpretation exceeds the nullification implied by Sergio's interpretation, which held that people did not experience any benefits and consequently were disinterested. Hence, Carla disqualifies Sergio's interpretation, moving dissatisfaction further away from the program itself. People are not discontent with the program; they are rather discontent about not being *more* engaged in the program. The consciousness-raising campaign thereby springs as a public service initiative demanded by the citizens themselves, who want to know more about the opportunities the program extends. To construct this argument, Carla puts one of the persuasion techniques of the campaign to work within the negotiation of the campaign itself, the narrative of economic circulation. Just as the short film was intended to illustrate, Carla argues that people are already experiencing everyday economic benefits, for which they are appreciative of the program.

To accomplish this argument, she animates an original source infused with a wider representation than the source animated by Sergio.[8] The statement that "*they* are very *conscious* that [the program] *does* benefit the tourist sector" is corroborated by an original source that responds directly to her analysis: "*Yes, we are conscious* because we continue to sell products." This leads to the conclusion that "all, um, concurred that [the program] does benefit them, because more tourists arrive."

Key in that argument is the complete attribution of local tourism to the Magical Villages Program, as illustrated by the notion that the selling of groceries to tourists is an effect of the program. From this perspective, however, the short film no longer carries the purpose of convincing people that the program entails economic benefits. Rather, it is to craft a circulatory chart of local tourism economy that counters the common inference that hotel and restaurant owners are harvesting the revenue. Asserting that citizens want to "conserve" the tourism economy generated by the program, she points out how their lack of knowledge makes them work against their own aspirations. Notably, Carla argues, citizens inadvertently inflict harm on the tourism economy by failing to respect the urban image. According to Carla, the issue is not that locals do not experience the economic benefits of the program, but rather that they have not yet discovered that conservation of the urban image is a central component of a successful community tourism economy. From this perspective, their task is thus to regulate citizens by showing how their conduct related to the urban image impedes the tourism economy they themselves desire and already find beneficial.

Recursive regulation in the meeting

Departing from the sketched interpretational disagreement, the chapter now highlights the recursive aspect of social technologies; they lead to self-government not in first instance within the target group, but within the group exercising the technologies. This recursive quality in social technologies may indicate why cooperation between local government and civil society – a pro Magical Villages group (SECTUR 2006:1) – figures so centrally in the program. The pro group needs not just to be active in shaping tourism within their community; they need to share the perspective on tourism offered by the program. The municipal government is responsible for shaping a functional pro group consisting of exemplary citizens who can function as local program ambassadors to mold the citizenry in the image of the program. A special class of citizens is implied: resourceful opinion-makers and successful tourism entrepreneurs. In Cuetzalan, they belong to the mestizo elite and middle class.

Embarking on what initially appears to be a corroboration of Sergio's interpretation, the hotel owner refers to local citizens who refute the claim that the Magical Villages Program is the source of local tourism and that the program has brought about benefits:

> **Hotel owner:** I have heard the fact that they say that Cuetzalan was already a tourist site when they gave it the title of Magical Village [. . . and] that it does not benefit them at all whether it is a Magical Village, because it was already a tourist site when it was nominated.
>
> **Marcelina:** Yes . . . but . . .
>
> **Hotel owner:** . . . these ideas flow around in many places.

Marcelina initially attempts to interrupt the hotel owner, but stops as she realizes that the hotel owner is merely animating, not condoning, a widespread idea. Rather, the hotel owner criticizes Sergio for transmitting an idea they are working to overthrow, because it hinders people from recognizing their own (community) interest in preserving the urban image, which is what they "live off." Such carelessness is dangerous, she stressed, because when locals fail to recognize the urban image as a program benefit and even the municipal authorities lack commitment to protecting the urban image, outsiders, attracted by the prospects of setting up a tourism business, will have free rein to violate local construction norms. Subsequently, the teacher emphasizes that it is difficult for the municipal government to enforce the regulations given that these violations happen so frequently, which is why the best solution to the problem is to raise people's consciousness. During the discussion, the hotel owner and teacher place Sergio within the problem group by pointing out that his analysis transmits the idea that the program is not *yet* benefiting people and how this idea contributes to a disregard of the urban image. Sergio is thereby brought forward to epitomize the magnitude of the problem and his interpretation is seen to testify to the need of working on the consciousness of citizens. Citizens simply lack the objective knowledge needed to attribute the flow of tourism to Cuetzalan's participation in the program. The significance of this perspective came across later, when Sergio interrupted himself to clarify local discomfort with the program:

Sergio: Oh yeah, pardon, I was asked to what extent the villagers feel proud, right?[9] Here exists, let's say, a resentment that Cuetzalan was *not* the one who, um, let's say, asked for the title of Magical Village. That is, Cuetzalan was given the title of Magical Village. And what we want to bring back is that *with* or *without* the title, Cuetzalan is magical. In other words, it has always been so, right? So, this pride does not exist on behalf of the villagers. To be precise, the [urban] image is not protected.

To defend his view, Sergio elaborates local critique, describing how some people emphasize that Cuetzalan neither applied for nor desired inclusion into the program. On that basis, he suggests a persuasion technique that guides attention to the symbolic recognition the program has bestowed on Cuetzalan. Seeing the inclusion into the program as a consequence of Cuetzalan's "magical" essence (rather than vice versa), he argues that regardless of "the title" of Magical Village, Cuetzalan has accurately been recognized as a "magical" place. A focus on Cuetzalan's "magical" quality, in his view, may cultivate a sense of pride among citizens that will make them protect the urban image. This way, he seeks to demonstrate that his perspective would not compromise program policies about the urban image, but instead direct the attention of citizens to the particular urban environment that makes Cuetzalan "magical." The persuasion technique thus employs an idea that few locals would dispute, namely that Cuetzalan is "magical."

Although such a persuasion technique circumvents the question of whether the program is benefiting locals, the perspective was deemed impermissible for rendering the program as irrelevant to Cuetzalan and its tourism industry. The negative reception of this strategy shows that the campaign should not just make people *act* in accordance to program policies and *think* in line with the perspective of the program; they also need to *know* that tourism increases through program policies. Hence, the campaign is successful only if it makes people see the program as the cause of tourism. The teacher soon reasserted the main point of the campaign to reject Sergio's line of argument, a statement that Marcelina immediately supported:

Teacher: And basically that is it, right? To look around a bit and accept that it is a Magical Village and accept the development that this entails.

Marcelina: [Interrupting] And to make them, to make them note the fact that we did not apply, or that the title of Magical Village was not applied for, but that, *yes*, it was given to them and that is because of the magic that Cuetzalan has. But that *today* it is something which is very important, which should be *conserved*. That you "could not care if they take it away from me?" Well, that "they won't take it? It's the same for me if they don't!" On the *contrary*, that it is a title that we should conserve and that we should be *proud* of.

The teacher dissociates the consciousness-raising campaign from Sergio's interpretations by declaring that regardless of how Cuetzalan came to be a Magical

Village, making people "accept that it is a Magical Village" and "accept" the developmental strategies of the program is a nonnegotiable aim of the campaign. Signaling in this way to Sergio that his interpretations are neither institutionally desirable nor relevant, she closes that part of the discussion and requests him to revise his perception of the problem. As the prime representative of the Magical Villages Program, Marcelina substantiates the problematization of Sergio. By embedding statements attributed to Sergio, she confronts him with himself, animating his negligent attitude and illustrating how he comes to question the value of the program. Doing so, she carves out a representation of him, dramatizes his position, and prompts him to reflect on the legitimacy of his claims. In effect, the teacher and Marcelina sanction Sergio by isolating his interpretation from the campaign, assigning it instead to the mode of thinking that is to be acted upon. As a result, Sergio is made aware that he does not (yet) fully think in line with the program, and therefore cannot be its proponent without revising his view – raising consciousness of the target citizens is impossible as long as he shares their consciousness. Marcelina, however, also offers him a lifeline and path to re-enter the campaign by refining his persuasion technique so it does not reproduce critique of the program: she proposes that the campaign publicly affirms that Cuetzalan did not apply to receive nomination as a Magical Village; it never needed to because it was selected due to "the magic that Cuetzalan has." This way, Marcelina naturalizes and renders uncontroversial Cuetzalan's participation within the program, while ascribing importance to the role the recognition plays "today." Although Cuetzalan's "magical" quality is the cause of the recognition, and citizens may recognize Cuetzalan as "magical" regardless of the recognition, the recognition has a wider significance to Cuetzalan.

Privatized participation and the unitary community

The analyzed session took shape from two institutional frameworks, as seen in the way the teacher combined her professional role at the university with her presidency of the Magical Villages Committee: the "Pro Magical Villages Group" conceived to secure "community participation" in political processes (SECTUR 2006:1). Magical Villages meetings constitute an institutionalized forum for organizing local government authorities, citizens, service providers, and, in this case, a higher education institution around the task of implementing program objectives. The session thus constituted a university exercise with didactic purposes and a political platform with operative consequences beyond the educational setting. The campaign was mobilized, and several students subsequently entered the Magical Villages Committee. This synergy between the two institutional frameworks illustrates how such meetings function as didactic platforms, stressing a core program function; the Magical Villages Program teaches communities how to do tourism.

Being the local embodiment of the program, Marcelina worked as the authoritative scribe, centering gravity in the official reading of the program by distributing legitimacy among the participants according to their ability to perform institutionally authorized interpretations. Marcelina thus assisted the students in crafting an appropriate consciousness-raising campaign, while simultaneously conveying to them that the campaign was of strategic communal concern. During the meeting, interpretational limitations protruded, as Sergio failed to achieve narrative recognition from other participants.

On close inspection, the main problem identified by the teacher is not a lack of involvement in the program by society, but rather that Cuetzalan does not meet the program criterion "*about* 'involvement with society,'" which figures centrally in SECTUR's annual evaluations (SECTUR 2009:3, 10). Consequently, the identified problem is one pregiven by the program and one that threatens Cuetzalan's participation in it because failure to comply with program criteria may invoke sanctions by SECTUR, the ultimate of which is exclusion. Notably, the solution to the problem – consciousness-raising – is equally premeditated (SECTUR 2009:13), and numerous Magical Villages have designed consciousness-raising campaigns to inform citizens precisely about the importance and benefits of being a Magical Village, sometimes on recommendation following evaluations (Madrid Flores and Cerón Monroy 2012).

In this paradigmatic case, university students – some of whom are also service providers – were mobilized to solve the double task of ensuring local involvement in program activities and instrumenting a consciousness-raising campaign to inform the community of the benefits of being a Magical Village. On a mere performative level, the students solve these problems for local authorities, since their activities demonstrate the active citizenry the program requests and the very launch of the campaign fulfills the requirement of using consciousness-raising techniques to consolidate program practice.[10] Moreover, from the perspective of the program, public exaltation campaigns springing from citizens in Magical Villages solidify the local community as principal of program policy. On a social level, the campaign is hoped to cultivate a more positive spirit in additional citizens concerning the Magical Villages Program and to make people respect the *urban image*. On an economic level, the initiative is hoped to boost tourism.

The meeting illustrates a totalizing institutional tendency, since the prosperity of local tourism is equated with the local prosperity of the program. Participation in the program, then, is not primarily a matter of raising the stakes on tourism, but rather a question of putting into motion the know-how and practices that the program envisions will foster tourism. To follow program instructions means to generate (more) tourism. Conversely, not following program instructions is thought to jeopardize tourism.

One apparent consequence of institutionalizing the Magical Villages Program in Cuetzalan is that it constructs two distinct classes of people, which protrude eminently through the participation framework of the campaign; there are recipients in need of having their consciousness raised and there are transmitters whose moral duty it is to perform the consciousness-raising. The groups are arranged according to their alignment with the program, and only citizens who align with the program can claim to know about tourism.

Within program doctrine, tourism is not just a collective community task, but also a moral obligation, and, since the program is equated with tourism, the community is morally obliged to work for the program. The major schism of such community-based vision of tourism is that economic participation in tourism is a strictly privatized matter, and, since the program concentrates its efforts on central Cuetzalan, the mestizo elite residing there is the major economic participant. Unsurprisingly, those residents are most eager to preserve the urban image. The campaign's focus on the urban image reflects a struggle over central public space between inner-city residents with hotels, restaurants, and shops and incoming vendors with petty commerce. Backed by the program and local authorities, a fight is waged against incoming vendors, who are understood to harm the urban image and hamper tourism and commerce. What the campaign partly requests is that incoming vendors realize how their vending activities damage a community effort. To achieve this objective, the campaign charts a social order that renders hotel and restaurant owners as local patrons who collect and redistribute the economy in a trickle-down sense to the benefit of the community as a totality. The aim of making people accept the program is therefore not an invitation to the citizenry to enter tourism, as Sergio seems to think, but to prevent locals from countering program aims and regulations. Reaching the desired end purpose therefore entails circumventing, rephrasing, and converting local critique of the program.

The meeting participants thus belong exactly to the class of citizens who benefit the most from tourism. This group emerges as the total community, when there is no forum for alternative positions. The Magical Villages Program has thus created a platform for organizing private business holders in central Cuetzalan in the name of the community. The classed positions of the members of the pro group fade from view as the concept of community-based tourism discursively severs their privatized interests in tourism from their participation in program processes.

Given that the meeting revolved around citizens in Cuetzalan, and seeing this divide within the town, it may be anticipated that possibilities for Nahuas in the surrounding area to participate in tourism are slim. Participation by Nahua communities surfaced once during the meeting. A student suggested that when hotels employ an indigenous woman as a receptionist or maid, "why not dress her in the traditional vestments?" given that this will both preserve indigenous heritage and help sell the image of Cuetzalan. A social order thus emerges in which mestizo elite businesses are seen to create jobs through tourism and donate employment to the larger community, while Nahuas are granted a participatory role as cultural objects and beneficiaries.

Notably, the program's vision of a thriving national *multicultourism* emerges as a manual of tourism that the community "itself" is responsible for putting into motion. Securing the program's success therefore becomes the duty and moral obligation of citizens upon which the fate of the nation and the community rests. To secure the program's success, citizens in favor of the program are morally compelled to exercise technologies of citizenship on 'apathetic' or 'resistant' citizens to make them capable of grasping and terminating their irresponsible conduct. However, in attempting to regulate the conduct of others, the meeting participants equally reflect on and regulate their own conduct. The obligatorily recurring Magical Villages meeting may thus be seen as a didactic activity that introduces local citizens to the mode of thinking integral to the program. Adding the label of Magical Village to meetings concerning multifarious aspects on local tourism creates the impression of a unitary community cooperating to achieve a collective goal. The recurring meeting, as an activity type, thus has the performative effect of testifying to and renewing the sensation of a concerted community effort, an active citizenry, and social policy in motion.

Notes

1 This hunch was substantiated when I found the ethnography *Mismo Mexicano pero Diferente Idioma* (Castillo Hernández 2007) displayed in the dossier Marcelina had elaborated for SECTUR in 2012 to demonstrate local efforts to promote Cuetzalan "as a true Magical Village" (Ayuntamiento de Cuetzalan del Progreso 2012).
2 This area corresponds to the historic town center, where buildings are of a colonial, neoclassical style, with sloping terracotta tile roofing (Yanes Díaz 1994:305–307). The students' focus on this area reflects the program's focus on that same area, which is where tourists are predominantly accommodated.
3 It is indicative that this research agenda circulates in several Magical Villages. A study of Cuitzeo (Michoacán), for instance, focuses on the "opinions" of the citizenry toward tourism and the Magical Villages Program, concluding that "local development" "from below" is hampered due to "an indifference from citizens toward the resources and local potentialities" (García Vega and Guerrero García Rojas 2014).
4 Extemporized and presented to an audience that knows about the Magical Villages Program, this passage holds several half-finished phrases and implicit points.
5 The "cheapening" of the program was a topic of debate in national media (Armenta 2013).
6 Likewise, restaurant owners remarked that ambulant food vendors were hindering a tourism-induced community economy by selling food to tourists at low prices. Stressing that the program does not tolerate ambulant commerce, they therefore maintained that local government should have them removed from the town center.
7 Cascades are locally important sites of ecotourism, and Las Brisas near San Andrés Tzicuilan is considered the prime cascade site within the municipality.
8 The embedded source addresses her directly to give her a discouraging piece of information ("To be frank with you") and a collective animator ("we," "us") emerges to corroborate her category of analysis ("they," "people," "all"). The embedded source animated by Sergio ("I," "me") is thereby subverted by a quantitatively more representative original source that appears to engage directly with Carla to confirm her analysis.
9 Nobody had asked him about this, but by making an unspecified meeting participant principal of his remark ("I was *asked*") and requesting confirmation by participants ("right?"), he manages to challenge Carla's interpretation, while presenting his comment as benign and disinterested.
10 A subsequent evaluation applies the campaign exactly in this performative sense, stressing how Cuetzalan's Magical Villages Committee and Municipal Council of Tourism have conducted the campaign to "raise consciousness of the inhabitants in general about what it means to be a Magical Village" (BUAP 2013:61–62).

References

Armenta, Gustavo. 2013. "Los Abaratados Pueblos Mágicos." *Periódico Viaje*, March 15. Retrieved January 10, 2014 (http://periodicoviaje.com/opinion/1245/Los-abaratados-Pueblos-Mágicos).

Asmuß, Birte, and Jan Svennevig. 2009. "Meeting Talk: An Introduction." *Journal of Business Communication* 46(3):3–22.

Ayuntamiento de Cuetzalan del Progreso. 2012. *Expediente: Cuetzalan Pueblo Mágico*. Cuetzalan: Administración Municipal 2011–2014.

BUAP. 2013. *Agenda de Competitividad de los Destinos Turísticos de México: Estudio de Competitividad Turística de Cuetzalan Pueblo Mágico*. Puebla: BUAP.

Castillo Hernández, Mario Alberto. 2007. *Mismo Mexicano pero Diferente Idioma: Identidades y Actitudes Lingüísticas en los Maseualmej de Cuetzalan*. Mexico City: INAH and UNAM.

Cruikshank, Barbara. 1999. *The Will to Empower: Democratic Citizens and Other Subjects*. Ithaca, NY: Cornell University Press.

Drew, Paul, and John Heritage. 1992. "Analyzing Talk at Work: An Introduction." Pp. 3–65 in *Talk at Work: Interaction in Institutional Settings*, edited by P. Drew and J. Heritage. Cambridge: Cambridge University Press.

García Vega, Diego, and Hilda R. Guerrero García Rojas. 2014. "El Programa Pueblos Mágicos: Análisis de los Resultados de una Consulta Local Ciudadana – El caso de Cuitzeo, Michoacán, México." *Economía y Sociedad* 18(31):71–94.

Goffman, Erving. 1981. *Forms of Talk*. Philadelphia, PA: University of Pennsylvania Press.

Gubrium, Jaber F., and James A. Holstein. 2009. *Analyzing Narrative Reality*. Thousand Oaks, CA: Sage.

Levinson, Stephen C. 1992. "Activity Types and Language." Pp. 66–100 in *Talk at Work: Interaction in Institutional Settings*, edited by J. Drew and J. Heritage. Cambridge: Cambridge University Press.

Louwerse, Max, and Willie van Peer. 2002. "Contents and Contexts: Section 1. Thematic Approaches." Pp. 213–216 in *Thematics: Interdisciplinary Studies*, edited by M. Louwerse and W. van Peer. Amsterdam: J. Benjamins.

Madrid Flores, Francisco and Hazael Cerón Monroy. 2012. *Evaluación de Desempeño de los Destinos Turísticos en el Marco de los Convenios de Coordinación en Materia de Reasignación de Recursos (CCRR): Análisis del Desempeño Turístico Local – Modelo de Satisfacción de los Turistas*. Mexico City: SECTUR, CESTUR, and CONACYT. Retrieved January 15, 2014 (www.sectur.gob.mx/wp-content/uploads/2014/09/IDT_DoctoMaestro_12.pdf).

SECTUR. 2006. *Criterios de Incorporación al Programa "Pueblos Mágicos": Versión Final 31 de Julio 2006*. Mexico City: SECTUR. Retrieved September 6, 2012 (www.sectur. gob.mx/work/models/securing/Resource/14192/CRITERIOSDEINCORPORACION ALPROGRAMAPUEBLOSMAGICOS.pdf).

SECTUR. 2009. *Reglas de Operación*. Mexico City: SECTUR. Retrieved September 6, 2012 (www.sectur.gob.mx/work/models/sectur/Resource/99fbd793-a344-4b98-9633-78607f33c b8f/Reglas_de_operacion.pdf).

Yanes Díaz, Gonzalo. 1994. "The Case of Cuetzalan and Yohualichan Puebla, Mexico: Archaeology and Tourism – Should They Be Integrated?" Pp. 303–312 in *Archaeological Remains: In Situ Preservation – Proceedings of the Second ICAHM International Conference, 11–15 October*. Montreal: ICOMOS.

6 Multicultourism in the Magical Village

Setting temporality and translocality

Upon arrival to Cuetzalan, I had given little thought to how the Magical Villages Program had evolved and processually constituted itself there. Neither did I realize how some of my queries departed from the image of stasis mediated of and by the program. Nonetheless, I did wonder why people tended to construct generalized accounts or point to recent events in response to questions such as: "How did you react when Cuetzalan was nominated as a Magical Village?"

Of course, in 2002, when Cuetzalan became a Magical Village, the program was not in motion in the ways it came to be later. The town was never *publicly* nominated. Celebratory inauguration ceremonies were not standard program practices or media events before the Magical Villages had been embedded in a narrative of recognition and the inclusion procedure had been (discursively) reversed (see Chapter 4). Entry into the program in 2002 was therefore little noteworthy, neither the cause of a news story, nor of particular public concern, as later it has come to be. It was first and foremost a political decision. The event and moment I was requesting interviewees to (re)construct had never occurred. Cuetzalan did not become *magical* by a stroke, but was inscribed into a cumulative process of transformation.

Expanding the historicization of the Magical Villages Program, this chapter analyzes how the politically promoted term *magical* has managed to assert itself as a primordial condition of social reality and become a natural way for inhabitants to think and talk about town life. Emulating Cruikshank's governmentality analytical framework (Cruikshank 1999:6), how has the program constituted a terrain of strategic political action that goes largely unacknowledged as a field of politics?

Constructionist approaches to narrative and interaction analysis stress the inseparability of narratives and the settings within which they come into being (Gubrium and Holstein 2009:123–197). In a compelling article, environmental historian William Cronon (1992) shows how differing interpretations of environmental change in the Great Plains are implicated by the disparate narrative settings within which they appear. As Cronon demonstrates, the narrative settings work as enclosures that facilitate certain narrative paths, and consequently certain ways to act in and on the environment, while closing off others.

This chapter extends such analytical order by examining how Cuetzalan's physical urban environment has been modified and infused with signage and narratives to produce a narrative setting revolving around a recognition framework with distinct temporal and translocal underpinnings that organize how citizens think and talk about the town. First, the chapter shows how the urban environment has been adapted through Cuetzalan's participation in the Magical Villages Program. Next, the chapter analyzes a travel magazine that celebrates the town's decennial anniversary as a Magical Village to show how mediation of urban space and social life accentuates the tendencies identified in the physical environment. Finally, the chapter illustrates how individual accounts relate to the recognition framework and mobilize the temporal and translocal constructions previously identified.

Through analysis of a Magical Villages meeting, Chapter 5 illustrated the existence of a narrative environment constructed around the notion of *magical* and institutional practices through which such narrative environment is fostered, sustained, and made to exceed its institutional origin. Yet for such meetings to work as a mobilizing factor and organizing principle, the concept of being a Magical Village must have been granted a weighty, collective significance a priori. This chapter therefore spotlights how the introduction of institutional conventions into the urban setting has topicalized Cuetzalan's status as *magical* and made the concept a natural way through which to experience the town and its social life. The chapter argues that program modifications of the urban environment feed into a narrative setting in which the notion of *magical* comes to organize how people conceptualize and narrate about the town's past, present, and future.

Remaking the urban environment

One crosscutting feature of the Magical Villages Program throughout its history is a focus on "conserving" and "improving" the "urban image" (SECTUR 2001:168, 2005:9, 2009:9). The majority of program funding has been destined to such conservation and infrastructural work, and is the most direct way in which the program asserts to be generating tourism. The program thus operates within a larger international framework that developed in the last half of the twentieth century, in which the idea of historic towns as heritage sites has been accompanied by a growing focus on urban conservation and increasing tourism to historic towns (Orbaşli 2000:1–3). From 2002 through 2014, eight so-called stages of "improvement of the urban image" were carried out in Cuetzalan, the seven first of which cost a total of nearly MXN 58,000,000 and demanded a municipal funding of a little over MXN 20,000,000 (SECTUR 2014). The project stages have made use of methods for limiting "signs of contemporary urban life" and installing artifacts that promote a "historic image," which are well-known conservation procedures in Spanish-colonial city centers recognized by UNESCO as world heritage (Nelle 2009), including those applied in Puebla City (Jones and Varley 1994:38–40).

The first three stages, which were carried out between 2002 and 2004, focused on infrastructure, restoration work, and relocation of ambulant and semi-fixed commerce. Facades were modified, repaired, and painted.[1] Overhead cables were moved underground and 'heritage' lanterns replaced the existing lampposts. The cement-tiled plaza and church atrium were repaved with a rustic rock pavement that was in use in the main streets, and the same pavement was extended to surrounding streets and sidewalks. A small building on the top tier of the three-tiered plaza was redesigned to host flower vendors, and – at a safe distance from the plaza – a two-story building was assigned to house a "gastronomic" market with greengrocer stalls downstairs and food stalls upstairs.[2] Moreover, a cultural center, housing the ethnographic museum and the municipal archives and library, was refurbished (Domínguez 2003, 2004).

Allocating buildings for specific commercial activities was intended to clear the center of most of the ambulant and semi-fixed vendors. Ambulant vending is a recurring topic of conflict in Cuetzalan and other Magical Villages. Since 2006, the program has formally instructed participant towns to reorganize commerce to eliminate ambulant vending in key tourist sites (SECTUR 2006:2). Municipal regulations ban ambulant vendors from occupying public spaces, since they and their stalls are seen to harm the urban image and the "typical scenery" (Ayuntamiento de Cuetzalan del Progreso 2012). Contemporary tourism initiatives show a propensity to cleanse public spaces of "petty commerce" (Baud and Ypeij 2009:3–4), and, incidentally, many of these vendors are Nahuas (and Totonacs) who travel in from the surrounding area to participate in regional economic life.

Certainly, the ongoing reworkings of the urban topography have had an effect on how citizens experience their town. However, the significance of these modifications lies not solely in the modifications themselves, but just as much in correctly attributing the changes in the urban environment to the Magical Villages Program and regarding them as an effort to bring back the golden age of Cuetzalan. The installation of new 'heritage' lanterns and rustic rock paving in streets and public spaces, as well as the attempt to clear the plaza of ambulant vendors and semi-fixed stalls with tarpaulin covers, is to be seen as a return to how Cuetzalan once was.

Corresponding to the chronology sketched in Chapter 4, the process of attribution began in 2006 with the fourth stage of program intervention. At this point, the program had begun to position itself as a brand and transmit a narrative of recognition. During this stage, the plaza park was redesigned by replacing modern-looking fences with antique-looking ironwork fences that corresponded in design with the 'heritage' lanterns and new 'heritage' style benches and trash cans (Notimex 2006; see Figure 6.1). In 2013, some locals were still upset about the restoration of the park, and would recount how the general public had not been properly informed about the plans, discovering one day to their disbelief construction workers damaging and discarding allegedly antique water fountains and old trees, and how citizens stormed to the rescue when the kiosk was to be demolished. When asked about the urban environment, however, most people would say that nothing has changed and that the town looks the way it always has, although some sarcastically granted that the Magical Villages Program has had the buildings of the main street repainted.

In March 2013, the park was completely remodeled for a second time during the sixth stage of "improvement of the urban image." Locals were shocked and infuriated to discover construction workers discarding the allegedly old ironwork fences, benches, and water fountains. A Citizen Front in Defense of Cuetzalan's Cultural Heritage was mobilized to limit potential damages (Hernández Alcántara 2013). People who a few months earlier had recounted how the heritage in the park had been previously destroyed now saw their heritage being destroyed once more. Keeping in mind that the concept of heritage can be a forceful source of identification and an effective means for mobilizing local communities against top-down paternalist politics (Smith 2007), seven years still seem to constitute a remarkably brief time span for projecting the heritage furniture into time immemorial. Nevertheless, some locals were outraged to find their heritage disappearing and others feared an inconsistent townscape, so much so that newcomer Lucinda spontaneously decided to email me illustrated reports (see Figure 6.2) that document the damage inflicted:

> **Lucinda (April 2013):** [T]he local and state authorities decided to remodel the plaza!! So one Thursday afternoon, an official event was held at the atrium; it was about the remodeling of Cuetzalan. The governor, mayor, local officials, and school children were present but no one from the community. The next day, a bulldozer in the plaza began breaking the stone from the floor while workers were removing the fences, benches, and fountains!! Next day, the kiosk, and later, even the big tree and some palm trees were removed . . . Criminals!! [English in original]

As heritage literature has long shown, the perceived age of objects does not depend on their actual age, but rather on the assumption of the objects as antique. Hence, notions of antiquity can be mediated by exploiting aesthetic and material conventions that correspond to contemporary imaginations of the past (Lowenthal 1985:242; Tunbridge and Ashworth 1996:10–11). Lucinda's reaction to the removal of the fences, benches, and rock pavement and the rise of the citizen front show how a group of locals have ascribed a significant temporal depth to these recent objects, making these citizens perceive their removal as a violation of town heritage and a disregard of town history. Given that these antique-looking objects are materially and stylistically framed in a style broadly perceived as 'colonial,' memorizing them as recent is simply counterintuitive, and would require remembering and understanding the context of their installation.

Yet the "perceived pastness" of objects also depends on the context within which they appear (Holtorf 2005:127–129). In this case, the objects were situated in the plaza, the heart of communal social life, and the founding space around which the old town developed, as seen across towns and cities in Mexico (Nuñez 2007:32–44). Locals who recounted the reworking of the park in 2006 focused mainly on the destruction and removal of old, "original" features and less on the installation of new features, and once the installation of these heritage objects is no longer remembered, they easily pass as antique in a town space, which is imbued with the deepest sense of community continuity.

Figure 6.1 The park as it looked from late 2006 to early 2013 with its heritage fences, benches and trash cans

Source: Photo received from former interlocutor, Lucinda, April 2013

Figure 6.2 Photograph documenting absence of fences, benches, and fountains, and damages to the rocky pavement and kiosk

Source: Photo received from former interlocutor, Lucinda, April 2013

As Goffman argues, human ability to determine what is going on in social set-tings depends on the capacity to "correctly [connect] acts to their *source*" [original emphasis] (Goffman 1986:516). However, since deeds and acts inevitably "come to us connected to their source," receiving deeds and acts is not a matter of draw-ing up connections, but rather of identifying the connectives that accompany such acts. This means that connectives – the linking of source and action – constitute a particularly vulnerable aspect of experience, since they tend to be received with "unguarded security," for which reason the management of connectives holds great opportunities for fabricating experience (Goffman 1986:479–480). Hence, once installed in the plaza, the heritage furniture denies its own novelty, gradually working its way into the collective memory of how the old town was. And if the rock pavement in the plaza, atrium, and streets was not exactly remembered as *the* original material pavement, it was perceived as *identical* to the one that had originally been in use. As municipal chronicler Cecilio stated regarding the new rock pavement in a seminar that gathered the chroniclers of Puebla's Magical Villages: "In a way we saw again the Cuetzalan of the early nineteenth century."

Framing the setting through narrative and signage

Nevertheless, while the comprehensive installation of features pointing to days past have extensively transformed the urban environment and local experience of it, the transformations themselves do not self-evidently lead to an expe-rience of urban space as contemplated by local authorities and the Magical Villages Program. Additional framing work is required to establish a con-nection between heritage furniture and the view on the past mediated by the program. Such framing of the setting began during the fourth stage, as pink and yellow street name signs, tourist signs, and display boards with the Magical Villages logo came to dot the town. In 2013, the colors on the street and tour-ist signs had turned pale, and some signs had disappeared. Yet even partly dismantled and worn by weather, the program signage still provided testimony to Cuetzalan's status as a Magical Village by weaving the local setting into a broader national history. Town history thus emerges as national history, mov-ing Cuetzalan from the geographical peripheries of the nation to the center of metropolitan nationalism.

The key display board flanked the park and carried the title *Cuetzalan* (see Figure 6.3). The title may be seen to refer both to the location of the display board and to the subject matter of its two accompanying texts, which expound the topo-nymic etymology and town history. Between the texts, a map marks out the town and its historic center, and at the top of the display board an encircled logogram is highlighted by the same yellow color that figures at the base, where the logo-gram reappears alongside the Magical Villages logo. The pink color, white font, and yellow base with the two symbols form the design template of all the display boards and street signs (see Figures 6.4 and 6.5).

The logogram has two intertwined origins and significances. It is copied from and represents the municipal shield as it looked in 2006. The municipal shield

Figure 6.3 The park as it looked from late 2006 to early 2013 with its display board in front

Source: Photo received April 2013 from former interlocutor, Lucinda

Figure 6.4 Cuetzalan's Aztec place sign

Source: Casper Jacobsen, February 2013

Figure 6.5 Program logo on display board

Source: Casper Jacobsen, February 2013

in turn is copied from an Aztec toponymic sign that occurs in the early colonial manuscript *Codex Mendoza*, which is widely celebrated as a key source to the study of the Aztecs.[3] *Codex Mendoza* consists of three pictorial sections produced by scribes from the Aztec capital Tenochtitlan with primary knowledge of the pre-Hispanic era, accompanied by glosses and explanations in Spanish and Classical Nahuatl (Anawalt 2001). The manuscript mentions a town by the name *Cueçalan* once in each of the two first sections (Berdan and Anawalt 1992:fol. 6r, 37r), which provide a chronicle of city state conquests attributed to individual rulers and a list recording the tribute collected from conquered city states within the imperial provinces (Anawalt 2001). The logogram adorning the display board and the municipal shield derives from the tribute section.

The etymological account on display is divided into two parts, introduced by the statement that Cuetzalan "has two meanings." This remark reflects the existence of two locally competing interpretations. Nevertheless, on the display board, the favored interpretation is doubly asserted by splitting it into two collaborating analyses with minuscule variation. One construes the etymology of Cuetzalan through linguistic analysis of the Nahuat toponym, and the other through epigraphic analysis of the Aztec toponymic sign:

It is derived from Nahuatl QUETZALLI, shining, beautiful and clear thing;
TOTOTL, bird, and the final diction LAN expresses together, near or among;
in consequence, QUETZAL-LAN means "among the beautiful birds or
together with the precious birds called quetzal"
    QUETZALLAN = Quetzal-Lan. A bundle of red feathers with blue tips
provide the phonetics, quetzalli, on top of the suffix tlan or lan, expressed by
two teeth "place in which the quetzal birds abound" or near them

The level of accuracy in this etymological reading is pertinent here only insofar
as it illustrates the means through which local toponymic etymology is made
relevant to a national audience. Common to both analyses is the assumption that
the first morpheme must originally have been *quetzal-*, referring to the plumage
of the colorful quetzal bird, rather than *cuezal-* as indicated in *Codex Mendoza*
and *cuetzal-* as the toponym occurs today. An earlier form of the toponym is
thus asserted in reference to the toponymic sign from *Codex Mendoza*, which
partly consists of four "red feathers with blue tips," and the first analysis inserts
"TOTOTL" (bird) into the toponym to qualify a translation revolving around
the quetzal bird.

Placing the Aztec sign at the top of the display board ensures that the reader
proceeds along the same deductive line that transforms the contemporary
toponym "Cuetzalan" into the 'pre-Hispanic,' Aztec toponym "Quetzallan."
First, the Aztec sign visually mediates the feather component, and then the text
specifies the component to be *quetzal* feathers. Thus, a connective is established between the toponym, the interpretation on display, and the Aztec place
sign, and an imagined pre-Hispanic environment "in which the quetzal birds
abound" is fused with the present-day environmental surroundings, which are
widely celebrated as extraordinarily green, fertile, and with a rich flora and
fauna (cf. Merlo Juárez 1995:11–16).

The preeminently placed Aztec sign plays a double framing role, though, since
the very state of possessing an Aztec place sign firmly inscribes "Quetzallan"
into the national legacy of Aztec culture and imperial history. The etymological
exercise therefore equally constitutes a public performance of insiderness, which
fuses contemporary local culture with major legacies of Aztec culture through
a demonstration of continuity in cultural identity, knowledge, and language
practices. This pre-Hispanicization of the local landscape creates a desirable
narrative environment from which Cuetzalan may emerge as a central location
within metropolitan nationalist narratives.

Municipal chronicler Cecilio lamented this tenacious folk etymology and its
centrality in official town history, since it disregards another, more plausible,
interpretation revolving around the scarlet macaw (Campo 1979), which does not
depend on reconstructing allegedly altered phonemes, but departs from the toponym as it occurs in the *Codex Mendoza*.[4]

When, as was the case, no one else mentioned this interpretation, it is not just
because the quetzal interpretation has long been in vogue.[5] Rather, the scarlet
macaw interpretation would hamper a town narrative rich in national symbolism.

Although both species are widely known due to their vividly colored plumage and used as icons in Mexico, the quetzal presents an obvious advantage; the almost one-meter-long tail feathers of the male quetzal bird were highly esteemed luxury items in several pre-Hispanic Mesoamerican societies, including among the Aztecs, who procured these feathers in vast numbers through tribute impositions on subjugated provinces. Hence, the quetzal bird gained an emblematic status, and, due to its close association with elite goods, the quetzal feather has become the pre-Hispanic and Aztec feather par excellence (Smith 2012:96), rendering the plumage from other colorful lowland birds of secondary importance. The special symbolic status of the quetzal feather is not the least due to being a componential feature of the pan-Mesoamerican feathered serpent god Quetzalcoatl (Nicholson 2001:246), who, with the surge of the indigenist movement and the Mexican-American Chicano movement, arguably became *the* pre-Hispanic culture hero of Mexico (Read and Gonzalez 2002:223–228). Since the same narrative resources are not available with the alternative interpretation, it is not surprising to find that the interpretation centering on the quetzal has more appeal. A basis for this claim may be found in the display board's section on local history:

The town of Cuetzalan has its origins from the time that the Tenochca empire expands; from the year 1475 the emperor Axayacatl converts the region of the Northern Sierra to tributary of the Great Tenochtitlan, *placing Quetzalan as a center for the collection of quetzal feathers.* [. . .] Later, in 1552, it is subjugated by the Spaniards and catechized by the Franciscans and by the year 1555 it is nominated San Francisco Quetzalan due to its important socio-economic activity.[6]

According to this text, Cuetzalan *originated* as a result of Aztec incursion into the Northern Sierra during the reign of Axayacatl, who made the region "tributary of the Great Tenochtitlan." Thus, "Quetzalan" *arose* as a consequence of imperial invasion and administrative planning with Axayacatl instituting the town "as a center for the collection of quetzal feathers." The foundation of "Quetzalan" is thus linked directly to Aztec imperial presence in the Sierra, and since Aztec imperial expansion is posited as cause of origin of the town, it may be inferred that the founding citizens were Aztecs relocated from Tenochtitlan and that the town played a crucial role as an imperial outpost in frontier land. Moreover, as "a center for the collection of quetzal feathers," "Quetzalan" is portrayed to have played a crucial part in the imperial economy, dispatching luxury goods to the Aztec elite. The display board thereby constructs a genealogy that links local citizens – most obviously the Nahuas within the municipality – to the invading Aztec imperial forces, thus framing local citizens as direct descendants of the Aztecs from the imperial capital Tenochtitlan and marking Cuetzalan as an Aztec town.

Notably, the *Codex Mendoza* does not enlist *Cuezalan* as a town conquered by Axayacatl or among those dispatching quetzal feathers to the imperial center. Nonetheless, the display board projects the interpretation into the early colonial era, as the Franciscans arrive in 1555 to name the town San Francisco Quetzalan "due to its important socio-economic activity." The text thus draws in the Franciscans as firsthand witnesses to the town's involvement in the quetzal feather trade, as testified by their sanctification of the toponym.

Departing from the Aztec place sign, the display boards carve out a concise regional pre-Hispanic history, which endows Cuetzalan with a central role within the Aztec empire. The feathers in the Aztec place sign are interpreted as quetzal feathers, facilitating a reconstruction of the toponym as "Quetzalan." In translating the toponym, the quetzal feathers become a quetzal bird that is inscribed into local ecology, thus increasing the likelihood of Cuetzalan having been established by Aztec emperor Axayacatl as a major distributor of quetzal feathers to Tenochtitlan.

Following through each step of the deductive process, it is evident that the guiding interpretational principle of such history writing is to angle local history so it becomes pertinent to a national audience. Not only is Cuetzalan portrayed as having played an important part in the Aztec empire; the town is also centered in contemporary Mexico by virtue of being an enclave of descendants of the imperial Aztec capital. As such, Cuetzalan is inscribed firmly into the nation, as the nation is inscribed firmly into Cuetzalan, and it should come as no surprise that an interpretational twist has occurred at the very beginning of the deductive sequence; the Aztec place sign of the *Codex Mendoza* refers not to Cuetzalan (Puebla), but to Cuetzala (Guerrero) (Smith and Berdan 1996:299).[7] Sorting out the *Codex Mendoza* from the history on display, the remaining empirical building block is the bare toponym. The challenge of writing grand, national history from within the confines of a small town is illustrated time and again in local writings, which draw on colonial sources dealing with Cuetzala (Guerrero) to provide the vital historical detail that corroborates an Aztec origin to the town.

The display board's Aztec place sign and accompanying historical narrative give the impression that the historical events described have taken place in that location, and consequently that the visitor is standing in a town space with origins stretching back to 1475 and the arrival of the Aztecs. Placing the town map between the two texts corroborates this notion by demarcating the spatial setting for the historical narrative. The center of the map presents an area of white polygons representing ensembles of buildings, and in between them named streets are marked out. This area corresponds to the government-certified zone of historical monuments, *the historic center*, composed of colonial-style buildings, and it constitutes the so-called Magical Villages polygon where the program has been working on the urban image. The remainder of the town is represented by streetless and buildingless blanks. By mapping the most remarkable places and routes, the program display board seeks both to shape visitors' movement through town and to delimit the part of town, which may credibly work to anchor the historical narrative on display. This way, the map indicates a temporal continuity in spatial terms, indicating the location in which visitors can find themselves placed at the center of an extensive and ongoing history. To this end, the display board is strategically located so that upon viewing it and reading the text, the visitor is standing on the plaza, facing the church and the atrium with its *voladores* pole and the green and hilly natural backdrop. The spatial outline of the town center with its plaza and atrium is paramount in mediating the sensation of spatial historical depth, since this architectural convention constitutes a nationally widespread model for organizing urban space, closely identified with the early colonial era (see Chapter 8).

The display board and its framing of local history and setting corresponds with the 'heritage' furniture, since the colonial-style ironwork benches and trash cans included into their design plaques showing Cuetzalan's Aztec place sign (see Figure 6.6). Form, material, and symbolic content are thus synchronized framing conventions that collaborate in this 'heritage' furniture to mark the objects as indeterminately old and push them into community memory.

From 2006 to 2013, the place sign appeared everywhere in Cuetzalan together with the Magical Villages logo. The visual juxtaposition of the Aztec place sign and the program logo tied the Magical Villages Program to the deepest sense of the past in Cuetzalan. Moreover, by marking all public historical narratives with the program logo, the signage framed such narratives as testimony to Cuetzalan's *magical* qualities and its status as a Magical Village. The Magical Villages Program thus emerges as an authenticating and recognizing organ, literally signing the narratives

Figure 6.6 Heritage bench

Source: Casper Jacobsen, February 2013

and framing what may count as testimony. The signage and narratives are therefore both performative paratexts that frame Cuetzalan as a Magical Village through public recognition and didactic devices that instruct locals as to what counts as proper history, what makes the town *magical*, and consequently how locals may assist in contributing to such identity work.

Departing from the analysis of how the Magical Villages Program has framed the urban environment, the chapter now turns to show how mediation of town space and social life in official promotional material accentuates the frames identified in the physical setting to further consolidate a narrative environment that ties together Cuetzalan, indigeneity, and notions of the past.

Mediating the setting

In March 2012, the municipal government and the Puebla-based travel magazine *Enlázate* printed a 32-page special edition in Spanish to celebrate Cuetzalan's decennial anniversary as a Magical Village. Officials of the municipal government co-produced the content, and the municipal department of tourism distributed the magazine to visitors during 2012 and 2013. Thus, the magazine can be taken to embody Cuetzalan's official on-site promotional strategy during those years. Printed in color on coated paper and richly illustrated with photos and a map pointing out the main attractions, the magazine is likely to have served as the prime source of information for domestic tourists in 2012–2013.

In six sections, the magazine covers topics such as local history, ecosystem, ritual dances, Cuetzalan's fiesta, architecture, and gastronomy. The accompanying photos show emblematic colonial-style architecture from Cuetzalan, pre-Hispanic ruins from nearby Yohualichan, natural scenery, and, above all, indigenous people dressed in ritual and traditional clothes.[8] Strikingly absent in most photos are material features that refer unequivocally to contemporary life. A single photo showing a typical, sloping street reveals a few distant cars, and another photo includes a white tourist wearing a bandanna, jeans, and jacket beholding a river.[9] Photos showing indigenous agents apply close-up and worm's-eye view techniques and are cropped closely around the human objects, isolating desired scenes from undesired features. By cleaning the illustrative material of references to contemporary life, the magazine employs and accentuates the *in situ* framing of the physical environment that the Magical Villages Program has been fostering. Moreover, the photos selected to illustrate town life predominantly derive from the patron saint fiesta in 2011. At this annual occasion, indigenous presence is high and traditional dances are performed. By selecting these images, 'everyday' Cuetzalan is portrayed as indigenous territory and as ritual space, and indigenous agents are primarily shown to be engaged in cultural and religious activities. Thus, the magazine effectively "under-communicates" Cuetzalan as a mestizo town, while "over-communicating" (cf. Eriksen 2002:29–32) indigenous presence and indigenous engagement in ritual activity. The magazine opens with an editorial by the municipal president, who presents a brief synthesis of life in the municipality that tourists can expect to experience:

Here you will find a variety of information that will bring you to know diverse aspects that represent the strong heartbeat of our quotidian life; a multicolored mosaic that has *the tradition* as a central component; a tradition that brings to the present beliefs, practices and collective sentiments that were constructed in the past; and recreated in the present. [Cuetzalan's] dances, patron saint fiestas, its gastronomy, its handicrafts, its abundant flora and wild fauna, its architecture, but, above all, its important number of indigenous residents that inhabit the municipality, all together they represent an important legacy in which the pre-Hispanic melts together with the Hispanic and the indigenous with the mestizo in an important exchange of uses and customs that have been fortifying our sense of belonging day after day [original emphasis].

(Baez Carmona 2012:3)

The municipal president presents "quotidian life" as Cuetzalan's main attraction, substantiating the presentation by stating that it revolves around a tradition of beliefs and practices with roots in the past. By giving special mention to the indigenous people and their number, the municipal president makes indigenous locals the prime agents of *"the tradition,"* which they bring to life in the present through their mere pursuance of everyday activities. This representation, which projects indigenous agents and their everyday life into history by stressing them as "legacy" of "pre-Hispanic" tradition, is strengthened by the accompanying photographic material. Rather than portraying everyday life, the magazine employs photos from the annual fiesta that show indigenous agents in public space exclusively engaged in ceremonial and religious activity, dressed in colorful ritual and traditional clothing, performing *"the tradition."* Thus, the textual presentation of local everyday life as "a multicolored mosaic" revolving around *"the tradition"* cooperates with the photographic portrayal of indigenous people engaged in ritual activities and dressed in colorful ritual clothes to produce a ritualization of everyday indigenous behavior.[10]

In an equally figurative manner, the magazine employs symbols of indigenous culture when describing everyday life. To this end, the text anchors indigenous life to rural Cuetzalan and the "pre-Hispanic" past, and conversely the text equates mestizo citizens with "Hispanic" and contemporary urban Mexico. By pointing to the melting together of "the pre-Hispanic" and "indigenous" with "the Hispanic" and "mestizo," the municipal president evokes the ideal of (multi)cultural mixing expressed by the ideology of *mestizaje*, which has been at the core of Mexican nationalism since the revolution (Knight 1990: 84–87). He thereby promises the tourist an experience of Mexico in the making by highlighting Cuetzalan as a place where an authentically pre-Hispanic indigenous culture prevails to infuse mestizo nationals with "a sense of belonging." Throughout the magazine, indigenous life is temporally severed from contemporary and majority Mexico by portraying indigenous people as in opposition to or incompatible with modernity:

It will suffice to walk the paths and royal roads or enter the houses of the Cuetzaltec territory to find oneself with boys and girls, women and men proudly dressed in their attires and speaking in the Nahuatl tongue, or masehualkopa, as it is known in the region, practicing their quotidian tasks impregnated with culture and identity and resisting the changes that the modernization processes try to impose on them.

(Fernández Lomelín 2012:30)

By "practicing their quotidian tasks," or simply by speaking their first language, the indigenous locals are seen to resist modernity. Modernity is articulated as a threatening force that encroaches on indigenous space, yet as something that can be deflected as long as indigenous communities retain their cultural practices. Indigenous cultural identities and languages thus emerge as premodern resources through which to resist modernity. By extension, indigenous locals become both principals of antimodernist sentiments and identity resources for visiting mestizos, whose urban life is conceived as less rooted and less authentic. In anthropologist Johannes Fabian's terms, the text constructs a social evolutionist "Typological Time" that dichotomizes rural, indigenous locals versus urban, mestizo tourists through spatial and temporal distancing (Fabian 2002:15–23). The effect is a "denial of coevalness" (Fabian 2002:31–32) that creates a temporal disjunction between otherwise contemporary indigenous Nahuas and mestizo tourists. The social evolutionary underpinnings of this temporal disjunction protrude from the idea that indigenous communities are able to counter modernity by maintaining their cultural practices; the existence of the described cultural practices are thus taken as indexical of a premodern stage in the evolutionary chart, whereby cultural differences signify evolutionary differences. Indigenous locals are taken to embody a past way of life, which the mestizo tourist can experience through "shared Time" (Fabian 2002:31–32), which allows them to observe indigenous people practicing "their quotidian tasks impregnated with culture and identity." Space conflates with time, and visiting mestizos may thus 'return' to such a perceived earlier evolutionary stage. In heritage tourism, traversing space is habitually equated with time travel (Källén 2015:103–128), and travel to Cuetzalan is subtly framed within a social evolutionist tale that relegates Nahuas to an earlier civilizational stage. Through such temporal othering, the magazine strategically employs indigenous presence in public space to symbolically situate Cuetzalan in a distant historical or mythologized national past.

The magazine 'premodernizes' indigenous citizens further by inscribing them into nature and marking their ecological engagement as unaffected by modern, polluting technology. The perceived symbiosis of indigenous people and nature, which is pervasive to cultural tourism and ecotourism, comes to symbolize a sense of lost sacredness in the secularized, materialist world of the mestizo traveler with which indigenous life is contrasted (cf. Taylor 2001; Badone 2004). Again, quotidian tasks are specified to place the indigenous locals in opposition to modernity and render them as integral to nature:

Cuetzalan, a municipality full of culture; with its beautiful women wearing their attire as white as their spirit and those embroideries as colorful as the nature that surrounds them. [. . .] The communities of Cuetzalan are those that still preserve their indigenous essence almost at 100%. They all walk to work, they cultivate their crops without fertilizers, they prepare the nixtamal [maize dough] to make handmade tortillas, they transport the water from wells by means of irrigation channels, they manufacture their clothes, and many other things that the mestizo has forgotten about and exchanged for the immediacy of things.

(Cortés Sandoval 2012:18)

The excerpt belongs to a section that celebrates Cuetzalan's first 10 years as a Magical Village. The text appears beneath a photo from the *huipil* ceremony of the annual town fiesta (see Chapter 8) and alongside photos showing a dripstone cave and a cascade surrounded by green vegetation.[11] The photos, which juxtapose natural scenes and indigenous women wearing white traditional clothing with colorful embroideries, thus interact with the textual description that describes indigenous women in similar terms. In the magazine, the traditional clothing, which is worn for the occasion of the *huipil* ceremony, becomes indexical of local indigeneity and provides an x-ray view of the inner state of indigenous women; the embroideries become extensions of nature and the white color points to the purity of "their spirit." The natural setting is thus constructed as the habitat of indigenous women, and nature is equally seen to reside inside the women, a symbiosis pointing to the pure ways of life "the mestizo has forgotten about." This sense of purity is linked to "indigenous essence," which consists in preindustrial relations to nature evidenced by their propensity to "walk to work," "make handmade tortillas," "manufacture their own clothes," and refrain from using "fertilizers." The magazine again evokes Fabian's "Typological Time" (Fabian 2002:15–23) to create a temporal divide between rural indigenous Cuetzalan and urban mestizo Mexico. The present lifeways of local indigenous communities belong to the past of the mestizo, who is understood to lead a materialist life and to have "forgotten" about the authentic, previous, and indigenous way of life. As often seen in Third World tourism (Bruner 1991; Badone 2004), travel to certain destinations is constructed as a spiritual homecoming for the tourist, whose journey is also portrayed as a return to an evolutionary stage, where mankind is closer to the original and natural state of the world.[12] This notion of spiritual homecoming is consolidated in the final paragraph that justifies Cuetzalan's 10 years as a Magical Village:

Secluded from the urban way of life, Magical Village Cuetzalan – which conveys day after day the value of friendship, of receiving those who visit [the town] and get to know the life of people who live in a completely different social context, with their indigenous communities so alive, as part of the national Mexican identity – is the reflection of our ancestors and of the magical culture that encloses this beautiful corner of the Northern Sierra of Puebla.

(Cortés Sandoval 2012:19)

The magazine constructs particular temporal relations between local indigenous people and the visiting mestizos, yet the inescapable context of these relations is the translocal frame of the nation: indigenous communities do not merely represent a previous social evolutionary stage, but a nationalized, pre-Hispanic past. Extending the *in situ* framing of the urban environment, indigenous presence and heritage is employed in the magazine to further situate Cuetzalan in a historical and mythologized *Mexican* past. A narrative setting is thus created in which Nahuas become live signifiers of a nationalized primordiality, and consequently figurative ancestors to mestizo travelers wanting to explore and recuperate their lost pre-Hispanic selves. As a result, Cuetzalan becomes a metonym for pre-Hispanic Mexico and emerges as the lost 'homeland' of mestizo travelers by its association with indigenous people. The indigenous Nahuas' perceived privileged knowledge of ancient tradition and their perceived relation to nature represent absences in 'modern,' urban, mestizo Mexico. A sense of loss of traditional society (Clifford 1986:112) intersects with "a mood of nostalgia" (Rosaldo 1989) captured in the traumatic colonial experience that produced the mestizo. Through text and images in the magazine, travel across space is thus temporalized, as Fabian points out (Fabian 2002:7), but it is also translocalized. The idea that contemporary indigenous locals are "our ancestors," that is, the old, original generation from which the young generation of mestizos partly springs, is only meaningful within a national frame that imagines a shared sense of kinship (Anderson 2006:5–7).

As illustrated, the physical urban and narrative settings collaborate in framing the destination as a medium through which metropolitan mestizo Mexicans are able to reconnect with precolonial rural Mexico and recuperate their pre-Hispanic selves. The promotional material thereby brings a perceived past to life by creating a setting in which Cuetzalan's inhabitants re-enact and re-actualize the past merely by carrying out their daily activities. Daily life is thereby constructed as a ritual activity through which Cuetzalan and its inhabitants keep the past alive in the present. Consequently, the promotional magazine creates a setting that, on the one hand, is temporally and geographically remote from 'modern' Mexico, but, on the other hand, contributes to the construction of the modern imagined Mexican community.

The next and final section analyzes an interview with a newcomer to show how the temporal and translocal frames identified in the physical and narrative setting intersect and give shape to complex mestizo self-narratives.

In the footsteps of Quetzalcoatl: pilgrimage to the origin of the nation

The narrative of recognition, which infuses a particular temporal and translocal order into the urban environment and into the narrative setting in official promotional material, also gives life to elaborate personal accounts, as reflected in an interview with cultural activist Ernesto. Ernesto grew up in Mexico City, where he earned a degree in social sciences. At the time of the interview, he was in his early thirties and had been living in town for about six years. Stressing his long-standing concern for indigenous rights issues, particularly environmental and territorial questions, Ernesto described his previous activities in other parts of Mexico. Ernesto visited Cuetzalan three times from 2003 to 2006. On the final trip, he participated in the Other Campaign of the Zapatista Movement, a political tour that brought him to San Miguel Tzinacapan. On that occasion, Ernesto decided to return to live there.

This account of how Ernesto came to Cuetzalan turned out merely to be his short version. Ernesto subsequently told me about his lasting interest in archaeology and anthropology, adding that for the past 15 years, he had been studying *Ce Acatl Topiltzin Quetzalcoatl* and other historical individuals from the pre-Hispanic era. Unexpectedly, he then tied his life story into an account of the life and whereabouts of Topiltzin Quetzalcoatl, thereby employing pre-Hispanic mythistory as an explanatory frame of his own life, which consequently explained his arrival in Cuetzalan.

Topiltzin Quetzalcoatl is surrounded by controversy in early colonial ethnohistorical documents and in contemporary research (Carrasco 2000). As is characteristic of Mesoamerican narration of the past, accounts on Topiltzin Quetzalcoatl are clearly interlaced with mythical events. Topiltzin Quetzalcoatl thus conflates with the deity Quetzalcoatl, and scholars disagree on whether or not Topiltzin Quetzalcoatl should be granted some degree of historicity. Notwithstanding competing interpretations and narratives, ethnohistorical sources report the Aztecs to have regarded Topiltzin Quetzalcoatl to be a priest and ruler of a grand metropolis referred to as Tollan, capital of a vast Toltec empire.[13] Aztec rulers legitimated dynastic rule by tracing their genealogies back to the Toltec dynasty, and Moteuczoma II, who ruled the Aztec empire in 1519 when the Spaniards first arrived to Tenochtitlan, was reported to claim a direct lineage to Topiltzin Quetzalcoatl. Equally, Tenochtitlan, the imperial center, was constructed in the image of mythical Tollan. The main plot in ethnohistorical accounts relates how Topiltzin Quetzalcoatl traveled to or founded Tollan to become ruler. In Tollan, he reshaped ritual practice by introducing autosacrifice and, according to some accounts, by eradicating the practice of human sacrifice. After ruling in Tollan for many years, Topiltzin Quetzalcoatl was confronted by enemies, in most sources directed by the god Tezcatlipoca. The conflict forced him into exile, and he traveled eastwards through the Valley of Mexico and Puebla to the shore of the Mexican Gulf, where he eventually either crossed the sea or was cremated (Nicholson 2001:246–247).

Before joining the Other Campaign, Ernesto had been engaged in environmental preservation and assisted in setting up a community museum in Amatlán (Morelos), a village that was dubbed Amatlán de Quetzalcoatl in the 1980s, after Mexican researchers claimed it to be the birthplace of Topiltzin Quetzalcoatl (Dubernard Chaveau 1982). Having been born in Amatlán, Ernesto explained, Topiltzin Quetzalcoatl went to Xochicalco (Morelos) to receive his education, before arriving at Tollan, where he reigned for many years. After Tezcatlipoca forced him into exile, he left Tollan on a "pilgrimage to spread the word of life." The route took "the shape of a serpent" and passed through "the most important cultural centers of pre-Hispanic Mexico":

Ernesto (February 2013): From there he had to come to Tlalocan. Cuetzalan is the ancient Tlalocan, which is the paradise or hell of water. And that has been written in Teotihuacan for 3,000 years. So, when this Mexica, Nahua, pilgrimage came here – it arrived more or less around 1470-something – the Mexica dominion was expanding. Well, they sent a great amount of people to settle in these lands, but the conquest – of being able to dominate this territory – was an idea they had acquired from the Teotihuacans; that is, to live in Tlalocan. Well, when the Mexicas arrived, which are the people, who are presently living here, they searched for and arrived at the earthly paradise, which they call Tlalticpac. And Tlalocan is a completely subterranean world consisting of caves and water. Nowadays, in any community, everybody knows what Tlalocan is, and who Tlalocan Nana and Tlalocan Tata are – who are the two gods that are governing that paradise. And one of the reasons why I have ended up in Cuetzalan is this, right? Because it is a mythical paradise of water and abundance. And it is written in the *Florentine Codex*, in the *Codex Borgia*, in a stack of pieces of history of pre-Hispanic Mexico. Ce Acatl Topiltzin passed by this place, because he had to pass by the sacred land of Tlalticpac Tlalocan before arriving to El Tajín. He left a significant footprint here, because *the first historical name this place has in a map is Quetzalcoatl*. Like Amatlán de Quetzalcoatl. [. . .] The first name in a map from 1600 says Quetzalcoatl. And it triangulates with Tlatlauquitepec and Jonotla, so there is *no* mistaking it.

Recounting Topiltzin Quetzalcoatl's "pilgrimage" across the pre-Hispanic landscape, Ernesto verbally re-enacts the pilgrimage, showing how he has been traversing the same sacred landscape by demonstrating his knowledge of these places. Ernesto's pilgrimage began at the legendary birthplace of Topiltzin Quetzalcoatl, where he dedicated himself to his service in a commemorative museum. In his path to and from Tollan, Topiltzin Quetzalcoatl visits Xochicalco (Morelos), Teotihuacan (Mexico), Cholula (Puebla), El Tajín (Veracruz), and Chichén Itzá (Yucatán). These sites are not just major cities of different epochs in the pre-Hispanic era, but are equally emblematic archaeological sites in contemporary Mexico.[14] While Cholula holds the world's largest pyramid, the rest are World Heritage Sites. Of equal importance to Ernesto's account, the architecture of all these sites display feathered serpent iconography, and, excluding El Tajín, all sites are organized around temples interpreted by archaeologists as dedicated to feathered serpent deities (Carrasco 2000:5).

In Ernesto's account, the itinerary of Topiltzin Quetzalcoatl's journey in the ethnohistorical account combined with the iconographic presence of feathered serpents in the same places bear witness to the historicity of Topiltzin Quetzalcoatl's pilgrimage; his historical presence has materialized in the architectural settings.[15] Yet the climax of Ernesto's story revolves around Topiltzin Quetzalcoatl's journey to find Tlalocan.[16] According to Ernesto, the imperial expansion into the Sierra de Puebla of the Mexica – the dominant ethnic group of the Aztec capital and empire – was a combined pilgrimage and conquest with the purposes of locating and populating Tlalocan. The Mexica had learned about Topiltzin Quetzalcoatl, his pilgrimage, and the location of Tlalocan in Teotihuacan, and had re-enacted his pilgrimage with the aim of inhabiting "the earthly paradise." Ernesto depicts Cuetzalan as the Tlalocan identified by Topiltzin Quetzalcoatl by referring to "a map from 1600" that asserts the first name of Cuetzalan to be Quetzalcoatl. "Like Amatlán de Quetzalcoatl," this toponymic reference testifies to the eternal "footprint" Topiltzin Quetzalcoatl left in Cuetzalan after his visit, just as the iconography of the archaeological sites referenced evidence his visits there.

In Ernesto's fusion of pre-Hispanic mythistory with his own life history and destiny, his travel to Cuetzalan constitutes both a symbolic re-enactment of a sacred pilgrimage and a concrete way of entering the sacred, original pre-Hispanic landscape and mythology represented by ideas of Tlalocan. Central to this experience is the presence of the local indigenous Nahuas, who, for Ernesto, bear witness to Tlalocan's existence as a concrete, physical place in the landscape. Moreover, to Ernesto, their very knowledge of Tlalocan certifies that the Nahuas are indeed the direct descendants of the Mexica. As seen in the conclusion of his self-narrative, the importance of the identification of local Nahuas as descendants of Mexica lies within its tie to the core mythology of Mexican nationalism:

Ernesto (February 2013): So the search for and discovery of culture that unfolds in Cuetzalan is – I believe – the most important one on a national level, because Mexico, the very name of this very country, is *in Nahuatl,* and it means place of the center of the universe. What I am getting at is that if people are looking for where the original and most pure representatives of all of Mexico are – these Mexica from Mexico – then here is the place. So, I arrived here due to all these circumstances; that here not only myth melts together with the history, but also because the culture still lives, walks, speaks, acts and all according to this ancient tradition. In that way [Cuetzalan] is one of the most important cultural – biocultural – bastions that exist.

Ernesto understands the modern nation-state as a continuation of ancient Mexico, the homeland of the Mexica from which the modern nation-state has derived its name. This understanding is possible because the core symbol of the modern Mexican nation-state, the coat of arms displayed on the Mexican flag, represents the origin myth of the Mexica and the foundation of their capital (Smith 2012:297–300). The mythology behind the coat of arms gives the nation-state the historical depth and mythological authority that allows it to exist as a natural and unquestioned form. Today, the Mexica homeland, their city Tenochtitlan and other Aztec city states in the Valley of Mexico, lie beneath Mexico City, and the people that inhabited these places have vanished.[17] Yet what Ernesto implicitly contends is that the Mexica never disappeared completely, because part of this people emigrated to Tlalocan, which he equates with Cuetzalan. Thus, according to Ernesto, the local Nahuas are the descendants of the Mexica, which is why he refers to them as "the most pure representatives of all of Mexico"; the local Nahuas are the most original *Mexicans,* since they derive from, represent, and thus give continuation to the original and ancient Aztec Mexico that, correspondingly, gave existence to the modern Mexican nation-state.

Thus, the climax of Ernesto's autobiographical account occurs as he embeds three narratives of mythistorical proportions into the local setting. First, throughout his life, Ernesto has been following in the footsteps of the wise and peaceful man-god Topiltzin Quetzalcoatl from which Aztec rulers and their mythical predecessors derived political legitimacy. Second, by doing so, he has come to inhabit the mythical space of Aztec Tlalocan, "paradise of water and abundance." Third, he has discovered a Mexica diaspora established just at 'the end' of the pre-Hispanic era, which, in contrast to the Mexico of Tenochtitlan, has not been eliminated through colonization.

Ernesto's account ties Cuetzalan into a national metanarrative that not simply sets the town on a par with some of Mexico's most treasured historical sites of the pre-Hispanic era, but makes Cuetzalan trump them. When Ernesto refers to Cuetzalan as Tlalocan and states that it "has been written in Teotihuacan for 3,000 years," he appears to be pointing to the iconographic scenes on the Temple of the Feathered Serpent in Teotihuacan, which show a feathered serpent in primordial waters. By doing so, he implies that the scenes portray Topiltzin Quetzalcoatl in watery Tlalocan and, as a consequence, that this central building in the most visited archaeological site in Mexico reveres and represents the sacred geography of Cuetzalan.

Ernesto's account employs notions of local history equivalent to the ones expressed on the display board, which also asserts that the town originated with the arrival of the Mexica. Additionally, his time frame ("1470-something") corresponds with that of the display board ("1475"), and the idea that Cuetzalan was previously called Quetzal(l)an, also expressed on the display boards, corroborates Ernesto's notion of the original place name as Quetzalcoatl.[18] Yet the major narrative building blocks are the intertwining conceptualizations of temporality and translocality that centralize contemporary Cuetzalan in a nationalized past. To this end, the contemporary Nahuas and the local natural setting protrude as relics of the past that facilitate 'modern' mestizos' return to 'their' Aztec past to overcome the trauma of colonization. As rural Nahuas are configured as figurative ancestors to urban mestizos, contemporary Nahuas are converted into pre-Hispanic Mexica, which provide the mestizo with a multilayered experience of return; return to the Mexica and Aztec Mexico, to the origins of the nation, to the mythical Aztec "paradise" Tlalocan, to a sacred location discovered by Topiltzin Quetzalcoatl, to their pre-Hispanic selves, all of which are resources through which metropolitan mestizos construct a sense of belonging. In the context of multicultourism, the Nahuas constitute live signifiers of a mestizo majoritarian national storytelling enmeshed in pre-Hispanic mythistory. As such, their contemporary lives are conquered and colonized as mestizo heritage.

Notes

1   The painting of facades is an ongoing project. Since 2012, the program colors in Cuetzalan have been white and red ochre, and were apparently elaborated by the national tourism fund FONATUR (Ayuntamiento de Cuetzalan del Progreso 2012).

2   The food stalls are a well-guarded secret, which I found out about thanks to newcomer Lucas, who suggested we could go there to get a hamburger. Alas, only the sandwich

stall was open. In 2013 and 2014, few stalls were active and there appeared to be little economic activity.

3 The *Codex Mendoza* is believed to have been commissioned around 1541 by the first viceroy of New Spain, Antonio de Mendoza, on behalf of King Carlos V (Anawalt 2001).

4 In this interpretation, the first morpheme *cuezal-* refers to the red feathers with blue tips of the scarlet macaw, which resemble those depicted in the toponymic sign in the *Codex Mendoza*. As opposed to the predominantly green (resplendent) quetzal bird, which is not known to have lived in the area (Peterson and Peterson 1992), the scarlet macaw was known to have existed in the area, Cecilio explained.

5 In the early 1970s, a quetzal bird appeared on the municipal shield (above Maya numerals), subduing a third interpretation (Arizpe Schlosser 1972:13).

6 "Tenochca" is the plural form of an ethnonym that refers to inhabitants of the Aztec imperial capital, Tenochtitlan.

7 The territory where Cuetzalan is located belonged to the tribute province Tlatlauhquitepec. According to the *Codex Mendoza*, feathers were not part of the tribute payments of that province.

8 Women tend to wear a white short-sleeved *huipil* blouse with colored embroidery from shoulder to shoulder on the back and front and a knee-length skirt. Men tend to wear white cotton shirts, pants, and often a white wide-brimmed hat. Ritual clothes vary according to the ritual, but most often they are ornamented, colorful, and include hats, headdresses, and sometimes masks.

9 Ads from hotels, restaurants, tour operators, and handicraft shops take up a third of the space, and some of these diverge from this tendency in the official promotional material.

10 The selective focus on ritual activity and "indexical dress" in photographic representation of non-Westerners is a widespread convention also found in a trendsetting magazine such as *National Geographic* (Lutz and Collins 1993:87–95).

11 In the *huipil* ceremony, young Nahua women from the surrounding area are engaged in a community queen contest and participate wearing traditional costumes. The photo shows the contestants standing in front of a backdrop of ornaments made from green, red, and yellow leaves. The backdrop is part of the open-air stage crafted for the occasion, which has been cropped out of the photo. The *huipil* queen is flanked by the additional contestants and shown seated in the center on a wooden throne decorated with plant ornaments and the headdress used for the *cuezali* dance.

12 This conception is related to a phenomenon referred to as roots tourism, where travelers set out to explore their (imagined) genealogical past. Such "homeland journeys" may pan out as pilgrimages constructed around visits to symbolic places and work as a transformative rite of passage that links identities to imagined pasts (Ebron 1999). In this sense, roots journeys take shape as an intertwined emotional and temporalized journey through which the traveler explores the "source" of self and inscribes lineage pasts into the landscapes visited (Basu 2007).

13 The facticity of Topiltzin Quetzalcoatl and the degree to which post-conquest accounts can be assumed to accurately mediate an (if there ever was *one*) Aztec view of Topiltzin Quetzalcoatl has been discussed at length (Carrasco 2000:1–62), but is not at issue here. Rather, these accounts of Aztec mythistory play a central role in Mexican nationalist narratives today and continue to be productive. Aztec mythology is thus an actively applied resource in modern history-writing in Mexico, geared to a national audience.

14 Their appeal is reflected in the number of domestic visitors, placing all sites in the top 15 that year: (1) Teotihuacan, (2) Chichén Itzá, (3) Cholula, (6) El Tajín, (14) Xochicalco (SIIMT 2013).

15 Due to the extensive time span during which the different structures have been constructed, Ernesto's interpretation is not the most evident one within an archaeological orientation. One currently influential interpretation is that the feathered serpent represents an institutionalized way through which urban elites in central Mexico, from Teotihuacan (CE 250) to Tenochtitlan (CE 1521) and other late post-classic cities, legitimized rule and

created authority for an urban-centered organization of social life (Carrasco 2000). Yet it seems that Ernesto is not looking to construct history from a Westernized epistemological orientation, but rather emulates a mythistorical narrative style.

16 In Aztec mythology, Tlalocan is an otherworldly place of abundant water, flora and fauna, and the subterranean home of the rain god Tlaloc.

17 Or more precisely, there are in central Mexico no descendants to claim lineal descent from the Mexica.

18 Historian Bernardo García Martínez (1987:162–163) first introduced the tentative hypothesis that a town called Quetzalcoatl appearing in early colonial documents could be identical to Cuetzalan. The hypothesis consists of three pieces of information. First, Cuetzalan does not appear in the colonial record before 1563, when inhabitants declare they moved to the location 10 years earlier. Second, Quetzalcoatl appears in the early colonial record, but disappears later. Third, the two locations are geographically close to each other, and the relation between the two toponyms is "indisputable" (García Martínez 1987:162–163). Based on this hypothesis, García Martínez drafted maps that place Quetzalcoatl where Cuetzalan is located today (García Martínez 1987:47, map 1; 74, map 2). These modern maps are most likely the ones to which Ernesto is referring.

References

Anawalt, Patricia. 2001. "Mendoza, Codex." Pp. 205–208 in *The Oxford Encyclopedia of Mesoamerican Cultures: The Civilizations of Mexico and Central America*, vol. 2, edited by D. Carrasco. New York: Oxford University Press.

Anderson, Benedict. [1983] 2006. *Imagined Communities: Reflections on the Origin and Spread of Nationalism*. London: Verso.

Arizpe Schlosser, Lourdes. 1972. "El Municipio: Cuetzalan." Pp. 13–18 in *Artes de México*, vol. 155, *La Sierra de Puebla*. Mexico City: Comercial Nadrosa.

Ayuntamiento de Cuetzalan del Progreso. 2012. *Expediente: Cuetzalan Pueblo Mágico*. Cuetzalan: Administración Municipal 2011–2014.

Badone, Ellen. 2004. "Crossing Boundaries: Exploring the Borderlands of Ethnography, Tourism and Pilgrimage." Pp. 180–189 in *Intersecting Journeys: The Anthropology of Pilgrimage and Tourism*, edited by E. Badone and S. R. Roseman. Urbana, IL: University of Illinois Press.

Baez Carmona, Arturo. 2012. "Editorial." *Enlázate: Edición Especial – Cuetzalan Está de 10*. P. 3.

Basu, Paul. 2007. *Highland Homecomings: Genealogy and Heritage-Tourism in the Scottish Diaspora*. London: Routledge.

Baud, Michiel, and Annelou Ypeij. 2009. "Cultural Tourism in Latin America: An Introduction." Pp. 1–20 in *Cultural Tourism in Latin America: The Politics of Space and Imagery*, edited by M. Baud and A. Ypeij. Leiden: Brill.

Berdan, Frances F., and Patricia R. Anawalt, eds. 1992. *The Codex Mendoza*, vol. 3, *Facsimile*. Berkeley, CA: University of California Press.

Bruner, Edward M. 1991. "Transformation of Self in Tourism." *Annals of Tourism Research* 18(2):238–250.

Campo, Rafael Martín del. 1979. "Los Psitácidos Mexicanos y el Toponímico Cuetzalan." Pp. 15–23 in *Tercera Mesa Redonda sobre Problemas Antropológicos de la Sierra Norte del Estado de Puebla*. Cuetzalan: Centro de Estudios Históricos de la Sierra Norte del Estado de Puebla.

Carrasco, Davíd. 2000. *Quetzalcoatl and the Irony of Empire: Myths and Prophesies in the Aztec Tradition*. Boulder, CO: University Press of Colorado.

Clifford, James. 1986. "On Ethnographic Allegory." Pp. 98–121 in *Writing Culture: The Poetics and Politics of Ethnography*, edited by J. Clifford and G. E. Marcus. Berkeley, CA: University of California Press.

Cortés Sandoval, Jorge, ed. 2012. "Pueblo Mágico: Cuetzalan está de 10." *Enlázate: Edición Especial – Cuetzalan Está de 10.* Pp. 18–19.

Cronon, William. 1992. "A Place for Stories: Nature, History, and Narrative." *The Journal of American History* 78(4):1347–1356.

Cruikshank, Barbara. 1999. *The Will to Empower: Democratic Citizens and Other Subjects.* Ithaca, NY: Cornell University Press.

Domínguez, Amelia. 2003. "Concluye Secretaría de Turismo la primera etapa del programa Pueblos Mágicos." *La Jornada del Oriente*, June 6. Retrieved November 8, 2013 (www.lajornadadeoriente.com.mx/2003/06/06/puebla/cul1.htm).

Domínguez, Amelia. 2004. "Inicia el próximo mes la tercera etapa de Mejoramiento de imagen Urbana de Cuetzalan." *La Jornada del Oriente*, July 28. Retrieved November 8, 2013 (www.lajornadadeoriente.com.mx/2004/07/28/oriente.html).

Dubernard Chaveau, Juan. 1982. "¿Quetzalcóatl en Amatlán (Morelos)?" *Estudios de Cultura Nahuatl* 15:209–217.

Ebron, Paulla A. 1999. "Tourists as Pilgrims: Commercial Fashioning of Transatlantic Politics." *American Ethnologist* 26(4):910–932.

Eriksen, Thomas Hylland. 2002. *Ethnicity and Nationalism: Anthropological Perspectives.* London: Pluto Press.

Fabian, Johannes. 2002. *Time and the Other: How Anthropology Makes Its Object.* New York: Columbia University Press.

Fernández Lomelín, Luis Enrique. 2012. "Crisol biocultural: Cuetzalan." *Enlázate: Edición Especial – Cuetzalan Está de 10.* Pp. 30–31.

García Martínez, Bernardo. 1987. *Los Pueblos de la Sierra: El Poder y el Espacio entre los Indios del Norte de Puebla hasta 1700.* Mexico City: El Colegio de México.

Goffman, Erving. [1974] 1986. *Frame Analysis: An Essay on the Organization of Experience.* Boston, MA: Northeastern University Press.

Gubrium, Jaber F., and James A. Holstein. 2009. *Analyzing Narrative Reality.* Thousand Oaks, CA: Sage.

Hernández Alcántara, Martín. 2013. "Denuncian Destrucción de la Plaza Histórica de Cuetzalan del Progreso." *La Jornada de Oriente*, April 5. Retrieved November 8, 2013 (www.lajornadadeoriente.com.mx/noticia/puebla/denuncian-destruccion-de-la-plaza-historica-de-cuetzalan-del-progreso_id_22634.html).

Holtorf, Cornelius. 2005. *From Stonehenge to Las Vegas: Archaeology as Popular Culture.* Walnut Creek, CA: Altamira Press.

Jones, Gareth A., and Ann Varley. 1994. "The Contest for the City Centre: Street Traders versus Buildings." *Bulletin of Latin American Research* 13(1):27–44.

Källén, Anna. 2015. *Stones Standing: Archaeology, Colonialism, and Ecotourism in Northern Laos.* Walnut Creek, CA: Left Coast Press.

Knight, Alan. 1990. "Racism, Revolution, and Indigenismo: Mexico, 1910–1940." Pp. 71–113 in *The Idea of Race in Latin America, 1870–1940*, edited by R. Graham. Austin, TX: University of Texas Press.

Lowenthal, David. 1985. *The Past Is a Foreign Country.* Cambridge: Cambridge University Press.

Lutz, Catherine A., and Jane L. Collins. 1993. *Reading National Geographic.* Chicago, IL: University of Chicago Press.

Merlo Juárez, Eduardo. 1995. *La Sierra Mágica (The Magic Sierra).* Puebla: SECTUR.

Nelle, Anja B. 2009. "Museality in the Urban Context: An Investigation of Museality and Musealisation Processes in Three Spanish-Colonial World Heritage Towns." *Urban Design International* 14(3):152–171.

Nicholson, H. B. 2001. "Topiltzin Quetzalcoatl." Pp. 246–247 in *The Oxford Encyclopedia of Mesoamerican Cultures: The Civilizations of Mexico and Central America*, vol. 3, edited by D. Carrasco. New York: Oxford University Press.

Notimex. 2006. "Avanza última etapa de mejoramiento de Cuetzalan." *Turista Puebla*, December 4. Retrieved November 8, 2013 (http://puebla.turista.com.mx/article346.html).

Nuñez, Fernando. 2007. "The Interaction of Space and Place: The Mexican Mixture." Pp. 1–73 in *Space and Place in the Mexican Landscape: The Evolution of a Colonial City*, edited by M. Quantrill. College Station, TX: Texas A&M University Press.

Orbaşli, Aylin. 2000. *Tourists in Historic Towns: Urban Conservation and Heritage Management*. London: E & FN Spon.

Peterson, Amy, and Andrew Townsend Peterson. 1992. "Aztec Exploitation of Cloud Forests: Tributes of Liquidambar Resin and Quetzal Feathers." *Global Ecology and Biogeography Letters* 2(5):165–173.

Read, Kay Almere, and Jason J. Gonzalez. 2002. *Mesoamerican Mythology: A Guide to the Gods, Heroes, Rituals, and Beliefs of Mexico and Central America*. New York: Oxford University Press.

Rosaldo, Renato. 1989. "Imperialist Nostalgia." *Representations* 26:107–122.

SECTUR. 2001. *Programa Nacional de Turismo 2001–2006*. Mexico City: SECTUR. Retrieved December 5, 2012 (www.sectur.gob.mx/work/models/sectur/Resource/9795/PNT20012006_PDF.zip).

SECTUR. 2005. *Programa Pueblos Mágicos*. Mexico City: SECTUR. Retrieved February 27, 2014 (http://web.archive.org/web/20060213212910/http://www.sectur.gob.mx/wb2/sectur/sect_Pueblos_Magicos).

SECTUR. 2006. *Criterios de Incorporación al Programa "Pueblos Mágicos": Versión Final 31 de Julio 2006*. Mexico City: SECTUR. Retrieved September 6, 2012 (www.sectur.gob.mx/work/models/securing/Resource/14192/CRITERIOSDEINCORPORACIONALPROGRAMAPUEBLOSMAGICOS.pdf).

SECTUR. 2009. *Reglas de Operación*. Mexico City: SECTUR. Retrieved September 6, 2012 (www.sectur.gob.mx/work/models/sectur/Resource/99fbd793-a344-4b98-9633-78607f33c b8f/Reglas_de_operacion.pdf).

SECTUR. 2014. *Inversión turística privada y pública en Cuetzalan*. Mexico City: SECTUR. Retrieved September 18, 2015 (www.sectur.gob.mx/wp-content/uploads/2015/02/CUETZALAN-DEL-PROGRESO.zip).

SIIMT. 2013. *Reporte de visitantes a zonas arqueológicas, museos y monumentos históricos*. Mexico City: SIIMT. Retrieved May 11, 2016 (www.siimt.com/en/siimt/siim_actividades_culturales).

Smith, Laurajane. 2007. "Empty Gestures? Heritage and the Politics of Recognition." Pp. 159–171 in *Cultural Heritage and Human Rights*, edited by H. Silverman and D. F. Ruggles. New York: Springer Science.

Smith, Michael E. 2012. *The Aztecs*. Malden, MA: Wiley-Blackwell.

Smith, Michael E., and Frances F. Berdan. 1996. "Appendix 4: Province Descriptions." Pp. 265–349 in *Aztec Imperial Strategies*, edited by F. F. Berdan. Washington, DC: Dumbarton Oaks.

Taylor, John P. 2001. "Authenticity and Sincerity in Tourism." *Annals of Tourism Research* 28(1):7–26.

Tunbridge, John, and Greg Ashworth. 1996. *Dissonant Heritage: The Management of the Past as a Resource in Conflict*. Chichester: Wiley.

7 Networking/rooting

Ritual co-parenthood in Tzinacapan

Considering that the promotion of tourism to Cuetzalan depends on indigenous (symbolic) presence, yet is tightly focused on central, mestizo Cuetzalan, and that the Magical Villages program has been reorganizing the commercial space to minimize ambulant vending, which modes of participation in local tourism does this situation produce for indigenous people in the surrounding municipal area? How do Nahua handicraft vendors relate to the Magical Villages Program, tourists, and newcomers? This chapter shows how a group of female Nahua handicraft vendors from San Miguel Tzinacapan manage the ambiguity of being desired yet undesired participants in local Cuetzalan-centric tourism, and how they attempt to turn multicultourism to their advantage by forging ritual co-parenthood ties to visiting outsiders.

In Mexico, ritual co-parenthood (*compadrazgo*) denotes a widespread, institutionalized practice for forging or strengthening social relations between relatives or, most frequently, nonrelatives (Mulhare 2000:18–19).[1] These often long-lasting social relations take many non-sacramental forms and revolve around the tie between parents and co-parents rather than between co-parents and the sponsored child (Nutini 2001).[2] As the diverse literature on the topic illustrates, ritual co-parenthood relationships are multilayered and may involve economic, moral, and social obligations, and may also carry emotional, political, religious, and symbolic significance (Nutini 1984:400–418).

In Tzinacapan, ritual co-parenthood plays a key role to social organization by creating interpersonal networks between households. Since these relations tend to be passed on from parents and co-parents to their respective children, such household alliances may last several generations. The same goes for conflicts, and, since around 1900, Tzinacapan has been divided into three political factions with different socioeconomic standings (Haly 2000:186–187).[3] Yet creating bonds with people in other places is considered equally important (Lok 1991:83–84), and people of the better-off faction, for instance, share such ties with well-off mestizos in Cuetzalan. For those members of the poor faction who are vending handicrafts, forging lasting bonds with middle-class outsiders strengthens their social security network and mitigates the perennial harms of socioeconomic vulnerability. This way of engaging with tourists would appear to be going against the stream, since interaction between tourists and those who cater to them tends to be transient and unrepeated, and with few lasting interpersonal consequences (Cohen 1984; Lyon and Wells 2012:9). However, if multicultourism calques its symbolic matter from ethnography, as argued in the case of ethnic tourism (Van den Berghe 1994:18–19), the emergence of such relationships may not be so strange in a world of ever-increasing mobility and connectivity. It may seem even less strange in a place such as Tzinacapan, which has been the object of sustained anthropological research since the 1970s (Lupo 1998:266–267).

Analyzing how such relationships emerge provides a view to the assessments involved on the part of Nahua women in making such relationships attractive to tourists and newcomers. The movement toward formalized relationships should not be viewed as marginal preludes to the emerging relationships, since the initial process involves key identity transactions for both parties arranged around negotiations of class, culture, and ethnicity. Hence, the chapter follows the movement from the informal and least committal end of the continuum toward the most committal and formal part of the continuum.

The chapter begins with an autoethnographic return to the first week of fieldwork to explore how Nahua handicraft vendors engage with newcomers and to illustrate what I experienced as an accelerated collaborative relationship-building process through which my family and I rapidly became entangled with peoples and places. Building on interview material, the chapter subsequently analyzes the formation of a ritual co-parenthood relationship between a newcomer couple and a Nahua woman and her daughter from Tzinacapan.

Becoming one's own informant

Returning for the first time to the earliest of my field notes 20 months after writing them evoked in me a mix of emotions. Although I had decided to wait long enough to hopefully re-experience my first impressions of Cuetzalan, I felt irresponsible for having let the notes collect dust for so long. Ambivalently, I felt estranged from the text and its descriptive layer – and even disembodied from the author – and yet I felt deeply tied to the experiential layer that filled the descriptions. The sensation of reading afresh a text spun long ago over experiences still so familiar to me gave me a pronounced experience of a key point in Goffman's work on the presentation of self and interpretation of experience, namely that whenever we speak of another and ourselves, we carve out an image, author a character, hold forth a figure of that other and of ourselves (Goffman 1986:523–537). On reading the notes, I was stunned by the characters that emerged; all crystallizations incompatible with the characters I had in mind at the time of reading. Since the time of writing, I had been invested in an ongoing authoring of characters, permanently adjusted by subsequent experiences in the field and in the office. The figure of an enthusiastic researcher within the text was now a character within my empirical material, as was the author-commentator, who had been in charge of writing the field notes, carving out figures, selecting events, and how to report and understand them. This author-commentator was suddenly transposed to that of informant.

Scanning through the descriptions of the characters, events, and experiences with a different reading in mind made me realize that I had not single-handedly been authoring characters; if anything, the field notes capture a continuous coauthoring of figures emerging through intersubjective fields of interaction (cf. Rabinow 2007:153 155). What the chapter therefore asks of the early field notes is: How did the co-creation of figures take shape during the first week of interaction, and how did this process support mutual efforts to initiate and strengthen our mutual engagement?

Initial encounters

Field notes (January 12, 2013): Today, we arrived to Cuetzalan. [. . .] We came to a small market with many restaurants and stalls that sell handicrafts. We soon found a place outside to sit. When we were waiting for our meal, we were instantly approached by ambulant vendors selling wristlets, necklaces, tortilla cozies, and serviette dispensers with embroidered *voladores* and the like. [. . .] Many of the vendors were women, and many of them apparently Nahuat speakers. [. . .] At one point there were four to five ambulant vendors encircled around the table [speaking Nahuat], and I did grasp that they were commenting on Julius.

Field notes (January 13, 2013): At the café we also met a girl named Lila who lives in San Miguel Tzinacapan. She showed much interest in Julius and asked if we believe in the "evil eye." I asked what "evil eye" was, and she gave me a brief explanation about two madams that could remove Julius' face. If it were to happen, he would cry a lot among other things. A red wristlet the girl was selling would protect him against this. Lila also told us that she speaks Nahuat and that the majority in San Miguel Tzinacapan speak Nahuat. She was happy to be speaking Nahuat and told us that her school teaches in Nahuat, Spanish, and English. [. . .] I promised to visit one of these days. [. . .] I told her that I know some Classical Nahuatl, but that I was not familiar with the Nahuat of this region. She asked me to say something in Spanish, which she would then say in Nahuat.

Field notes (January 14, 2013): As we were sitting at the café in the morning, Francisca dropped by. She did not try to sell us anything, but just entered to greet us. Concerning names, she recalled only "Julio," and we repeated introductions. She also lives in San Miguel Tzinacapan and she asked us several times if we were really going to visit them and, if so, when? She also said that we already had many friends there.

Rereading the field notes, I was amazed to find that my vivid memory of an accelerated friendship-making process had minimized the speed by which acquaintanceships had actually developed. Starting the day after our arrival, we were approached and greeted as acquaintances by a number of Nahua saleswomen. Several individuals from San Miguel Tzinacapan invited us to come by for a visit, and weaver and textile vendor Ximena from San Andrés Tzicuilan would take me on a hike to the Las Brisas cascades near her town 10 days later. Many of the vendors remembered us after one encounter and paused to greet us and chat, while toning down their vending ambitions or ceasing actively to offer us goods for sale.

The excerpts render our initial encounters with Nahua women and children from Tzinacapan who walk the town to vend handicrafts. Since the highest density of tourists is to be found during weekends, Friday to Sunday are the days when all these vendors go to Cuetzalan, although some arrive occasionally on weekdays. The vendors we came to engage with sold colorful string-art keychains shaped like the headdresses used in the *cuezali* dance, string-art serviette dispensers with flora and fauna motifs, tortilla cozies with embroidered motifs, particularly *cuezali* dancer motifs, braided wristlets, and long necklaces carrying a *mucuna pruriens* seed imbued with the power to protect against evil eye. Similar handicrafts could easily be found in souvenir stalls and shops, which puzzled us initially. Nonetheless, the handicrafts assume a structuring position in the interaction between the women from Tzinacapan and tourists. If a tourist categorically declines purchase, the tourist by implication declines to engage in a prospective, extended interaction. However, the tourist may also decline for the moment or ask to see further goods, thereby welcoming further conversation. More than being material objects in a mere economic transaction, and beyond working as entry points to interaction, the handicrafts also assume performative functions as identity markers on each side of the interaction. Displaying their clearly handmade goods, the vendors signal that they are not just vendors; they convey their authorship of the displayed crafts. Portraying themselves as craftswomen of indigenous material culture, these Nahua women emerge as "carriers of tradition" (Yuval-Davis 1997:61). The handicrafts thus externalize the internal design of their possessor and work as testimonies of cultural and ethnic identity.

For tourists attracted to Cuetzalan by its indigenous image, the acquisition of indigenous handicrafts from indigenous vendors constitutes a transferal of the assumed cultural content contained by the handicrafts and a platform for recounting a personal narrative of a cultural encounter to friends and family. Nevertheless, far from all tourists show interest in the ambulant vendors and their handicrafts, and tourists may just as well turn to the many souvenir shops in town. When the vendors first approached us, they gathered around our table and spoke Nahuat to each other, thereby verbally performing their ethnicity and providing us with a taste of authentic indigeneity.

Communicating in Nahuat serves, of course, not merely performative functions directed at outsiders, but – by encircling us and letting the conversation pass over our heads while smiling and occasionally signaling at Julius – we were implicitly being invited to witness their lively conversation. Anthropologist Walter Little has highlighted such performative vending strategies among Kaqchikel ambulant saleswomen in Guatemala, who also catch tourists' attention by speaking the Mayan language Kaqchikel close to them. That way, the tourist is first in establishing visual contact, from which springs the ensuing verbal contact initiated by the Kaqchikel saleswomen (Little 2008:94–98). As the field notes demonstrate, the conversation in Nahuat did not go unnoticed and enthusiastically entered my notebook as an extraordinary experience worthy of report in itself. Such performative strategies have the advantage of detecting tourists who respond with positive interest to displays of indigeneity, and who are thus likely to engage in conversation with the vendors. Establishing contact and opening interaction in such an indirect way has the advantage of minimizing the vendors' economic intent, which is paramount in mediating to the tourist an "authentic" lifeworld that does not render indigenous vendors' behavior and presence dependent on tourism and monetary economy (Little 2008:92).

On another occasion, Lila initiated contact by attracting Julius' attention with hissing sounds and accompanying gestures. It was also via Julius that Lila first verbalized her 'cultural competence' as a springboard for offering her handicrafts. Babies are perceived to be particularly susceptible to evil eye, and Lila initiated our conversation by asking us if we believed in evil eye. Lila's question presupposed that we would already be somewhat familiar with the concept, which reflects that most visiting Mexicans are likely to have heard of it. By bringing up this topic, Lila signaled that evil eye is a topic of everyday concern to people in and around Cuetzalan. This way, she skillfully crafted an occasion for vivifying before us a cultural trait, which could be further expanded through autoethnographic description. In our conversation, my inquiry about evil eye triggered an explanatory description ending with Lila offering us a red wristlet for Julius that would protect him against evil eye, highlighting again the handicrafts as a mediating device between the two parties.[4] Later in the conversation, Lila proudly identified herself as a Nahuat speaker of Nahuat-speaking Tzinacapan. What did not occur to me then was that all that she was telling us about Tzinacapan carried the connotative sentence 'in contradistinction to Cuetzalan.' Whatever she was, Cuetzalan was not. Community identity in Tzinacapan is tightly bound to this cultural Othering vis-à-vis mestizo Cuetzalan. This binary opposition evoked in cultural terms is grounded in the shared economic and political history between these neighboring towns, the two largest in the municipality, which coincide with a mestizo (settler) and Nahua (colonized) divide. The regional hegemony enjoyed by contemporary mestizo Cuetzalan has been, and is being, gained at the expense of the surrounding Nahuas (Haly 2000:168). Had we imagined that Cuetzalan was an authentically indigenous village, Lila was informing us that it was not. By implication, we would have to go to Tzinacapan to experience authentic indigeneity. Sensing how strongly Lila felt about her village and her first language, I became anxious to signal my Nahuat competence and to demonstrate my sincere interest in her cultural background. Although I wanted to transmit the image of us as a regular tourist family, I was equally eager to differentiate myself from the 'standard' tourist. What was less clear to me was that by highlighting Nahuat as something of importance and by showing interest in experiencing an authentically indigenous village, I was expressing my support to a counter-discursive current in Tzinacapan, which refutes the indigenous image Cuetzalan presents to its tourists. By expressing interest in Tzinacapan, and later on by visiting the village,

I was taken to show loyalty to Tzinacapan, confirming a hierarchy that placed Tzinacapan above Cuetzalan on a scale of indigenous authenticity. My positive reception of topics such as evil eye and the predominance of Nahuat in Tzinacapan clearly made me a tourist of special interest, and that impression was confirmed by my immediate acceptance of Lila's invitation to visit her hometown.

As the field notes demonstrate, the earliest encounters are bound together by the handicrafts, which function as mediating devices between the two interacting parts. Or, more concisely, the interaction emerges embedded in a transaction framework. When, on the third day, we met Francisca for a second time, she invited us to Tzinacapan and prompted us several times to make the journey by stressing our many friendships with people there. In that encounter, Francisca made no attempt to sell us handicrafts, which we found striking, since, after all, that was her (main) errand in town, and we were three of very few tourists there at the time.

Nahuatizing tourists

Friday that week, I went to Tzinacapan to pay Lila and Francisca a visit. Upon arrival, the plaza and streets were empty, and I soon found myself alone in the church staring at Baby Jesus lying on an altar surrounded by colorful Christmas baubles, tinsel, animal figurines, toys, and a complex acoustic milieu knitted out of three overlapping Christmas carols in greeting card edition. Afterward, I asked for directions to Lila's house, and turning around the first corner, I saw a girl in a green tracksuit walking toward me. It was Lila. This time, she seemed different – shy – and wondered where Louise and Julius were. As I was trying to explain the reasons for my lone excursion, I noticed that she kept gazing toward a group of men working next to a pile of rocks. I asked what they were constructing, and Lila, sliding in the opposite direction, replied, "They are constructing a road. My uncle is up there; he is drunk. Where do you want to go?" As we crossed the plaza on our way to Francisca, Lila met her friend Patricia and asked her to tag along. Attentive to Lila's tacit plea of molding what could be interpreted as an illegitimate rendezvous into a less problematic three-person constellation, Patricia joined the excursion:

> **Field notes (January 18, 2013):** At Francisca's place we had coffee and bread. Francisca asked us several times if the coffee was too cold or too hot. While we were sitting there, I tried to play the role as ethnographer fully and wanted to steer to the topic of *voladores* poles. [. . .] Francisca quickly turned to the topic of co-fathers and co-mothers. She explained that, for instance, Patricia and Lila have co-parents from Mexico City and Yucatán, tourists that had visited Cuetzalan and San Miguel. Perhaps the intention was that I should take the bait and become co-father to Francisca's son? I asked what it implied to be co-father to a child from San Miguel. [Francisca:] A co-father goes on occasional excursions with his sponsored child and sponsors clothes, schooling, and the like. [. . .] We also touched upon the topic of tourists. Apparently, there

are different categories. They use the well-known term gringo. Additionally, there is the term *güero*. [Francisca's explanation:] "A *güero* is someone who does not buy tortilla cozies because they eat bread instead of tortillas. They do not buy serviette dispensers. They buy nothing, except perhaps for a wristlet." [. . .] After we had visited Francisca, we moved on to Patricia's house. Lila could not join, as she had to return home to grind maize, but she would come afterwards. [. . .] As we walked further down the road, Patricia suddenly turned to the right and I quickly found myself inside a one-room plank house with beds, comal griddle on a fireplace, altar, chickens, and a family. Patricia's mother [Angelica], uncle, and a few siblings were present. And a little later a woman and her daughter also entered and sat down. Startled [to see me], the woman exclaimed, "Coyotzin?" Coyote is a term for mestizo among Nahuat speakers of the area. [. . .] Nahuat was very vividly spoken in the house, and I tried to catch as much of the conversations as possible, but it was difficult. I only caught bits of it. Nevertheless, I sought to demonstrate that I knew some. We ran through the numerals and Angelica tested me. [. . .] They gave me a tortilla to munch and Angelica asked Patricia to apologize to me that they had not yet any food to offer. All in all, she asked Patricia to translate quite a few things, although she did manage Spanish herself.

These excerpts from my first visit to San Miguel Tzinacapan again point to the speed by which relationships developed. The transient encounters with Francisca and Lila were the crucial lifelines that kept me from feeling like a nosy intruder or a tourist out of place, and without which I would have no sensible undertakings in Tzinacapan. Illustratively, meeting Patricia for the first time, I soon found my excursion dependent on my frail relation to her, as we left Francisca's place and Lila went home to do household chores. This frailty vanished from view as I became a guest in Patricia's humble home. Being received in such a friendly manner was reassuring in the light of my vulnerable out-of-place situation, and, in a sense, the very combination of unreserved hospitality and the frailty of our relations quickly made our relation seem anything but frail. That sense of the situation was momentarily disrupted when another guest arrived and pointed out the farfetched nature of the situation by spontaneously singling me out as "*coyotzin.*"[5] Rereading my field notes, I was surprised to discover a change in my behavior after this labeling incident. To handle the crisis introduced into the interaction arrangement, I began to signal my knowledge of and interest in Nahuat. I thereby challenged the "*coyotzin*" label and carved out a less straightforward position for myself from which the strengthening of the relationship could be sustained. Patricia's mother, Angelica, fittingly responded with a code-switch from Spanish to Nahuat when addressing me, putting me to a friendly test and entertaining a simple conversation, a situation that would allow me to demonstrate the ability to which I could comprehend and speak the language. By arranging our interaction around Nahuat, we collaborated in loosening my attachment to the category of coyote and their attachment to the utterance that had produced the crisis. So, while the "*coyotzin*" incident initially disrupted the scene by problematizing the figures, positions, and relations we were carving out for each other, the disruption came only to accentuate the already initiated process.

Something similar had happened at Francisca's place when I had asked about the types of tourists the vendors meet. Francisca mentioned "gringos" and "*güeros.*" The word gringo was reserved for North Americans, and I remember asking what exactly *güero* should be taken to mean, noting in Lila's face a slight disquietude with the topic, indicating that the category could well apply to me.[6] Francisca nonetheless proceeded with a description that was open for escape, and therefore inoffensive to me. It appears that my being in Tzinacapan marked me out as a particular kind of tourist. And my going there to ask about the *voladores*, the annual town fiesta, and other culture-related themes only confirmed that impression. Being aware that I would be staying in Cuetzalan for some time, Francisca introduced the topic of co-parenthood relationships between tourists and people in Tzinacapan.

Clearly, Francisca was spot on in her observations. After Lila's account on evil eye and her passionate talk about her town and the widespread use of Nahuat there – supplemented by a live demonstration – it now seems like I *had* gone to Tzinacapan to experience more of that sort of 'authentic Nahua space' Lila had vivified before me.

Why the use of the adverbs "suddenly" and "quickly" to describe our entrance to Patricia's "plank house with beds, comal griddle on a fireplace, altar, chickens, and a family" that was "vividly" speaking Nahuat? A drastic change of scene seemed to be implied, qualified by a description pointing out the use of Nahuat and the presence of a home altar, fireplace and comal griddle. The description almost shoots me into a microcosm of alternative reality. Conversely, Francisca's sparsely furnished concrete house did not find its way into the description, and the scene in the field notes departs instead from the serving of bread and coffee and is fixed to our conversation on *voladores*, the town fiesta, co-parenthood, and tourists, the first two topics launched by myself.

Likewise, rereading the notes made me wonder why I immediately steered from the bus to the church. Seeing how my account chains together descriptions of saints, relics, and flower arrangements with the "special feeling of having the church to oneself, when one feels that perhaps one should not have been there at all," it now appears that an inconspicuous collaboration took place between two figures of self: explorer and author. Having seen from the bus a Nahuat phrase on the backside of the church, that setting seemed to be a sure bet for the explorer in search of an 'authentic space' to feed to the author. Afterward, the explorer searched for Lila rather than Francisca. After all, Lila was the one who had mentioned evil eye and enthusiastically launched a conversation in and about Nahuat. At Francisca's place, the explorer sought to arrange the conversation around the topics of *voladores* and the fiesta, and the author assisted by sorting out the empty concrete house from the description. The explorer, then, appears to have sought out different kinds of 'authentic spaces' around which the author structured the text. As seen in the author's frame-breaking comment about the explorer playing "the role as ethnographer fully" by purposively directing the conversation to the topic of *voladores*, the 'authentic space' is something that cannot merely be arrived at, but something in need of crafting. Yet, as the field notes equally show, this crafting took place in collaboration with the handicraft vendors. The day after the visit to Tzinacapan, we met Patricia and Angelica, who were vending in central Cuetzalan:

> **Field notes (January 19, 2013):** Julius was in the carrier on my back saying "*ja*" ["yes" in Danish, Julius pronouncing it "iyah"]. Patricia heard it as "*tiyaz, tiyaz!*" "You will go, you will go."

As Patricia's interpretative account shows, an identity channel had opened between Patricia's family and me. By accepting the kind invitations to visit Tzinacapan, I had expressed an interest in getting to know the vendors and their way of life. This move opened a collaborative effort to release me from the categories of coyote, conventional tourist, and explicit outsider, and relations tying me to Tzinacapan began to form. When Patricia met Julius for the first time, she expanded the already existing identity channel. Hearing stories about his impatient character and his wanting to be on the go, she linked that piece of biography to our previous encounter in which Nahuat had played a significant role, when she interpreted Julius' utterance to signify "tiyaz." By making Julius a (potential) Nahuat speaker, she actively helped to negotiate a position for all of us outside the category of coyote. By extension, Patricia began to refer to Julius exclusively as "*Tiyaz*" ("Where is *Tiyaz?*"). The appellation tied in with Julius' biography performatively and descriptively; it expressed his (coming) capacity to speak Nahuat, and marked out a feature of his personal character. When other vendors asked why she called him *Tiyaz*, the appellation thus created occasions for telling this twofold narrative. Sharing such narrative connected us biographically, linguistically, and socially, while also adding temporal depth to our relationship.

The chapter now turns to analyze the formation of a ritual co-parenthood relationship between newcomers Lucas and Olivia and the Nahua handicraft vendor Maria and her daughter Yolani from Tzinacapan.

"More than a tourist"

I first met Lucas and Olivia in January 2013. Both have university degrees and their moving to Cuetzalan was linked to their careers. Olivia had arrived from Puebla City a month earlier, but originated from another part of Mexico. Lucas had arrived from Europe in mid-2012. During our first stay, they were developing a friendship, and upon our return in September 2014 they had become a couple and were living together. Two months earlier, they had also become educational co-parents to Yolani from Tzinacapan, the 6-year-old daughter of Maria. In 2013, I had told Lucas and Olivia of my inkling that tourists occasionally come to be educational co-parents to children from Tzinacapan, so when I phoned Lucas upon arrival in 2014 he excitedly presented the big news, and, as appetizers to the account in store, emphasized the ceremonies and rituals they had attended to enter their new roles. During a joint excursion later that week, Lucas and Olivia stressed individually that while co-parenthood relationships are chiefly formalities elsewhere in Mexico, in this region, and in Tzinacapan in particular, such relationships involve much more sincere and extensive commitments and are conceived of as ritual kinship.

A few days later, I met Lucas for an interview. Before getting to business, he wanted to tell me about Arturo, a man who had moved from Mexico City to Tzinacapan some years back, a story that came to tie in with the interview. In Mexico City, Arturo had formed part of a *Concheros* dancing troupe, which had existed "for more than 100 years" and which "recreates" "original Mexica dances," Lucas told me.[7] When Arturo arrived in Tzinacapan, he wanted to teach people there to dance these 'original Aztec' dances. Yet Arturo encountered little enthusiasm for his idea, and he sought instead to become part of already existing dancing troupes in Tzinacapan. Arturo eventually succeeded and had since managed to start a *Concheros* group there. Lucas not only thought I should talk to Arturo, but employed the storyline as a springboard to express his own perception of Tzinacapan:

> **Field notes (September 23, 2014):** Thereupon, Lucas stressed how late the Spaniards had gained ground in the Northern Sierra – not until around independence [1821] did mestizos and Europeans begin to flow to the area due to government policies of attracting "civilized" citizens to the country. In that respect, Lucas emphasized that these circumstances mean that San Miguel Tzinacapan is probably the most authentically indigenous village one can find – in the area as well as in Mexico.

Lucas' historical reading serves several purposes. Making the case for Tzinacapan as probably "the most authentically indigenous village" in Mexico, Lucas challenged Arturo's initial presupposition of who would be capable of teaching whom about authentic indigenous dances. Furthermore, the reading worked to explain why Arturo had faced such problems; in Tzinacapan, an exceptional sociocultural cohesion exists, which provides the basis for resistance to external influences, thereby securing sociocultural continuity. To become part of Tzinacapan society, certain intrinsic sociocultural paths must be traveled, Lucas was telling me, the key one being ritual co-parenthood. From this contextualizing remark, it is evident that the significance of the newly established relationship, for Lucas, exceeds his concrete attachment to Maria and Yolani. Rather, the relationship reflects Lucas' beginning attachment to Tzinacapan as a place of authentic indigeneity, a place that was never really colonized, which only recently came into contact with mestizos, and which has preserved an authentic, that is, pre-Hispanic, way of life.

To set off the interview, I asked Lucas how the idea of him and Olivia as co-parents had emerged, and from whom the initiative had sprung. He told me that he had known Maria and Yolani for a long time, along with their close friend Suyapa, all of whom sold handicrafts in Cuetzalan when he first arrived. Lucas explained that their friendship had been growing and becoming increasingly confidential for quite some time. In the beginning of 2013, their friendship was well underway. When, once, I went to Tzincapan with Lucas, Maria invited us inside her modest plank house for a bowl of *quelite* herb soup with tortillas and coffee. Afterward, her husband accompanied us on a walk around the area in search of an old sage whose age increased steeply during our futile search for him. Suddenly, Maria's husband recalled a forgotten errand and urged Lucas to spare him five pesos. With the coin in his hand, Maria's husband charged up the steep dirt road as if his life depended on it, much to our immediate amusement. As we were chuckling, bright 8-year-old Eugenia appeared behind our backs and said disapprovingly, "Did you just give him five pesos? Now he has gone to buy himself a glass of aguardiente." Our amusement having been transformed into guilt and concern, Lucas asked how large such a drink would be. Eugenia showed with her hands that such a drink could be rather large, although not quite as large as a 10-peso drink, and she added that she had recently seen him "tossed" in the ditch, unconscious from drinking. Later on, Maria's husband caught up with us, sweaty, wheezing, and incoherent, asking for another five pesos, instantly doubling the requested amount. As we left for Cuetzalan, Lucas expressed his concern, but also saw how this episode made some pieces fall into place for him. The discovery of Maria's husband's alcoholism appears to have led to an intensification of Lucas' relation to Maria and her daughter Yolani.

Later that year, Suyapa approached Lucas to let him know that perhaps Maria would put forth the proposition that Lucas and Olivia could become educational co-parents of Yolani. Suyapa, being, in the words of Lucas, an "intimate friend to Maria," had gleaned that she was considering that Lucas and Olivia could be the right co-parents for Yolani. Lucas then asked Suyapa what such a relationship would involve:

> **Lucas (September 2014):** So, [Suyapa] told me what this exactly meant in the *macehual* culture, in San Miguel, exactly. She told me that this was something, well, *serious*. That they would make a formal invitation, that they would come to my house one day, that they would make a proposition, the two of them, mother and daughter. And then they would leave it in my hands to think it over and make a decision.[8]

Suyapa additionally explained that educational co-parenthood relationships begin when a child leaves preschool and end when the studies of the sponsored child are brought to completion. The relationship would involve educational and pedagogical responsibilities such as supervising Yolani's progress in school, aiding her with her homework, and motivating her interest in learning. Suyapa also explained that a co-parent, although not obliged, tends to sponsor tuition fees and materials required at school, such as uniforms, schoolbags, and booklets.

Prior to the formal proposition, Suyapa thus served as the mediating entity between the two parties. Lucas never discussed the matter with Maria and Yolani, since Suyapa, to his understanding, was briefing him on classified information to prevent a situation in which Lucas would stand unprepared and perhaps respond inappropriately. Lucas thus 'signs' an interactional contract presented by Suyapa; he agrees to preserve a situation of insulation between the two parties on the matter at hand. Through this interaction format, Suyapa creates a situation in which Lucas needs her to enhance his information state on the sociocultural and practical significance of co-parenthood in Tzinacapan. Discussion of the topic is therefore submerged in a cultural context that exceeds the concrete relationship that has made the topic pertinent to Lucas. Negotiation of the ensuing relationship takes place with *macehual* cultural tradition in Tzinacapan as a principal, while Suyapa merely assumes an animating role. A year prior to the formal proposition, Lucas thus entered a process of role preparation, and Suyapa assumed a didactic role vis-à-vis Lucas.

In Lucas' account, the first thing Suyapa stresses is the *seriousness* of such a relationship in the *macehual* culture of Tzinacapan. This aura of seriousness is equally performed by embedding their conversation on the topic in a collusive arrangement. Thereby, Suyapa sets a mood of formality through which to discuss the topic, and by highlighting the centrality of co-parenthood relations to *macehual* culture in Tzinacapan, she adds a ritualistic dimension to the relationship:

> **Lucas (September 2014):** It means that you have a kinship, through this ritual, a degree of kinship with the family. And with the rest. As much with the biological as the ritual family [. . .] So, as you form this tie, you make yourself part of this family or this community to a degree, right?

By emphasizing ritual co-parenthood as an extensive kinship relationship that will attach Lucas and Olivia not only to Maria and Yolani, but to the community at large, Suyapa also signals that despite the couple's friendship with people in Tzinacapan, a divide exists between them that may only be bridged through a co-parenthood relationship. Suyapa thus, almost unseeingly, points out that Lucas and Olivia are outsiders, but that they may become cultural insiders. The ritual co-parenthood relationship thus becomes something worth striving to achieve since it will entail their consecration into *macehual* culture in Tzinacapan. Suyapa, Maria, and Yolani thereby constitute entry points for Lucas and Olivia through which to obtain privileged access to 'authentic' indigenous culture. Suyapa thus constructs and mobilizes a desire in Lucas to belong to their community and become an initiate to authentic *macehual* culture.

Incidentally, Lucas also came to experience *macehual* culture in action around that time, as he was invited to participate in a ceremony that celebrated the graduation of two young men from Tzinacapan in which the educational co-parents symbolically devolved their sponsored child to the parents and formally concluded their co-parental responsibility. Lucas described how he had witnessed orations in Nahuat, followed by a banquet for around 100 guests. To his luck, Suyapa also attended the ceremony and came to his side to explain what was going on and paraphrase the speeches. At the time of the interview, Lucas seemed to have forgotten that he, back then, had emailed me a brief description of the ceremony, including a reported conversation between himself and Suyapa on the topic of educational co-parenthood. Lucas was told that usually – as demonstrated by the ceremony – local co-parents would be chosen due to their physical proximity and their knowledge of the tradition, but occasionally people from larger Mexican cities were elected, or even people from far-off places. Significantly, preparing Lucas for his role as educational co-father may have begun before Suyapa introduced the idea that Lucas might become one. In Lucas' account, he intertwines the ceremony and Suyapa's topical elaboration to show how he came to realize the solemnity of co-parenthood relationships:

> **Lucas (September 2014):** I then began to understand what it means to be a co-father [. . .] A banquet with so many musicians and such, all that is difficult for these people. It is a huge endeavor. That also gives you proof of a very great importance, because these people cannot afford to splash out nor to squander, and they also make you understand the degree of importance, right, to do all of this. [. . .] So I said, "Ouch! This is *serious*." [. . .] With what Suyapa was telling me, and what I was seeing through that [ceremony], I think that [in that moment] I began to understand what educational co-parenthood involves and what it exactly means in the *macehual* community.

As Lucas exclaims, "Ouch! This is *serious*" in reference to the ceremony, he illustrates a revelation that brings him "to understand what educational co-parenthood involves and what it exactly means in the *macehual* community." Lucas mirrors the reported words of Suyapa, who told him "exactly" what "educational co-parenthood" means "in the *macehual* culture" and highlighted the relationship as a "serious" matter. This way, Lucas communicates a personal transformation through which he has come to share the cultural horizon of Suyapa and the *macehual* community of Tzinacapan. At the time of narration, the personal transformation has been completed, as Lucas has become someone who can tell others of the solemnity of educational co-parenthood. Significantly, when asked how his new role has influenced his relationship to Maria, Yolani, and Suyapa, Lucas emphasized a change in his relation to the community in its entirety:

> **Lucas (September 2014):** Arturo, this guy who tried to integrate himself thoroughly with the people of San Miguel, admitted to me that the effective way [to integrate himself] was in the end really through one of the existing, strong standards of integration; it was through co-parenthood. That was what made him see that he now formed part of the community of San Miguel. [. . .] And I have noted, for instance, a certain change of attitude in the other women from San Miguel, who go to [Cuetzalan to] vend. They are no longer going to classify me as a tourist [. . .], they know that I am the co-father of Yolani, that I have this relation to Maria. So they know that I have a relation to the community.

For Lucas, the relation to Maria and Yolani grants him membership of the town and *macehual* culture. After formalizing the co-parenthood relationship, other villagers have changed their way of engaging with him, and he now feels as part of

San Miguel Tzinacapan. This sense of belonging is confirmed by his encounter with Arturo, who, after trying for years to "integrate himself thoroughly with the people of San Miguel," found co-parenthood relationships to be "the effective way" to make himself part of the community. Lucas' interpretation that Arturo "admitted" co-parenthood to be "the effective way" of becoming part of the community illustrates that achieving a degree of belonging to Tzinacapan was something Lucas had been aiming at achieving. The introduction to the interview, then, serves also as a springboard to the climax of his account: like Arturo, Lucas himself had come to realize that to make friends and access social life in Tzinacapan, the only way is to commit oneself to the community through a binding and enduring co-parenthood relationship. In this sense, Maria and Yolani become resources to a cultural rooting sought for, since they provide access to "*macehual* culture" in "the most authentically indigenous village one can find."

Common features mark the reported undertakings of newcomers Arturo and Ernesto (see Chapter 6). Both migrated from Mexico City and were attracted to the area due to Tzinacapan, and both discursively tie the town and its inhabitants to the Aztec Mexica past. On the face of it, Lucas' doings differ from their doings in the very sense that Lucas is not a Mexican national, and hence is not looking to forge ties with figurative ancestors. Nonetheless, exactly the idea about authentic, pre-Hispanic Mexico is what connects Lucas' doings to those of Arturo and Ernesto; as much as they are, Lucas too is exploring and learning about what it means to be Mexican. Having left his family and friends behind in Europe and starting a new life in Mexico with Olivia, he is forming relations that make him capable of belonging in Cuetzalan. Yet he is simultaneously forging ties to core constituents of the Mexican nation, and his endeavor is therefore not just about forging concrete social relations to people around him, but, by creating figurative links to the authentic Mexican nation, equally about him finding a place in Mexico. This activity strengthens Lucas' belonging to the cosmopolitan crowd in Cuetzalan, as he engages in meaningful conversations with other newcomers, who are able to confirm his ability to integrate with "Deep Mexico" (Bonfil Batalla 1989). Lucas' belonging to a group of cosmopolitans, who are on a quest to reconnect with their Mexican roots, then, includes Lucas into a larger national project that exceeds the concrete place in which he currently lives. Thus, the experiences Lucas shares with other cosmopolitans in Cuetzalan, when mediated through personal accounts, are resources that grant him a genuine sense of belonging in Mexico. Like other cosmopolitans, Lucas too is undergoing a cultural transformation that makes him feel 'more' Mexican.

The chapter now turns to show what the ritual co-parenthood with Lucas and Olivia and friendship relations with tourists signify for Maria and Yolani.

"City-friendships" as networking strategy

Ambulant vending in the Global South tends to be something resorted to when people have no other feasible income alternatives (Hansen, Little, and Milgram 2013:7–8). The people from Tzinacapan who go to Cuetzalan to vend are part of a group in town who face harsh economic conditions. During fieldwork in 2013, Maria was vending handicrafts full-time, but in 2014 she had found part-time employment and restricted vending to weekends. Sometimes I tagged along to see how vendors interacted with tourists and to get an impression of how much they were selling. Seeing how apparently little they sold made me wonder why many of them sustained their efforts to sell handicrafts. Part of the answer is that the vendors usually have no other or sparse income, so even days without sale do not constitute a direct loss, provided they walk the approximately five kilometers back and forth. Yet another part of the answer is that vending handicrafts is not all they do. Contrary to other ambulant vendors, this group is actively looking to network with tourists and newcomers. Their preference for vending handi-craft merchandise is therefore not coincidental, since these wares are 'natural' pretexts for engaging with tourists. Since tourists' average stay lasts 36 hours (BUAP 2013:136) and tourism concentrates on weekends, being on the spot in central Cuetzalan to meet tourists early on is crucial to enhance the possibility of attracting tourists to Tzinacapan on a flying visit. The main mission of this group appears to be to convey to tourists that Cuetzalan is really a mestizo town, and that they are Nahuas from nearby Tzinacapan. The vendors thereby signal to tourists attracted to Cuetzalan by its indigenous image that they have not reached their desired destination and that they would have to go to Tzinacapan to accom-plish the goal of their travel. If tourists cannot fit a visit to Tzinacapan into their schedule, the vendors give them a reason to return on a second trip, inviting them to pass by their place, so they can show them the village.

Maria dubs these relationships "city-friendships" and laconically states, "We meet, we make friendships." This was how Patricia encountered her co-mother. On her first trip to Cuetzalan, she met Patricia, and on her second trip Patricia's family took her to Tzinacapan:

> Maria (September 2014): They invited her to the house, they prepared mole for her, they ate, and in that way, little by little, friendship, friendship, friendship. [. . .] Then, afterwards, she became a co-mother. And another madam from Mexico [City], from Xochimilco, was also co-mother to her siblings.

The serving of mole poblano, the Pueblan signature dish, is indicative of the significance ascribed to these relations. Being an expensive and complex dish with many ingredients, mole poblano is reserved for times of festivity – and for co-parents. The meal thus has a symbolic significance, and the serving of mole by Patricia's family illustrates the effort made to court to the visitor. As I experi-enced myself, being met with such hospitality by people who face obvious hard-ship is likely to make a lasting impression on the visitor. Moreover, for urban, mestizo Mexicans, witnessing the grinding of maize on a *metate* quernstone, seeing handmade tortillas make their way to the comal griddle on top of the fire-place, while being surrounded by a household of Nahua speakers, is arguably a cultural performance set to impress and send them on a figurative journey to pre-Hispanic Mexico. In my own visit to Patricia's house, described earlier, a "more than 100-years-old" *metate* quernstone was soon brought forth for inspection and I was encouraged to touch it, which most likely demonstrates that visitors before me had ascribed to it a relic-like quality. On a later occasion, another vendor, Isabel, invited me and my family to the first communion of her daughter. Upon arrival, we were escorted past the main room with the additional guests and straight to the kitchen, where we were served mole poblano and could observe middle-aged and elderly women serving, cooking, and chatting in Nahuat.

In addition to Yolani, Maria has a 20-year-old son, Eliseo, who lives in Puebla, where his educational co-father, Pablo, is also based. As a child, Maria's husband was vending handicrafts and established contact with Pablo when he visited Cuetzalan as a tourist. Although their relation was never formalized, Pablo helped finance Maria's husband's schooling, and subsequently helped him find accommodation and employment. Pablo still supports him, but, as Maria puts it, now her husband "just drinks."

The co-parenthood relationship between Eliseo and Pablo has not produced the results hoped for either. Eliseo dropped out after elementary school and, to Maria's despair, has declined Pablo's offer of financing a microbusiness for him. Crucially, Maria situates Pablo's ongoing support within the co-parenthood relationship, regarding his efforts as a revised strategy to help Eliseo "be somebody in life." Maria thus regards educational co-parenthood as something beyond patronage of educational expenses and, more broadly, as a commitment to Eliseo's professional future. To Maria, the relation presents an opportunity for Eliseo to exit the poverty cycle into which he has been born, the aim being for him not to face a life with the same fragile living conditions and material poverty as Maria. Despite everything, the relationship between Pablo and Maria is undiminished in strength, and it is still of value to Maria, who stresses Eliseo's co-father for being "responsible," since he keeps an eye on her son and will help him out, should he face financial difficulties. Maria too can still rely on Pablo to house her, if she would need to go to Puebla City, and, should Yolani need hospital treatment there, she can count on Pablo to cover the medical bills. Maria's relation to Pablo thus exceeds Pablo's immediate commitment to Eliseo and his schooling, since the relationship additionally provides Maria with accommodation in Puebla City and, in case of emergency, with an ad hoc health insurance. By means of the relationship, Maria acquires a degree of financial, social, and geographic mobility that would otherwise be beyond reach for her.

Having seen her son leave school prematurely, Maria stresses that apart from financial support, Yolani's co-parents are to supervise her schooling, make sure she puts an effort into her homework, and provide extra tuition. Inquiring about what Maria expects from the relation, Maria flipped the issue, pointing to the expectations with which Lucas and Olivia have entered into the relationship:

> **Maria (September 2014):** Well, they expect that the girl can manage in school and that I also help the girl to work hard so that the girl also learns and to give the girl advice so she ends school well. For example, that she becomes somebody in life, a [Olivia's profession] or a [Lucas' profession], somebody, just not nobody.

The central issue, according to Maria, is not what she and Yolani wish for. She has transferred responsibility for the course of education to the co-parents, and their task is to facilitate a personal transformation in Yolani; they are to shape her in their own image. How this change is achieved in concrete terms Maria cannot know with certainty, but by nurturing their relation Maria activates Lucas and Olivia in formative roles vis-à-vis Yolani. Through this process, they will inevitably pass on the knowledge and values that have brought them where they are today. The aim of the relationship, for Maria, thus seems to be that Yolani ends up with an education and profession such as those of her co-parents. In achieving this aim, co-parents are helpful, as Maria illustrates by citing Pablo, Lucas, and Olivia to stress the importance of being "somebody in life," meaning to lead a life that resembles more the life of the co-parent than that of Maria. By linking herself and Yolani to Lucas' and Olivia's educational experience, the bond provides an 'esoteric' expertise that will guide Yolani in the right direction. Maria thus ascribes greater significance to moral and didactic support than financial sponsoring of tuition fees and school materials. The co-parents, who both hold university degrees, are thus drawn in as resources to Yolani's course of education and as role models that embody a desired end point for Yolani. The specialized resources the co-parents bring to the relationship stem from their positions as accomplished professionals, who are to help Yolani make the right choices and achieve the skills needed to do well in the educational system. Maria's expectation and hope, then, is that the co-parents will take charge of Yolani's educational formation and become live signposts of her potential future. After formalizing the relation, Maria expressed her expectations in negative form to Lucas, as reflected in my interview with him:

> **Lucas (September 2014):** Maria remarked not so long ago, "Well, in a few years, school is over with. Then she will start vending, right?" [. . .] But I told her, "Look, do not think that way, because your daughter is very bright and, in reality, we are in charge of her education and we want her to study as much as she is capable of and wants." And it was as if [Maria] thought, "Ouch!" She did not reply, but we told her that we are ready to help her, so the girl studies as much as she likes. [. . .]. When the mother insinuated that in a few years [Yolani] would leave [school], I said, "Excuse me, but I am the *co-father* and I want her to study this much! She is a very bright girl. She can do many things and we will take charge of that so she achieves more, studies for more years [. . .]. Through you she can learn all about the *macehual* culture, but she can also learn about world culture. Just as she is learning Spanish she can learn, perhaps, English. She can study elsewhere. She can study in Mexico [City] or in another country and afterwards the girl will have many more options." And the mother simply did not reply. She thought that we were right in giving her an opinion in that respect.

Clearly, Maria has *not* chosen Lucas and Olivia as educational co-parents with the mere expectation that they will cover educational expenses until Yolani leaves elementary school and may contribute to the household economy by

vending handicrafts. Rather, by expressing her ambitions for Yolani in negative terms to Lucas, Maria portrays herself as having a limited outlook, which
debilitates her ability to offer a responsible parental care. Thereby, she indirectly
prompts Lucas to manage the educational situation and to step firmly into the
co-parenting role, making him concretize the more ambitious plan he has for
Yolani. Maria thereby directs Lucas into a position of superior expertise on
Yolani's life and future, casting Lucas as prime adult role model by casting herself
as an 'unwittingly negligent' mother figure. In Goffman's terms, Maria's skillful
maneuver makes Lucas assume principality of the co-parenthood relationship
("I am the *co-father*") and strive to make *his* vision of Yolani's future materialize
("I want her to study this much!").

Thus, while Maria and her fellow vendors may never know what specifically
will emerge from a city-friendship, they have a precise idea of what such relationships entail in general terms; the relationships link their marginalized existence
to a network of better-resourced urban, middle-class citizens who help them avert
the worst harms of poverty and bring hope of social mobility in their direction. In
Mexico, middle-class life is predominantly urban-based and it is indicative that
"city-friendships," when formalized as co-parenthoods, tend to revolve around
education, which since the 1960s has increasingly become the path to middle-class
life in Mexico (Gilbert 2007:25–30). Additionally, educational co-parenthood
relationships can be maintained from a distance, since stable physical presence
is less necessary than in sacramental co-parenthood relationships that require the
co-parent to take the child to church. Supervision and tuition may be offered via
telephone, as in the case of Eliseo's co-father, and the calls perfectly fulfill the
equally important performative task of having middle-class agents repeatedly
stress education as the key trait the child should strive to acquire.

Not everyone in Tzinacapan is pleased about such city-friendships, however,
as Maria stresses through her story of a tourist from Mexico City who stayed
overnight in her house:

> **Maria (September 2014):** In that way we make friendships with the tourists.
> But not everyone! Because some companions [. . .] do not like it. We are not
> all alike. [. . .] Other people distrust a person who comes from the outside. And
> I say to her, "No, he [tourist] is not a bad person. He will sleep in the house."
> [. . .] Next day, he probably came to me, because he heard the conversation
> the other madam was saying – as if he was feeling bad – but [I said], "Do not
> worry, nothing will happen to you." He says, "It is just that madam, thank you
> so much for having a good heart, because *I am*," he says, "*from the city*. For
> a town," he says, "I am a stranger." [I said], "Yes, for them, but not for me."
> [. . .] And these persons come to visit because Cuetzalan is a Magical Village
> and we vend handicrafts. We have to converse! Because if we don't . . .

Maria positions herself vis-à-vis other groups in Tzinacapan, who are suspicious
of relationships with outsiders and whose lives appear not to depend on socializing
with tourists. Maria and the other handicraft vendors, however, cannot afford not

"to converse" with tourists, since selling handicrafts alone is not a feasible way of making a living. Tourists who visit the area are channeled into Cuetzalan due to the Magical Villages Program, as Maria points out, and the major part of tourism expenditure flows into hotels, restaurants, and tour operators in Cuetzalan. Since Cuetzalan constructs itself as a Magical Village through strategic displays of temporality and translocality tied together by a nationalized concept of indigeneity, the only marketable asset the handicraft vendors have is their ethnicity mediated in cultural terms. However, lest their efforts benefit business owners in Cuetzalan by adding a crucial performative spice to the experience of the *magical* environment, the vendors need to displace Cuetzalan, redirect tourists to Tzinacapan, and insert their encounters with tourists into an alternative economic cycle that sends profits their way. As this chapter has shown, this is an arduous and in many regards impossible task. To this end, the strategy employed by the female handicraft vendors reflects the realistic estimation that they will not be able to pull themselves out of poverty through tourism or otherwise in just one generation. Instead, they attempt to tie themselves and their children into a wider social security network to fend off the more serious harms of socioeconomic marginalization, and they hope to forge a network that will remove the perennial effect of poverty by creating conditions through which their children may take a step up the social ladder. As illustrated, the handicraft vendors thus apply an identity-based long-term networking strategy that looks to craft enduring social relations with urban middle-class tourists and newcomers on behalf of their children, whom are thus spun into a web of relations that transcends their (ethnically based) social class and social networks in Tzinacapan, and bypasses Cuetzalan.

The encounters between handicraft vendors from Tzinacapan and middleclass newcomers and tourists involve a central identity transaction through which both parties get liminal access to each other's distant worlds. This process revolves around an exchange of identity-based notions of traditional, rural, indigenous versus modern, urban, mestizo Mexico. Both groups thus acquire more 'Mexicanness' through the relationship. While one part creates or 'restores' lineage roots to pre-Hispanic, indigenous Mexico, and explores the indigenous Other as a lost, primordial, authentic self, the other part creates ties to urban middle-class mestizos, the central figures around which the Mexican labor market and state institutions are configured. The relationship is thus tied together by a transaction of the traditional and the modern, supported by mestizo fantasies about the past and the future.

Paradoxically, multicultourism is, it seems, the vendors' most apparent way out of the multicultourism into which they are currently inscribed. Cuetzalan is the meeting place for handicraft vendors from Tzinacapan and tourists, and their interaction gravitates around the notions of temporality and translocality espoused by the Magical Villages Program. The encounters thus articulate a degree of ambivalence since they situate themselves both within and outside the Magical Villages Program. The encounters are not envisioned by the program itself and in certain ways articulate critique of the multicultourism it espouses, and yet the vendors employ multicultourism to their advantage in the hope of escaping from it.

Notes

1 *Compadrazgo* was introduced into Latin America in the sixteenth century by the Catholic Church, and was in its initial European form connected to sacramental ceremonies (Nutini 2001:245).
2 The literature on *compadrazgo* is vast and tends to split into functional and structural analyses (Mendoza Ontiveros 2010). For an insight into the variegated shapes these relationships may take, see Nutini (1984:3–16). For a historical overview of *compadrazgo* in Europe and Latin America, see Mintz and Wolf (1950).
3 Timothy Knab's (1995) ethnographic account revolves around this once violent conflict and demonstrates how it still divided the town in the late 1970s.
4 Other vendors practiced this "evil eye" sales strategy on me at later occasions.
5 I take her use of the honorific suffix -*tzin* to indicate that no offense was meant. The term coyote refers not exclusively to ethnicity, but also to linguistic competency, since it denotes an individual who speaks only coyote language, i.e. Spanish (Castillo Hernández 2007:100).
6 *Güero* typically denotes a light-skinned person, sometimes with the connotation of urban, middle class, the last of which was hinted at in Francisca's comment about *güeros* having abandoned the tortilla in favor of white bread. In urban environments, the maize tortilla, which is part of the indigenous staple food in Mexico, is sometimes replaced by white sliced bread.
7 The *Concheros* tradition is said to have originated in the Bajío area of central Mexico, but from around 1900, as migration to Mexico City intensified, *Concheros* groups began to emerge there (Rostas 2009:165–166). According to anthropologist Susanna Rostas, *Concheros* groups increasingly see themselves as warriors in a symbolic struggle to reconquer Mexico by recovering, reasserting, and reinventing a pre-Hispanic, mainly Mexica-centered, cosmology and social order. These *Concheros* refer to themselves as Mexica, purify the dance of post-conquest features, and often aspire to learn to speak (Classical) Nahuatl (Rostas 2009:205–206).
8 *Macehual* (plural: *macehualme*) is the term Nahuas in the area employ to refer to themselves (Castillo Hernández 2007:58).

References

Bonfil Batalla, Guillermo. 1989. *México Profundo: Una Civilización Negada*, 2nd ed. Mexico City: Grijalbo.
BUAP. 2013. *Agenda de Competitividad de los Destinos Turísticos de México: Estudio de Competitividad Turística de Cuetzalan Pueblo Mágico*. Puebla: BUAP.
Castillo Hernández, Mario Alberto. 2007. *Mismo Mexicano pero Diferente Idioma: Identidades y Actitudes Lingüísticas en los Maseualmej de Cuetzalan*. Mexico City: INAH and UNAM.
Cohen, Erik. 1984. "The Sociology of Tourism: Approaches, Issues, and Findings." *Annual Review of Sociology*, 10:373–392.
Gilbert, Dennis L. 2007. *Mexico's Middle Class in the Neoliberal Era*. Tucson, AZ: University of Arizona Press.
Goffman, Erving. [1974] 1986. *Frame Analysis: An Essay on the Organization of Experience*. Boston, MA: Northeastern University Press.
Haly, Richard. 2000. "Nahuas and National Culture." Pp. 157–192 in *Native American Spirituality: A Critical Reader*, edited by I. Lee. Lincoln, NE: University of Nebraska Press.

Hansen, Karen Tranberg, Walter E. Little, and B. Lynne Milgram. 2013. "Introduction: Street Economies in the Global South." Pp. 3–16 in *Street Economies in the Urban Global South*, edited by K. T. Hansen, W. E. Little, and B. L. Milgram. Santa Fe, NM: SAR Press.

Knab, Timothy J. 1995. *A War of Witches: A Journey into the Underworld of the Contemporary Aztecs*. San Francisco, CA: Harper San Francisco.

Little, Walter E. 2008. "Living within the Mundo Maya Project: Strategies of Maya Handicraft Vendors." *Latin American Perspectives* 35(3):87–102.

Lok, Rossana. 1991. *Gifts to the Dead and the Living: Forms of Exchange in San Miguel Tzinacapan*. Leiden: CNWS, Leiden University.

Lupo, Alessandro. 1998. "Los Cuentos de los Abuelos: Un Ejemplo de la Construcción de la Memoria entre los Nahuas de la Sierra Norte de Puebla, México." *Anales de la Fundación Joaquín Costa* 15:263–284.

Lyon, Sarah M., and E. Christian Wells. 2012. "Ethnographies of Global Tourism: Cultural Heritage, Economic Encounters, and the Redefinition of Impact." Pp. 1–18 in *Global Tourism: Cultural Heritage and Economic Encounters*, edited by S. Lyon and E. C. Wells. Lanham, MD: Altamira Press.

Mendoza Ontiveros, Martha M. 2010. "El compadrazgo desde la perspectiva antropológica." *Alteridades* 20(40):141–147.

Mintz, Sydney W., and Eric R. Wolf. 1950. "An Analysis of Ritual Co-Parenthood." *Southwestern Journal of Anthropology* 6(4):341–368.

Mulhare, Eileen M. 2000. "Mesoamerican Social Organization and Community after 1960." Pp. 9–23 in *Supplement to the Handbook of Middle American Indians*, vol. 6, edited by J. D. Monaghan. Austin, TX: University of Texas Press.

Nutini, Hugo. 1984. *Ritual Kinship, Volume II: Ideological and Structural Integration of the Compadrazgo System in Rural Tlaxcala*. Princeton, NJ: Princeton University Press.

Nutini, Hugo. 2001. "Compadrazgo." Pp. 244–246 in *The Oxford Encyclopedia of Mesoamerican Cultures: The Civilizations of Mexico and Central America*, vol. 1, edited by D. Carrasco. New York: Oxford University Press.

Rabinow, Paul. 2007. *Reflections on Fieldwork in Morocco*. Berkeley, CA: University of California Press.

Rostas, Susanna. 2009. *Carrying the Word: The Concheros Dance in Mexico City*. Boulder, CO: University Press of Colorado.

Van den Berghe, Pierre. 1994. *The Quest for the Other: Ethnic Tourism in San Cristóbal, Mexico*. Seattle, WA: University of Washington Press.

Yuval-Davis, Nira. 1997. *Gender and Nation*. London: Sage.

8 Regenerative fiesta

Ritual configuration of history, identity, and society

Julius and I were watching a group of *Concheros* dancing in the church atrium of San Miguel Tzinacapan when an old lady smilingly approached to greet us, "I have seen you in Cuetzalan. *Thank you* for coming to the fiesta of San Miguel! This is my village." Although we had not previously met, the old lady apparently knew of our extended stay in Cuetzalan. Based on that source of intelligence, she thanked us for coming to her hometown to experience the fiesta. Her remark transmitted an unequivocal sense of pride in her village. But why *thank* us? Notably, a clue may be found in an identity-configured political struggle between metropolitan Cuetzalan and surrounding Nahua communities, which escalates during Tzinacapan's and Cuetzalan's consecutive fiestas. Our presence in Tzinacapan, despite our residence in Cuetzalan, was taken to express our sympathy for Tzinacapan, deeming the fiesta worthy of foreign attention. Bypassing Cuetzalan in this way, we unwittingly assisted in challenging the cultural, historical, and political centrality afforded to Cuetzalan and *its* fiesta within the region.

This chapter analyzes the role of Cuetzalan's fiesta in a translocal configuration of identities. The chapter first sketches how the fiesta is popularly conceived within an evolutionary scheme, before proceeding to show how this conception is structured by and activates settler versions of local history, which feed into contemporary local politics and social reality. In condensed form, the chapter highlights a pervasive metropolitan depoliticization strategy that naturalizes asymmetrical power relations by culturalizing the indigenous as the Other, and thereby rationalizing the mestizo Self (cf. Brown 2006:17–24).

Next, focus is turned to the community queen pageant called the *huipil* ceremony, a core activity within the fiesta in which young women dressed in traditional indigenous clothes, a *huipil* blouse inter alia, represent the surrounding Nahua communities.[1] The chapter examines how the ceremony becomes ritually bracketed in space and time, how these ritual brackets anchor and structure the activity, and how the social setting is calibrated to frame the event. The analysis shows how the identity configurations that emerge from the evolutionary narratives are integrated in the frame and organization of the *huipil* ceremony, and how the seance ritually re-actualizes these narratives. The accomplishment partly consists in constructing a cyclical, self-repeating event that is constructed and perceived as significantly organized by Nahua political authorities and communities even as it is situated in the municipal capital and organized and mediated by the municipal administration. The focus on ritual bracketing renders visible the inconspicuous ways in which the organization of a public performance oriented toward indigenous cultural traditions is structured from above to mediate the reverse impression of an event springing from below. The analysis thus shows how the frame of the event structures the production format and participation framework in ways that require young women from indigenous communities to engage in a self-culturalization to emerge as live "carriers of tradition" (Yuval-Davis 1997:61). As the women become central objects in a public assessment of indigeneity, the regulatory and "repressive" aspect of authenticity (Wolfe 1999:163–214) comes to the front, as it enforces and normalizes the depoliticization of indigenous issues and subjects in public space. The *huipil* queen candidates and Nahua authorities thus become embedded "autoethnographic" (Pratt 2008:9) sources of the authentic, cultural, and religious indigene – the counterpart of a settler *homo economicus* – and the *huipil* ceremony works to corroborate the mestizo representation of indigenous life as guided by self-contained culture.

The evolution of the fiesta: four sequences, three components, two characters, one line of view

There are structural similarities between the answers I received when asking locals about town life and about the town fiesta. In both cases, the responses sketched an evolutionary development that fed directly into contemporary social structures. The evolutionary narrative of the fiesta is structured around four chronological sequences that are understood to map three distinct components of the fiesta, each of which is identified with a particular group. The first, and core, component is referred to as the fiesta of the patron saint. As the municipal official in charge of organizing the *huipil* fair in 2014 expressed:

> **Aureliano (September 2014):** Well, [the Franciscans] establish themselves and establish 4 October as the principal date to celebrate the patron, which coincides with the fiestas dedicated to Xochiquetzal, which our predecessors celebrated 4 October. They coincide. And well, here these fiestas have been carried out continually from that time up to our days; that is the patron fiesta. [. . .] So, imagine that here in Cuetzalan all these [different] dances are gathered, and they all have the same line of thought; to please God. Prior to the arrival of the Spaniards, to please Quetzalcoatl, Tlaloc and all those you would like me to mention. After the arrival of the Spaniards, it is about pleasing Jesus Christ, the Virgin, San Francisco. But it continues to be the same line, a religious one.

The first sequence is located in the pre-Hispanic era and attaches an indigenous origin to the fiesta, which is seen as a *religious* celebration of one or several Aztec gods. The second sequence is located in the colonial era and relates how, upon arrival, the Franciscans realized how the indigenous religious celebration coincided in calendar and symbolism with the Catholic celebration of San Francisco. Two festivities with distinct origins thus came to constitute Cuetzalan's fiesta, as they were fused through the patronage of San Francisco by the Franciscans, who discovered their shared religious essence.

The second component arose when Cuetzalan had passed from being an indigenous village to a coffee-producing mestizo town. In 1949, the mestizos introduced a market fair, tending to run from September 27 to October 5, which was dubbed the coffee fair in celebration of the economy that resulted from the growing coffee industry. Correspondingly, its principal activity is the coronation of a coffee queen – once a means of financing the fair – but which nowadays takes the shape of a beauty pageant. Because of its original (discursive) ties to the coffee industry, the fair is understood by locals to have added an *economic* dimension onto the *religious* fiesta.

In 1963, the third component appeared when the municipal president introduced the *huipil* fair or *huipil* ceremony as it is frequently named. As Coronado argues, the *huipil* fair is often articulated as an altruistic attempt by mestizo society to preserve authentic indigenous culture, customs, and traditions, and to serve as an extended hand to the indigenous communities that were coming to feel "displaced" from the fiesta due to the coffee fair (Coronado 2000:130–132). The *huipil* fair is then taken to join the interests of two discrete groups by adding an explicit layer of cultural preservation to the fiesta, which, due to its tourist appeal, is seen to strengthen the existing economic dimension.

The narrative sequences thus delineate three disparate components that extract and segregate the diverging characteristics of two groups of citizens. The religious component – the patron fiesta – is seen as indigenous in its origin and indigenous participation in the fiesta is seen as religiously motivated. The economic component – the coffee fair – was installed around the patron fiesta by coffee-producing mestizos who discovered unexploited commercial opportunities. The cultural component – the *huipil* fair – was also invented by the mestizos who saw that the fiesta was parting into two and that indigenous participation was decreasing. To show their appreciation of the Nahua communities and to include them in the fiesta, the mestizos created an event through which indigenous customs and traditions could be displayed, celebrated, and perhaps preserved.

As the chapter will now illustrate, this plot about *the evolution of the fiesta* is doubly geared to *the evolution of the region*, the generic plot within local mestizo history-making. The former works both as a *pars pro toto* version of the latter and as a reinforcing component within it by procuring new testimony to the plot and its characters.

Tenacious anti-conquest: locating the discursive in(ter)ventions of settler seeing-man

Anthropologist Elizabeth Furniss argues that historical consciousness and identities across settler societies tend to be constructed around the foundational metaphor of the frontier (Furniss 1999:16–22). To Furniss (2005), the term frontier denotes both an imagined colonial setting and a mode of encoding concrete territories, and it equally points to a transitory process, as the frontier is always being pushed into the horizon as civilization moves forward. According to anthropologist Patrick Wolfe, the notion of the frontier is informed by a binary conceptualization with the performative effect of facilitating invasion and colonization, since diverse groups of settlers are conjoined by their shared mission and opposition to indigenous inhabitants (Wolfe 1999:165–167). Wolfe's observation on the performative effect of the frontier myth is instructive because it highlights a productive aspect: narratives of frontier land have informed social reality and inspired Europeans to leave their homeland and settle in far-off places. Therefore, while it is valid to claim that the notion of the frontier has skewed research on colonization processes – certainly, a European point of view is integral to the term (Pratt 2008:8) *and* it represents an ideological construction rather than an accurate account of the colonial situation – it is equally valid to claim that abandoning the idea of the frontier altogether will similarly skew scholarly understanding of colonization processes and contemporary dynamics in settler societies. The idea of the frontier is pervasive in settler-colonial storytelling, and has therefore played a vital role in settler colonialism. While settler narratives vary across time and space, they are invariably progressionist and centered on land use and territorial possession (Furniss 2005:28–29). In the characteristic scheme of settler colonialism, land is central, and indigenous labor is portrayed as superfluous because, rather than to exploit an indigenous workforce, settlers were interested in removing indigenous presence from the lands to be acquired (Wolfe 1999:27–29, 163). Frontier narratives therefore describe New World territory as vast, basically unoccupied, and rich in resources awaiting extraction. The frontier, then, becomes an imagined space in which binary opposites meet, and settlers emerge as pioneers of civilization, who subdue savage man and nature to construct towns and modern society (Furniss 2005:29–30).

According to Coronado, the mestizo construction of history in Cuetzalan centers on depictions of how mestizos arrived to transform a natural landscape into productive land, including a planned town, by constructing infrastructure and introducing cash crops (Coronado 2000:86–87). I experienced just how central such historical narrative continues to be for local identity when it was served to me time and time again. At first, I failed to comprehend the local fascination for the construction of roads and the introduction of coffee. Nevertheless, I since noticed that this fascination was particularly vivid in the historical accounts I received from descendants of settlers, and for some reason I often found myself talking to them. As historian Trevor Stack has similarly experienced in towns of west Mexico (Stack 2003:196), I ended up receiving accounts of local history from members of the "old" families. In Cuetzalan, the "old" families are descendants of the early waves of settlers and they are granted supreme authority in town history-making. Locals referred me to them constantly and the municipal government appoints its chroniclers from that branch of citizens. Hence, as Stack (2003) shows, town history and family histories intertwine and members of "old" families become privileged town historians due to their biographical links to the founding citizens who figure as protagonists of what is recognized as official town history. Dodging settler versions of history, politely or otherwise, becomes difficult because "old" family members are known to know more about town history than other citizens. This impression was underpinned in my interview with municipal chronicler Hernando. Benito from another "old" family had persuaded me to meet Hernando and arranged for it to happen. Hernando turned out to be the great-grandchild and grandchild of two protagonists of town history who are credited with the local introduction of coffee and the construction of the highway running from Zaragoza to Tuxpan. As we sat down, Hernando insisted on presenting "some historical data" that would be "convenient" for me to know prior to "our talk." This initiated a dizzying 50-minute monologue (interrupted only by the serving of coffee), beginning with the arrival of two groups of mestizos to the area in 1856:

> **Hernando (February 2013):** These people who arrived in Cuetzalan arrived with a *different vision*. [. . .] And above all, well, they fell in love with the region, they fell in love with this zone. And they loved it as the natives of this place love and loved it. In this place, there were indigenous people. Upon arrival, the mestizos straightaway began to integrate with the indigenous class. They were fusing in a way so that they could accomplish many things. [. . .] Communication with other towns was very difficult. Cuetzalan was *incommunicado*! [. . .] There were trails, *muddy* trails, due to the quantity of rain precipitated in this place. [. . .] Due to this, the paths were always *muddy*, they were always *difficult to access*. [. . .] [The clerics] neglected to arrive to Cuetzalan and said that this was because Cuetzalan had the worst roads. And they knew nothing about most of what was going on here. That kept the town *isolated*. But with the arrival of these people, *other horizons* began to open. For example, and I will tell you soon, the production of unrefined whole cane sugar begins. Moreover, they made stills to produce spirits. [. . .] They brought it all the way to Poza Rica, Tuxpan, and to Zacapoaxtla and to other towns such as Mazatepec, so that they could make commerce. [. . .] And they also began to implement *shops – bakeries, blacksmiths*. [. . .] But that is another way; yes, *commerce* was realized. [. . .] That happened in the 1880s and prior [original emphasis].

The settler within this evolutionary narrative is not unlike the *seeing-man* that emerges from literary theorist Mary Louise Pratt's reading of colonial travel accounts. The traveling *seeing-man*, "he whose imperial eyes passively look out and possess," is the protagonist of what Pratt terms the "anti-conquest," a class of narrative strategies through which European exploration writers managed to simultaneously declare European superiority *and* safeguard their innocence despite their entanglement with the planetary project of imperial economic and political expansion (Pratt 2008:9). A habitual mode of securing such innocence was a descriptive segregation of humans from geography, which constructed vast landscapes as devoid of human activity, yet as abounding in passive assets that invoke prospects of a colonial future (Pratt 2008:50–66). This mode of representation, which Pratt traces to the classificatory scheme of the natural sciences, places explorer and explored in liminal positions to the described territories. However, while for the explorer invisibility facilitates an allegedly benign appropriation and re-signification of territory through an advantageously reduced role as mere observer of geographical settings, invisibility for the explored becomes a step toward dispossession, *deterritorialization*, and *dehistoricization*. What situates the descriptive undertaking, then, is the identification of resources and possibilities that may expand European presence in the colony. So, descriptions of colonial landscapes legitimize impositions of an imperial vision that identifies resources, which require the transformative intervention of industrious European settlers and imperial technology.

Hernando describes mestizo arrival to a desolate landscape governed by a natural (dis)order in need of intervention to compose social and economic order. Upon arrival, the settlers "fell in love with" the land and immediately "loved it" as do and did the indigenous inhabitants. This benevolent portraiture of hostile encroachment into indigenous territory, which joins settlers and indigenous inhabitants in their mutual love of the region, is fulfilled by the 'fusion' of the two groups "so that they could accomplish many things." A shared love of the lands becomes synonymous with a confluence of interests, and the indigenous inhabitants are narratively obliterated through total absorption. After the settlers "integrate with the indigenous class" at the outset of the account, no further mention of them is needed, and they vanish from the account as settler history unfolds, "other horizons open," and "different visions" are implemented. This narrative strategy resembles what anthropologist Mark Rogers (1998) has encountered in his study on festivals and community identities in two regions of Ecuador. As he argues, mestizo identity stands for the totality, while indigenous identity is partial and specialized, which places mestizos in a commanding position of panoptic overview (cf. Foucault 1977).

Preceding indigenous societal forms are equally denied when the chronicler points to a lack of (infra)structure, subsequently delivered by mestizo settlers. The region was "isolated," "incommunicado," and "difficult to access," and to remedy this situation the settlers needed to act upon the landscape. Sequestered houses become a planned town with shops, new products, and a variety of specialized occupations. Fragile, unproductive, subsistence agriculture is substituted for a strong commercial and industrial economy through the introduction of new cash crops, goods, and instruments. A region disconnected from the surrounding world receives infrastructure such as electricity, roads, and a highway, and enters a wider commercial network. All these mestizo transformations of the natural landscape work to restrict continuity with previous ways of life; they are seen as new inventions and social substitutions of a natural order, a narration of how a non- or pre-place became the place it is today, and entered into first a regional and later a national project of modernity. Having described how settlers inserted Cuetzalan into a regional market system, the chronicler depicts how, beginning with the Mexican Revolution in 1910, the settler community established connections to shifting Mexican presidents, and how due to this Cuetzalan became a key point on the oil route from Veracruz to Mexico City.

It is this plot of a hitherto ungoverned, isolated territory – a natural order of which the invisible indigene is inherently part – that implicitly constitutes the privileged right of the industrious mestizo settlers to these lands. In short, mestizos brought progress to the area by introducing social order per se, leaving the Nahuat toponym as the only gesture of continuity between the pre-place and the place. Tellingly, the progressionist narrative about new mestizo Cuetzalan, disconnected from past indigenous Cuetzalan, was subsequently inscribed into the name of the municipality by adding the modifying clause *del progreso* to the Nahuat toponym.[2] The narrative makes no mention of the conflicts that accompanied the mestizo invasion of indigenous lands. This silence contrasts sharply with historical documents and contemporary indigenous accounts of local history, which emphasize interethnic conflict, dispossession of fertile land, and forced incorporation into coffee cultivation (Thomson 1991; CEPEC 1994; Knab 1995:147–184; Coronado 2000:93–95). But then again, the issue here is not the accuracy of settler history, but rather its persistent framework from which the mestizo emerges as *homo economicus* through implicit antithetical comparison with the ostensibly natural pre-societal Nahua.[3]

Keeping in mind the generic anti-conquest narrative, one may see how the narrative of the coffee fair reifies a plot organized around the notion of progress and the industrious settler protagonist. The mestizos have crafted an order they found to be lacking and created a void in demand of their intervention; they produce an *economic* and *rational* dimension to what ostensibly was a purely religious celebration. The narrative of how the mestizos invented the coffee fair thus portrays the original indigenous (and Catholic) fiesta as purely religious and procures (re)new(ing) testimony to the idea that mestizos brought progress and social order to the region by skillfully introducing commerce and industry. However, as early colonial sources convey, Aztec fiestas were far from purely religious events. In Aztec society, politics and religion were intricately linked and interdependent ideologies (Carrasco 1995:2), and fiestas of the imperial capital Tenochtitlan included not only the worshipping of specific patron gods, but also overt symbolic manifestation of political power through ritual display of imperial superiority (Brown 1988). Moreover, Aztec fiestas were geared to the market system. Not only did community fiestas and market days coincide so that surrounding communities would attend fiestas and their accompanying markets, but many fiesta activities took place within the marketplace. Likewise, markets had their own temple shrines and representative deities. Therefore, markets were not mere economic institutions and fiestas were not mere politico-religious events (Hutson 2000:135–137; Hodge 2001). This combination of market fair and fiesta was a widespread practice in pre-Hispanic central Mexico, which continued in the colonial era and is also found today. This is not to say that Cuetzalan's fiesta *has* a pre-Hispanic origin, but to chart the historical reasons why it would be highly unexpected to find a fiesta in central Mexico without links to the market economy.

Fiestas are social events that bring together people from different towns and such social gatherings generally involve commercial activities.

Correspondingly, historian of religions Ian Reader argues that the success of pilgrimage destinations rests on strong links to the market (Reader 2013). Nevertheless, most academic literature on pilgrimages tends to demarcate the sacred from the profane, regarding the market as a parasitic entity that is nurtured by, rather than nurturing, the pilgrimage destination. This tendency to split sacred religious structures from profane commercial and economic structures is both widespread and long-lasting, even as proponents view the relation between religious and commercial activity as a modern condition (Reader 2013:11–24).

In sum, a mestizo view of self and indigenous society is reflected in popular accounts on the town fiesta. By representing the indigenous fiesta as a purely religious activity, its ties to the market economy are discursively severed. This segregation provides the basis of discursively superimposing the mestizo coffee fair on the indigenous fiesta, a strategy of representation that reflects and reinforces mestizo accounts of local history. Reflecting what Patrick Wolfe argues in the case of settler society in Australia (Wolfe 1999:178–179), the settlers' discursive and practical disruption of the preceding economic system and its "disembedding" from the political, religious, and social system in a struggle over land has placed mestizos and indigenous people in two discrete, non-conflicting spaces: an economic one and a religious one. An intense Othering, then, is at the heart of "repressive authenticity." It is repressive because it blurs the shared economic and political interest in land by authenticating an indigenous subject that poses a marginal threat to settler society economics and politics (Wolfe 1999:180).

Anchoring identities in the *huipil* ceremony: autoethnography in the contact zone?

The chapter now turns to analyze the *huipil* ceremony, the constituting event of the *huipil* fair. Paralleling Coronado's observation in 1997 (Coronado 2000:132–133) that coffee played no obvious role in the coffee fair, there is nothing outside of the *huipil* ceremony that suggests a central role of the *huipil* blouse in the *huipil* fair. The market stands include *huipil* blouses in their assortment, just as they include coffee, handicrafts, and other souvenirs, but such stands are always there on market days.

Since its inception in 1963, the *huipil* ceremony has changed, and the number of participants has increased. In its first year, there was only one participant, a mestiza from Cuetzalan, and in 1965 and 1967 a mestiza from Xocoyolo was crowned. The incorporation of indigenous participants into the ceremony thus demanded a decisive effort from mestizos in Cuetzalan. The organizers since came to employ the municipal political structures and it has become customary for the eight auxiliary councils in the municipality to contribute candidates for the ceremony. Once recruitment of participants turns into a recurring political assignment of the auxiliary councils, distinguishing voluntary from obligatory participation in any strict sense becomes difficult. This participatory ambivalence surfaced in my interview with an experienced organizer of the *huipil* ceremony, Aureliano, who stated that "a participant is requested" from the auxiliary councils by the municipal authorities, instantly adding "or those who want to." It would, however, be fair to say that auxiliary councils are expected to deliver a candidate each.[4] This is reflected by the equivalent expectation that auxiliary councils are to bring the dancing troupes that are introduced near the end of the *huipil* ceremony, and which subsequently take over the atrium to perform a variety of ritual dances. Aureliano told me that the fiesta in 2013 was the worst in his lifetime due to a meager attendance of dancing troupes, and that many dances were lacking, stressing that normally all auxiliary councils participate, except for San Miguel Tzinacapan:

Aureliano (September 2014): And now, curiously, the discrimination is coming from them toward us. They discriminate us.

Casper: By not coming to the fiesta?

Aureliano: Of course, there is a discrimination there too. And I don't complain, because, well, these are things. They are grounded in something. But, well, this is what is happening.

This rhetorical strategy resembles what anthropologist Charles Hale calls "reverse racism" (Hale 2002:515). Mestizos believe they have shed racist attitudes of the past through inclusionary principles of equality; however, when indigenous people dishonor such gestures of equality, this is taken as diagnostic of indigenous racism toward mestizos (Hale 2002:515). This theme is returned to later, but for now it may serve as a backdrop of the fiesta; while indigenous presence is warmly appreciated, encouraged, and celebrated, indigenous absence is indignantly and resentfully problematized. Participating and performing in Cuetzalan's fiesta is not just the cultural right of local Nahuas, but also their moral duty (cf. Scher 2014:92–96). Thus, the precondition for the visible cultural appreciation and recognition of indigeneity in the *huipil* ceremony is a tacit, repressing obligation to participate.

The auxiliary councils appear to have been included in organizing the *huipil* ceremony since the 1970s, and the ceremony has since incorporated participants from three additional towns. Onstage, the participants are to present the culture and history of their communities through three-minute speeches in Nahuat and Spanish, wearing traditional indigenous female vestments. The winner is elected by a jury, consisting of Nahua auxiliary mayors, also dressed in their traditional vestments, the reigning *huipil* queen and "outstanding" citizens. Nowadays, the event is broadly perceived as an indigenous ceremony, and popular descriptions of the event almost invariably describe the jury as comprised solely of Nahua authorities. This popular conception is illustrated in an interview with a frequent jury member, Manolo, a Nahua from San Andrés Tzicuilan:

Casper (February 2013): Are they *all* mayors, or?

Manolo: Mhm [affirmative].

Casper: So, the judges are the mayors?

Manolo: They are the mayors. There [in the *huipil* ceremony] the municipal presidency does not intervene in anything. They are just there as special guests to watch the event. But of course, they also sponsor what is necessary to make it all happen.

The perception that the jury consists only of Nahua political authorities corroborates the view that the municipal authorities are mere sponsors of an event organized by indigenous agents. This perception is not coincidental, but indicative of a tendency that sustains the widespread idea that the *huipil* ceremony is an indigenous event; it reflects how attention is guided toward that which is framed, rather than the framing. Likewise, integrating Nahua authorities into the planning of the ceremony substantiates the idea that the Nahua communities 'themselves' are principals of the event and its contents. Yet to plan such a commemorative event means to put oneself at the service of the returning frame template that is passed down the line from year to year, and to fulfill the expectations the audience can rightly entertain for a returning event. This frame governmentality both regulates Nahua authorities unseeingly and procures visible Nahua principals for the ceremony. A view of the event as springing from indigenous interests is produced together with the pervasive idea that indigenous interests are primarily culturally motivated, as illustrated in a television interview with a state delegate of the National Commission for the Development of Indigenous Peoples following the *huipil* ceremony in 2011:

> **Delegate:** [I]n this case we are sharing *our Pueblan traditions*, and in particular this traditional *huipil* fair together with the municipal president and with all the inhabitants of Cuetzalan as well as with all the tourists of national and international character that I am seeing here. So, for me, it was a pride to crown the queen, Roberta López López, who was – truly – very moved, because on account of her speech she is much helped, right? Above all, in what she conversed about; to speak of their traditions, of their typical dishes from around here, of the places, of the cascades, of all the cultural richness they have; it helped her gain the crown. For *her* it is a pride! [. . .]. So, it is part of coexisting and enjoying with *our indigenes* what is *for them* so important, as is *their culture*. We know that economic development is important [. . .] but even more important, I would say, is to preserve these traditions so that they shall not be lost [emphasis added].
>
> (SBC Noticias Zacapoaxtla 2011)

The delegate ascribes differing degrees of attachment to the ceremony to different groups of participants. The *huipil* fair is taken to represent both "*our* Pueblan traditions" and "what is *for them*," that is, "*our indigenes*," "so important, as is their culture." The *huipil* fair thus becomes an emblematic expression of both "*our Pueblan traditions*" and authentic indigenous culture. Mestizo majority society is in a position of mastery since they possess "*our* Pueblan traditions" and "*our* indigenes," while the indigenous people *are* their culture as expressed through the ceremony. The remark that the winning queen "was – truly – very moved," and the linking of it to the candidate's speech on Nahua "cultural rich-ness," works to stress the candidate's emotional involvement in the ceremony, which authenticates such culturalized expression of indigenous identity as the sum total of indigenous life. This, again, illustrates how mestizo identity is understood to encompass the totality, while indigenous identity is restricted to cultural narcissism (Rogers 1998). Such strategies of representation depoliticize indigenous subjects and sustain the discursive and temporal divide between the mestizo *homo economicus* and the indigenous *homo religiosus*.

The following sections show how the *huipil* ceremony is framed in space and time to construct the impression that the event is an indigenous tradition.

Spatializing the fiesta

The *huipil* ceremony takes place on the bottom level of the three-tier divide of public space in central Cuetzalan, in the atrium outside the church (see Figures 8.1–8.2). The 893-square meters of the middle tier constitute the largest plane space within the center, but since this tier holds the public park, the atrium is the largest readily available space and the most apt spot for a space-consuming event. Nevertheless, since 2002, a large stage has been mounted on top of the park during the fiesta, creating space for concerts and the coffee queen pageant. The continued placement of the *huipil* ceremony in the atrium highlights the clas-sificatory significance of the spatial boundaries to the types of events they encase. In Mexico, the atrium is characteristically a quadrangular forecourt that works as an exterior extension of the church nave (Edgerton 2001:46–47). This archi-tectural outline for churches and convents became the preferred one beginning in the early colonial decades of 1520–1530, partly because the open space could accommodate large-scale baptism, conversion, and other religious activities, and partly because friars sought to incorporate local indigenous conceptions of sacred space into Catholic ground plans. In pre-Hispanic Mexico, square precincts hosted public rituals such as dances and processions, and, adapting such activi-ties to Catholicism, friars encouraged their continuance in the atriums (Edgerton 2001:52–64). From its inception, this ritual space was not merely an outcome of the contact zone (Pratt 2008:7–8), but constituted in itself a prime contact zone between Catholic and indigenous religious practices. As an inherent feature of most Mexican churches, the atrium has been architecturally inscribed into the Mexican townscape as a venue known to host public indigenous rituals.

In Cuetzalan (as in surrounding indigenous towns), the *voladores* pole in the center of the atrium latently encodes the space as a significantly indigenous sacred setting, and it facilitates ritual activation of the space as such. Placing the *huipil*

Figure 8.1 Participant in the *huipil* ceremony performing speech

Source: Casper Jacobsen, October 2014

ceremony in the atrium therefore entails an employment of the symbolic synergies that flow from a permanent, architecturally established sacred space. By embedding the ceremony in a sacred setting that ordinarily circumscribes the types of activity that may take place there to that of religious ritual, the organizers employ a precoded public expectation of what constitutes an atrium activity. The location of the event therefore creates a transformational spillover effect that is enhanced by the strategic incorporation of ritual activities into the event and by the ritual dances that subsequently unfold in the atrium. As a permanent sacred setting, the atrium a priori transforms the character of public events performed there to that of *sacred* ritual. In contrast, the stage atop the park is visibly ephemeral and situated by the town hall, the municipal political center. This way of spatializing an 'indigenous' part of the fiesta into a 'sacred' atrium and a 'mestizo' part onto a 'secular' stage engages recursively with settler versions of history and the fiesta. The differentiated settings convey a taxonomy that codifies public perception of and appropriate response to the activities of the fiesta; indigenous activity is classified as sacred ceremony and mestizo activity is classified as secular entertainment. The spatial conventions therefore become laminations that encode and mediate indigenous and mestizo activities differently. As obvious as it is for citizens of Cuetzalan that secular activities such as the concerts or the coffee queen pageant cannot take place in

Figure 8.2 Overview of the three-tier central Cuetzalan

Source: Una Canger, March 2014

the atrium, the *huipil* ceremony cannot take place on the concert stage, since that would direct attention to the event as 'staged.' The authenticity of the ceremony, then, depends on spatial conventions; the indigenous event and its participants must be placed in their 'natural habitat.'

To enhance the sense of spatial sacredness, the northern half of the atrium was covered with pine needles, demarcating the ritual space. Within the ritual space, a small stage had been crafted for the ceremony – as is usually done – this year with an additional tarpaulin roofing. Also covered in pine needles, the stage was additionally adorned to match the decorations on the church, both applying red and green *heliconia* leaves and circular ornaments made from palm leaves, which are used in fiestas. Enhancing the ritualized setting, indigenous protagonists were concentrated in the inner sanctum. An indigenously dressed folk band and the *huipil* queen participants flanked each side of the stage, while the Nahua part of the jury and the reigning *huipil* queen were located in a distinguished position in front of the stage.

Temporal enclosures: building up an information state

The publicly disseminated program scheduled the *huipil* ceremony to begin at 10 a.m. In the municipal logistics plan, however, events were scheduled to begin two hours in advance, with the folk band playing regional music to "create an atmosphere." Forty-five minutes before 10, the fiesta was well under-way. Locals and tourists were strolling in the market, vacant spots in and around the atrium were becoming few, the *huipil* queen candidates and the Nahua jury arrived jointly, and children in traditional indigenous clothes were performing the *xochipitzauat* folk dance to the tones of the atmosphere-creating band.

The two-hour transposition of the scheduled versus the disseminated starting point facilitates the concealment of the external boundary of the social occasion. That is, organizers ensure that when people arrive, they witness only the organized social activity – a fiesta already flowing – and not the organizing of social activity – a band testing microphones and preparing to play. This retrospective indeterminacy of the fiesta's time span – the concealment of the external bracket – insulates the larger social affair from ongoing everyday activity of the environing world, and it signals the managerial imperative of having people experiencing the calibrated milieu rather than the calibrating efforts of management. The concealment of management thus becomes a central managerial concern. Together, the need to conceal the external boundary of the fiesta and the organizational logistics involved in arranging the *huipil* ceremony determine the possible order of events during the fiesta. Because the *huipil* ceremony occupies the atrium – the locus for dancing – the ceremony has to take place before the dances, since otherwise the organizing of the ceremony cannot be concealed. Hence, because the dances cannot predate the *huipil* ceremony – the atrium is not available – a spontaneous commencement of the fiesta is not possible. This produces the managerial task of subtly commencing the fiesta to maintain a sense of spontaneity; after all, it is supposed to be a town fiesta, not a politically organized event. This managerial effort signals the undesirability of launching the *huipil* ceremony at the inception of the continuum of events; it gains its naturalness only from a set of preceding calibrations of social reality, and it therefore needs to be safely embedded within the larger social affair of the fiesta. Such calibration is an organizational task that may be inspected through the management of the temporal brackets that enclose and structure the ceremony itself.

The temporal spaces within and around the *huipil* ceremony were administered by two masters of ceremonies (emcees) appointed by the municipal administration – one mestizo and one Nahua – who were speaking to the audience in Spanish and Nahuat, respectively, through a loudspeaker system. The distribution of their tasks, defined by their use of distinct languages of communication, readily signals a complementarity of roles, which is also signaled in the structured alternation between the speakers. Rarely, the mestizo emcee spoke without being followed by the Nahua emcee. Nevertheless, beneath this structured complementarity, the division by language also marks a hierarchical division of roles. The distribution of tasks grants the mestizo emcee supreme authority in matters of verbal representation since he holds the exclusive privilege of mediating the event to the visiting mestizo audience. Awareness of the pre-assigned asymmetry of role-integral capacities shows itself in the production format of utterances of the mestizo emcee. Similar to what Coronado (2000:139–141) shows in her analysis of the event in 1997, the mestizo emcee presents a supra-ethnic, municipal self. Such "totalizing municipal identity" (Rogers 1998) facilitates a speech position that has the advantage of effacing mestizo political involvement in the organization of the event, including his own role. With his monopoly on mediating the event to the external audience, the mestizo emcee implicitly claims to represent people within the municipality at large, rather than the municipal administration in Cuetzalan. From the supra-ethnic position, he emerges as a proxy cultural insider; he does not pretend to be an indigenous insider, only to appear in their image, possessing the knowledge and the authority of mediating the cultural content of an internal indigenous event before an audience that he constructs as external by addressing them as "visitors" and by framing the audience as cultural witnesses. Within this production format, the mestizo emcee claims merely to be animating, not producing, the ceremony, and the Nahua emcee becomes an embedded source that corroborates the mestizo mediation of the event as internal and authentically indigenous. The participation of the Nahuat-speaking emcee testifies to the necessity of installing a proxy cultural insider, who will make the indigenous ceremony graspable to the external audience. As the event was about to start, the mestizo emcee increasingly calibrated the seance and setting as indigenous:

> **Mestizo emcee:** Cuetzalan, *Cuetzalan* is our municipality. [. . .] It has a population that exceeds 90% in regard to the indigenous people. *A population of more than 90% indigenous* and the rest of the population [is] mestizo. One sole, *one sole auxiliary council* to the south of the municipality, the highlands, Xocoyolo, is composed of mestizos.

The repetitive technique marks part of the information as spectacular for the visitor, and the ensuing comments by the Nahuat-speaking emcee work recursively as a strengthening testimony to the preceding portraiture of the municipality as indigenous.Through such pronouncements of 'factual' information that addresses the environing world rather than the ceremony itself, the audience is gradually prepared to witness an *indigenous* event and receive *indigenous* accounts from *indigenous* subjects. Significantly, then, articulating the municipality as indigenous works to enforce an authentic indigenous space that could otherwise be disturbed by the central presence of mestizos. The emcee's attention to this potential threat to the experience of the event protrudes through his emphasis on Xocoyolo as the "sole auxiliary council" with purely mestizo inhabitants. Highlighting this irregularity and articulating mestizo presence as marginal within the municipality, the mestizo emcee minimizes the significance of mestizo presence in the social affair, even as the event is hosted in and significantly organized by the mestizo municipal capital. He thereby assists tourists in eliding mestizo presence from their experience, and, by avoiding characterizing Cuetzalan as a mestizo town, he implies that it is indigenous.In this respect, he emphasized Cuetzalan as a municipal gathering point that attracts national and international attention and as one of the first Magical Villages, stressing that "there are at least 80 Magical Villages in Puebla, but Cuetzalan still holds first place." As Chapter 5 showed, emphasizing Cuetzalan as one of the first Magical Villages works to naturalize its nomination and to insulate it from more recently nominated towns that are perceived to devalue the category. Cuetzalan thus emerges as a prototypical Magical Village, and the ensuing *huipil* ceremony and ritual dances become the epitomes of what makes Cuetzalan a particularly magical Magical Village.

Immediately prior to the *huipil* ceremony, the emcee proceeded to explain the origin, purpose, and structure of the event. The question of origin in particular makes the communicative task a delicate one. Not only is the origin of the *huipil* ceremony traceable to 1963, but its inventor was also a leading mestizo politician, both of which may provoke the audience to question the authenticity of the event. This origin thus needs to be convincingly counterbalanced by measures that signal indigenous autonomy of the ceremony and reduce mestizo involvement to a liminal role of initiator and annual host. That is, sources that transgress the origin of the event must be relied upon to establish its authenticity; indigenous agents must figure as principals of the event. Such accounts of the origin of the *huipil* fair have been fluctuating for decades (cf. Merlo Juárez 1979:42; Coronado 2000:135–137). All versions are structured by two discrete agents: the safeguarding mestizo benefactor and the safeguarded indigene beneficiary.

According to one version, indigenous communities had come to feel that the secular activities of the coffee fair were overriding the traditional indigenous fiesta, due to which their participation in the fiesta was diminishing. Realizing this, mestizo society introduced the *huipil* fair to create an event that would appeal to indigenous communities and stimulate their participation. Mestizo authorities thereby succeeded in showing indigenous communities that their participation in the fiesta was important to Cuetzalan. As indigenous communities engaged in the event, indigenous participation increased, and so the traditional indigenous fiesta, including its "purity," was safeguarded. Another version holds that the *huipil* fair was instituted to safeguard indigenous vestments, which were dissipating due to acculturation processes. In this account, indigenous material culture is reappraised and recognized, giving indigenous communities a sense of cultural self-pride that helps them preserve their material culture. More broadly, the *huipil* fair is seen to safeguard indigenous cultural traditions. In recent accounts, the cycle is complete, as the *huipil* ceremony itself has become an indigenous tradition within the fiesta, and consequently an object in need of preservation. Nevertheless, all versions emphasize the *huipil* fair as a safeguarding measure that preserves the authenticity of indigenous culture, whether it be the fiesta, the vestments, or cultural traditions.

Given that the *huipil* ceremony has a point of origin in the figure of the mestizo benefactor, mediating the event as autonomously and authentically indigenous consists in dislocating the mestizo principal by visibly integrating indigenous principals into the structure and organization of the event. Notably, the emcee explained that the indigenous jury was composed of political authorities from the auxiliary councils, which had decided on a candidate each for the event. Here, the spatial and temporal brackets of the event are extended beyond the setting and the ceremony itself, thus initiating the event indeterminately in advance in the communities. The authorities, wearing their festive suits, were placed in a preeminent position within the ritual space, and anonymously behind them and outside the demarcated area were the "outstanding" citizen part of the jury in ordinary clothes. Likewise, the emcee avoided directly correlating the two groups, giving the impression that the back row was rather a group of distinguished spectators. Similarly, after the presentations, the indigenous authorities and the reigning *huipil* queen assembled in a circle by the stage to show that they were discussing their verdict (see Figure 8.3). Only afterwards, when the first dancing troupes were at the center of attention, did the reigning *huipil* queen collect the votes of the remaining jury. As the voting had closed, the main Nahua authority went onstage with the reigning *huipil* queen to declare the winner by throwing into the air ribbons of a color that corresponded to the ribbons on the winner's miniature baton of authority. Later, during the crowning, only the Nahua part of the jury was present in the scene. This centrality offered to the Nahua jury helps move attention away from their being outnumbered by the less visible jury.

Invested into the *huipil* fair is a sense of authenticity understood to transgress the origin of the ceremony. The origin of the ceremony may be recognized as recent, but the culture, traditions, and vestments presented through the event are pushed into time immemorial. The imperative of memorizing the event as an initiative that came from Cuetzalan stresses that the *huipil* fair was born into and still

Figure 8.3 Nahua jury and reigning *huipil* queen gathered in a circle to settle on the winner, while *voladores* dance in front of the crowd

Source: Casper Jacobsen, October 2014

maneuvers a difficult political climate in that it serves as a reminder of mestizo compassion for the indigenous communities and genuine mestizo concern over indigenous marginalization. The *huipil* ceremony reactivates a story of how mestizos acted altruistically in favor of the indigenous communities.

Repressive authenticity naturalized: from constriction to description to experience

The narrative of the origin of the *huipil* ceremony contains two contradictory views on indigeneity. On the one hand, the ceremony celebrates indigenous participants for their 'natural' authenticity – Nahuas know about their culture and follow their traditional lifeways – and, on the other hand, the ceremony is a strategy to secure the preservation of their 'natural' authenticity. The ceremony thereby portrays indigenous culture as at once central and liminal, vivid and endangered. These contradictions, which must be managed by the mestizo emcee, arise through an organizational procedure that moves the ceremony from prescription and proscription to description and performance. A few months in advance, the municipal government sends a letter of convocation to the auxiliary councils announcing the *huipil* ceremony and the criteria of participation. The criteria are pre- and proscriptive constrictions that delineate the desired participants through inalienable characteristics, cultural and gendered competence, and public performance. The criteria stipulate what the candidates *need to be* or *need to do*, and in the ceremony these requirements become resources for live description of characteristic indigenous behavior and cultural traits. Where the criteria state that the participants must wear "100% authentic" and "traditional" cotton vestments made on a waist loom, and cannot wear makeup, stockings, nor footwear, the emcee stated that the participants appear before the audience in their "traditional" and "authentic" vestments. Likewise, his remark that "all participants know how to work the waist loom" derives from the criterion that they must know how to work it, and the description of participants' features as "autochthonous" comes from a criterion that requests such. Translating constrictions into descriptions, the mestizo emcee informed the audience that the participants need to speak Nahuat and have the capacity to practice their "traditional culture," spontaneously evoking their ability to cook handmade tortillas. Due to this, he stressed, the audience should not mistake the *huipil* ceremony for a beauty pageant, since the purpose of the *huipil* ceremony was about being "the most traditional woman." To that end, each woman had been selected as representative of their community and would appear onstage to relate "the characteristics of their place of origin," first in Nahuat and then in Spanish. This is a critical moment of translation given that the criterion that guides the oral performance instructs the candidate to "confine herself to speak exclusively of the cultural and historical aspects of one's community." The instruction of producing community-centered cultural and historical accounts thus emerges as a naturalized indigenous genre in the description of the emcee, which in turn may be experientially and performatively confirmed through the ceremony. The emcee thereby appears to be authenticating the participants rather than regulating them, even as he conjures a particular type of indigenous subject through ethnographic description and prescription. While the descriptions delineate the participants as naturally authentic indigenes, the pre- and proscriptions constitute the safeguarding functions of the ceremony that seek to keep them (naturally) authentic. What in the selection process are requirements for participation are portrayed as natural traits in the context of the ceremony, and therefore notions of what the participants *are* and what they *should be* cannot be easily distinguished. The implication is that if participants do not produce a performance that honors the pre- and descriptive domain of the ceremony, they run the risk of publicly compromising their own and community authenticity and of being discredited as cultural insiders.

So far, the chapter has considered ways in which the *huipil* fair was framed in space and time in front of participants and audience. To further explore the framing of the event, attention is now turned to instances in the speeches of the candidates. These moments, when candidates assume the stage and become the center of undivided attention, constitute the most vulnerable moments of the ceremony, not just for the presenting candidates, who become objects of public scrutiny, but also for the organizers. Pointing in particular to disruptive moments in which attention is moved from the enclosed performance to the organizing frame of the event, the chapter analyzes both the implications of an accidental frame break and a more deliberate frame-breaking activism that seeks to destabilize and call into question the social occasion and its organizers.

Inviolable characters: the cultural Nahua and the traditional woman

The instructions requiring the candidate to speak with elegance, grace, and pride, and exclusively about the culture and history of their community, frames more than what is immediately apparent, as illustrated by a benign but significant frame break by a 17-year-old participant from San Andrés Tzicuilan. The candidate was noticeably nervous in front of the crowd, occasionally wriggling from side to side, struggling to keep her composure, stretching some syllables while searching for words. However, it was not until she delivered the following remark that her speech disintegrated and she became decidedly uncomposed:

> **Candidate, Tzicuilan:** I am studying in the school of Digital Diploma, which is located in the community of Cuautamazaco. I intend to continue studying so as to be able to help my community. My favorite pastimes are to dance, laugh, and have a good time without forgetting my mother tongue.[5]

On the surface, there is nothing obviously subversive about this remark. Yet upon delivering it, members of audience briefly scanned each other's faces for a reaction to the utterance, and serious nervousness took hold of the candidate as she froze for five full seconds before proceeding with a description of her community, now increasingly stumbling on words and restarting phrases. This instance is noticeable, considering that a few moments earlier she had delivered the same remark in Nahuat without throwing the event into the same state of disorganization. Nonetheless, the candidate struck the constricting frames of the event, causing an irreparable frame break that disrupted the event momentarily and made her fall out of character permanently.

The remark concluded the routine introduction in which the candidate acknowledges the presence of the audience and declares her name, age, community, and educational institution. In doing so, candidates may be seen merely to provide 'factual, biographical information' about themselves. Nevertheless, the standardized introduction is a role requirement that performs the important task of amalgamating the character projected onstage with a biographical entity, as well as anchoring it in a particular cultural community. This role-required conflation of person with community and character is aired by the emcees, who enclose each presentation with introductions and conclusions that mention the candidates by name, age, and community. The person–community–character conflation is also visually displayed by the traditional indigenous vestments candidates have to wear, and it is verbally evoked by having candidates speak first in Nahuat and then in Spanish, making the Nahuat speeches into performative preludes that support the Spanish introduction in which they declare their community of origin. The introductions (by candidates and emcees) therefore serve as liminal transition phases during which the singular animator overcomes individuality to emerge as insider and prime exponent of a particular cultural group. This change of gears can be read from the different production formats underlying the introductions and the presentations; only in the standard introduction may the candidates assume principality. After the introduction, the animation of a collective, community identity is requested. The candidates performed this shift by switching from singular self-referential forms to collective self-referential forms ("we," "us," "our," or "my community").

After the candidate from Tzicuilan had mentioned her school, the standard introduction had come to an end, terminating with it the legitimate space for animating a personal biographical identity, as it had been successfully linked to a community character. Stretching the initial production format beyond the standard form, the candidate transgressed the role rights that structure the performances and slipped into unwarranted animation of self-as-protagonist with personal emotions, intentions, and pastime preferences. Instead of expounding the cultural community identity of her onstage character, she loosened her personal attachment to the collective character that the occasion was requesting her to conjure. The candidate's remark about her "mother tongue" is telling, because it hints at her anticipation of a likely troubled response to the remark about "pastimes." The mentioning of her linguistic capacity may be viewed as a safety measure to protect the candidate by reassuring the audience that while said "pastimes" may seem to be all too familiar to them, conversation in Nahuat forms part of these everyday activities. Such anticipation points to the deep source of trouble; the phrase collides with the view of authentic indigenous culture that is integral to the ritual frame. The candidate signals in-group, community membership ("my mother tongue"), while rejecting reductive and inflexibly essentialist views of indigenous people as culturally managed and bound by ancient tradition, and she signals that indigenous women are not just domestic and pious "carriers of tradition" and "bearers of collectives" (cf. Yuval-Davis 1997:26, 61). By characterizing herself as one who likes to "dance, laugh, and have a good time," the candidate presents herself as little different from young mestiza women. Correspondingly, the very mention of "favorite pastimes" creates an undesired approximation to the coffee queen format in which candidates are supposed to speak about their pastime activities to give an impression of their individual character. Thus, the mention of pastime activity collapses a distinction between the identities to be conjured in the respective pageants, and counters the emcee's instructions to the audience that they were not about to witness a beauty pageant; the *huipil* ceremony was about coming across as the most traditional woman. The comment about pastimes therefore betrays the animated character doubly; the particular pastimes are incongruent with the activities a traditional indigenous woman is expected to engage in, and the very mentioning of pastimes highlight individual characteristics in a character that is supposed to be collective.

Signaling in-group identity through linguistic competency, then, was an attempt to direct the potential harms of the phrase toward the frame of the event. Yet in a public ceremony intended to celebrate indigenous *culture* and the traditional indigenous *woman*, there would appear to be little receptivity of attempts to reconfigure the constituting views on culture and gender. Nevertheless, the lasting problematic implications for the candidate's presentation arose from her violation of the production format. By animating a self-as-protagonist ("My favorite pastimes"), she created an illegitimate disjunction between person and community-character. Bringing in herself as the direct source of the nuancing attempt, the utterance may easily be isolated to apply solely to her, making the phrase vulnerable to refutation as a cultural description. Her remark may be read as the claim to be more, other than, and different from the cultural group she undertakes to represent, instead of an attempt of nuancing the idea of cultural belonging that structures the arrangement. This became doubly problematic, because the person–character disjunction cast into doubt not only whether she can rightly claim to be part of the cultural group she undertakes to represent, that is, whether she really is a 'cultural insider,' but also whether there is an 'inside' at all. Since a complete coherence between person–character–community is necessary to create a successful cultural description, it may thus be argued that within the production format of the ceremony, candidates primarily function as embedded sources to validate dominant mestizo conceptions of indigenous people and women as, above all, cultural and traditional beings. Requesting a loosening of their personal identity from the cultural character of which they are prime exponents is a request that is disciplined by the very structure of the event, as their credibility as indigenous, cultural insiders is compromised.

When the candidate distanced herself from the collective character, the audience response of immediate bewilderment and suspicion, then, constituted a public disciplining that made the candidate acutely aware of the limitations of what she can claim to be, that is, the degree to which she is *not* there as her 'own' person, but rather as a culturalized collective figure.

The winner

When the 18-year-old participant from Zacatipan finished her speech in Spanish, she received loud ovations for an enthusiastic and well-performed speech. Although she was only the third of 11 contestants, an old man behind me exclaimed, "This one will bring it home." What distinguished this performance from those of the other contestants was the candidate's ability to be in character from the outset of the speech:

> **Candidate, Zacatipan:** Welcome all my friends, let us embrace each other while we are here in the utmost precious land of the *huipil* where neither flowers nor songs can end. [. . .] Good morning all national and foreign visitors as well as all of my Cuetzaltec siblings, who are visiting us today in this grand national coffee and *huipil* fiesta of 2014. My name is [. . .].

The first phrase, which modifies the Spanish version of a well-known piece of Classical Nahuatl poetry, was a key to her success.[6] The phrase contains a stylistic device called *diphrasism* in which a couplet consisting of two separate items create a single metaphor (Garibay Kintana 1953:19). Although diphrasist metaphors are applied by speakers of many Mesoamerican languages, they are closely associated with Classical Nahuatl due to the influential Mexican scholar Ángel María Garibay Kintana, who labeled this feature in Classical Nahuatl literature and promoted it as a distinctive stylistic trait of that language (Garibay Kintana 1953:67). In the first phrase, the metaphor consists of "flowers" and "songs," which in juxtaposition mean "poetry." Within a public performance of indigeneity, this, in Mexico widely known, diphrasist expression works not only as a Nahua term for poetry in the literal sense; it also stylistically performs it. Therefore, the active use of such poetic construction in a public speech substantiates the claim that Nahua poetic traditions will persist, as the candidate signals cultural speakership competence to insiders and outsiders. By 'naturally' making use of such cultural resources in a performance set in the "land of the the *huipil*," the candidate evokes a sensation of cultural preservation and continuity. Designating Cuetzalan as the land of the *huipil* effectively links her performance to the cultural conceptions that underlie the ceremony, as the ceremony elevates the *huipil* to signify the continuity of traditions. This way, the candidate commences with a recognizably ethnocized manner of speaking that situates her comfortably within well-known conceptions of Nahua cultural traditions. Setting off her presentation this way, she minimizes the significance of her individual presence, emerging from the outset as "bearer of the collective" (Yuval-Davis 1997:26).

Organized disorganization: democracy as indigenous custom

Having argued that a successful performance in the *huipil* pageant is dependent on the cultural conceptions that frame the event, and that the candidates are brought in as community specimens and embedded sources of authentic indigenous culture, the chapter now considers instances of frame-breaking activism, deliberate attempts from below to disrupt an event organized from above. Since even benign frame breaks have the potential of destabilizing the event and the performances it encloses, a concern of frame-breaking activism is to challenge the event without inflicting harm on the activist. Hence, the structures of the event must be exposed and reversed. Two instances follow from the *huipil* pageant, before highlighting the wider existence and implications of this practice during the fiesta. Consider first the introduction by which the 16-year-old candidate from Xiloxochico launched her presentation:

> **Candidate, Xiloxochico:** Ladies and gentlemen, young ladies and young gentlemen, [male] masters and [female] masters, and above all, you, qualifying jury. To all of you I say: "Good morning." Today, 4 October, we find ourselves united in our municipality Cuetzalan. We come to greet our patron saint, San Francisco de Asis.

Here, the candidate acknowledges the presence of the audience, before unfolding a vertical relationship that places the Nahua political authorities of the jury in a preeminent position. She thus conveys that her speech is directed at the Nahua authorities, a stance that was reinforced whenever she introduced a new topic by repeating the address, "Gentlemen of the qualifying jury." By positioning the Nahua jury as the main recipient of her speech, the audience emerges as bystanding witnesses to an internal dialogue, which immerses the speech in an aura of authenticity and truthfulness that fits with the framing of the event as, essentially, an internal, indigenous ceremony. However, this participation framework is also what enables the candidate to convey dissidence while innocently fending off suspicions of bad faith. The candidate from Xiloxochico was one of few participants who avoided formally addressing the municipal president and the visiting state governor. By implicitly addressing them as part of the general audience, she marked them as less significant than the Nahua authorities, thereby delineating the hierarchy she is responsive to. This hierarchy is stressed in the opening remark, which embeds her participation in the common claim that "We come to greet our patron saint," which elaborates on who are not being 'greeted,' that is, municipal and state political authorities. Yet since the selective greeting of the patron saint fits with the framing assumption that indigenous participation in the fiesta is religiously motivated, the absent greeting of mestizo authorities cannot be straightforwardly categorized as disobedient.

After having described the vestments, fiestas, and traditions of Xiloxochico and recounted the history of the waist loom, the candidate concluded her speech in the following way:

> **Candidate, Xiloxochico:** Gentlemen of the qualifying jury, and all who are listening to my phrases, my speech, I invite you to visit my community. There you will be able to see a church of modern construction as well as the presidency.

And to finish, I want to tell you that to confront poverty – we can confront it with sustainable development. And with much pride I can say that we, the people of Xiloxochico, are similar to the additional seven auxiliary councils and that when we elect our governor we do so in a democratic manner, and we do not engage in proselytism. *Custom* of our ancestors, *custom* of my community [cheer and applause]. We, the people of Xiloxochico, will always welcome you with open arms. Thank you very much [applause].

Having safely emerged as a representative of indigenous culture in Xiloxochico and as a traditional, domestic woman who knows how to weave, the candidate engaged explicitly in political matters that break with the organizing instructions to speak exclusively about the culture and history of her community. By offering her opinion on how poverty can be dealt with, the candidate signals that poverty exists in the municipality and that it is a pressing issue for people in Xiloxochico. By publicly pitching the idea of "sustainable development" as a means for poverty alleviation, she furthermore signals that the political promise of sustainable development – which is often associated with indigenous lifeways (Muehlmann 2007) – is yet to arrive in the area. The double appearance of "confront" together with an almost doubled speaking rate indicates that the candidate is aware that she is moving into controversial terrain. Expanding her indigenous speech position, the candidate includes all indigenous communities in the municipality into her talk by stating "that we, the people of Xiloxochico, are similar to the additional seven auxiliary councils." Through implicit opposition to Cuetzalan, the political statement becomes a critique of politicians in the municipal capital, who, as she insinuates, proselytize and elect their leaders in non-democratic ways. The participant situates the ensuing couplet phrase ambivalently between the political statement and the closing remark that welcomes visitors to Xiloxochico, and subsequently it cannot be known with certainty whether she refers to democratic politics or hospitality as an indigenous "custom." Nonetheless, because she had previously concluded her uncontroversial account on weaving with a similar couplet structure (*"Pride* of my community, *pride* of my municipality"), she guided the audience into interpreting her to be claiming democratic politics as an indigenous custom that sets them apart from the dominant political system.[7] She thereby mobilized part of the audience to loudly demonstrate their appreciation of such bold claims, thus authenticating and legitimizing the notion of democracy as a communal, indigenous custom. What prevailed after the speech, then, was not a claim on the part of the candidate as much as a claim on the part of a group within the audience, which performed the interpretive work that chained together democratic politics and indigeneity.

While the critique remains ambivalent and not concretized toward specific agents, it is worth noting, again, that the audience response occurred during the Spanish version of the speech, which points to the mestizos as implied recipients. Moreover, by placing these claims at the end of her speech, she forces the audience into condoning her remarks through their compulsive, concluding applause.

Characterized by struggle

When the representative of San Miguel Tzinacapan entered the stage as the penultimate contestant, she delivered an explosive performance. In contrast to the other participants, she gave most of the speech in an indignant tone and moved about on the scene, whipping the miniature baton of authority rhythmically to stress her points:

> **Candidate, Tzinacapan:** Good morning to all females and males present, favorable qualifying jury: My name is [. . .], I am 14 years old and I study *in the distance education high school Tetsijtsilin* [audience applause and cheer], *and on this day I come to represent the auxiliary council of San Miguel Tzinacapan.* For hundreds of years, Tzinacapan has been characterized by being a town of struggle that does *not* permit injustices, [and] does not let our language, our traditions, such as the dances, stewardships, and communal ranks, die. Our community is characterized by being a people *proudly macehual.*

Loud audience response is not uncommon in Latin American pageants (McAllister 1996:115–116), but in this *huipil* pageant the audience generally restricted itself to a concluding applause after each speech. Nonetheless, as the candidate announced her school, she received an enthusiastic cheer from part of the audience. The timing of the cheer implies that it was not a spontaneous audience response, but rather a statement of support from a group of friends or family, who immediately sanctified the indignant performance. In the preceding Nahuat version of the speech, the candidate spoke more softly, and since the indignant tone and supportive cheer were attached to the Spanish version, it follows that both messages were directed toward the mestizo part of the audience. As previously illustrated, the audience may sanction performances thought to be inappropriate, and therefore some measure of control over audience response is crucial to frame-breaking activism. The early positive reaction to the confrontational attitude of the Tzinacapan candidate therefore has, in itself, a performative effect that promotes a reading of the performance as appropriate and just.

The cheer following the announcement of the school *Tetsijtsilin* also reflects the significance of this institution in Tzinacapan. The school is part of a larger cultural revitalization program run by a civil association called PRADE that was initiated in 1973 by two university professors from Puebla City (Almeida and Sánchez 1989). The school has achieved national and international recognition for its intercultural and locally grounded approach to teaching in an indigenous community, and the director articulates the school as a movement of resistance toward established cultural and educational paradigms (Morales Espinosa 2012). The zeal of resisting hegemonic ideology plays a central part in the school's history and self-perception, and the cheer that accompanied the candidate upon mentioning the school expresses the vitality of this tradition of resistance. Conflict is part of local interethnic history, and resistance toward mestizo Cuetzalan is central to community identity in Tzinacapan (Coronado 2000:182). The candidate expressed the themes of conflict and resistance by pointing to a several-hundred-years-long "struggle" and stressing that her town "does *not* permit injustices." This "struggle" refers both to general processes of colonization and to local conflicts over land with incoming settlers, whose descendants control the political life in the municipality and inhabit the municipal capital and regional commercial hub, where the *huipil* ceremony takes place.

Yet while subverting the peaceful and celebratory recognition arrangement, the candidate simultaneously manages to comply with the request to present the cultural "characteristics" and history of her town by portraying the "struggle" against "injustices" as a defining cultural characteristic of her community. Their continued struggle against dominant society is what keeps the cultural traditions and Nahuat alive in town, and thus the precondition for the statement that people in Tzinacapan are "characterized by being [. . .] *proudly macehual.*" Doing so, the candidate rejects the notion that her cultural identity is uncontroversial in contemporary Mexico, and thus refuses to contribute to the guiding sentiment that the *huipil* ceremony is an act of recognition that marks the conclusion of ethnic conflict and discrimination of indigenous citizens.

Paralleling the handicraft vendors (see Chapter 7), the candidate highlighted Tzinacapan as the superiorly authentic regional indigenous town, where cultural traditions are practiced most vividly:

> **Candidate, Tzinacapan:** I can tell you that Tzinacapan is the locality that counts on the greatest variety of autochthonous dances. We can mention the *santiagos, migueles, negritos, voladores, quetzales, toreadores, españoles, vegas*, and many other dances. Personally, I have participated in the dance of the *voladores*; a pre-Hispanic dance most definitely. I know that I have much left to learn, but today with little experience *I venture to invite the youngsters of my age that we continue walking with the pride and dignity that characterizes us macehualme* [applause and cheer]. On this day, I feel very proud of coming to represent the auxiliary council of Tzinacapan. *I do not feel ashamed to say that I am macehual, that I can speak the Nahuat language that our ancestors gave us. I feel very proud to speak it!*

The candidate not only drew visitors' attention to Tzinacapan as the center of regional traditional dances; she also reminded local authorities that to craft the desired fiesta for incoming tourists, they rely on dancing troupes from indigenous communities, Tzinacapan in particular, as she demonstrates by cataloguing the numerous dances practiced there. By stressing her commitment to the *voladores* dance and that she is not "ashamed" to be a Nahuat-speaking "macehual" who will "not let our language, our traditions [. . .] die," she emerges as a "carrier of tradition," setting an example that may inspire other "youngsters" to embrace their cultural and ethnic identity.

The fiesta in translocal politics

There are limits to what can be achieved through frame-breaking activism in the *huipil* ceremony. San Miguel Tzinacapan's candidate subverted the form by contesting the appreciative atmosphere surrounding the ceremony. Yet, paradoxically, by articulating a position of opposition to Cuetzalan as a place, where cultural traditions have disappeared, she emerges as exactly the kind of Other figure envisioned by the *huipil* ceremony; a young Nahua woman, who before the audience vivifies indigenous women as "carriers of tradition." The production format of the ceremony ensures this by requesting the candidates to produce inward-gazing community-oriented cultural descriptions. The ceremony thus reinvests indigeneity with culture-related content and localized positions that produce an image of indigenous communities as detached from and uninterested in the surrounding world. Indignant display of "defensive identity" (Castells 2010:64–70) does not undermine the ceremony, even though it emerges in opposition to urban mestizos. Rather, the defensive reaction strengthens the guiding assumption of the ceremony; that indigenous citizens are principally cultural beings. All candidates are thus caught in a frame trap, since they can participate only as embedded sources to authentic indigeneity as configured by majority society, and their appearances are evaluated according to their ability to conjure such authenticity.

The candidates are also caught within the confines of a political framework. As observed, the municipal chain of command is employed to recruit candidates for the ceremony. The candidates are preselected by auxiliary councils, and are therefore not primarily responsible for representing themselves, but are taken to represent 'their' community. Supplying the ceremony with apt candidates is the political responsibility of auxiliary councils, and the repercussions of unacceptable performances thus exceed individual candidates. This selection mechanism encourages sincere engagement in the ceremony and discourages absence and lackadaisical or clear-cut sabotaging performances, since political consequences could follow for the auxiliary council in question. Hence, within the production format of the ceremony, principality of individual performances is ultimately projected onto the auxiliary authorities who have screened participants. Indeed, for this very reason, several of the candidates' speeches were authored exactly by the auxiliary authorities they represented. Producing a proper indigenous performance is thus a thoroughly political task, and the speeches from Xiloxochico and Tzinacapan point to the strained relations between authorities in those auxiliary councils and in Cuetzalan.

Noting the history of conflict between mestizo Cuetzalan and the surrounding indigenous communities, Gabriela Coronado asks how Cuetzalan's fiesta, which depends on indigenous participation, is tied together in spite of these ongoing tensions (Coronado 2000). Coronado's main point is that an answer can be found only by inserting the fiesta into a wider social and political context. According to Coronado, collaboration by indigenous groups to create a scenery of harmonious interethnic coexistence and authentic indigenous spectacle, pleasant to the tourist eye, could be understood as passive compliance, if one were inattentive to their grounds for participating in the fiesta. Their helping hand in constructing for the mestizos a culturally vivid spectacle is a strategic maneuver to smooth out interethnic interaction, which may ease subsequent negotiations with mestizo authorities. Coronado thus highlights reciprocal exchange and interdependency; mestizos depend on indigenous participation to sustain local tourism, and indigenous groups depend on mestizo authorities who decide how to redistribute municipal resources. A further relation of reciprocity is embedded therein because in political negotiations with state and federal agencies Cuetzalan also requires the symbolic participation of "poor" indigenous groups to secure external funding for the municipality. In turn, economically and socially marginalized indigenous groups are reliant on mestizo authorities to acquire funds on their behalf through federal social programs. With such political interdependence, Coronado argues, there is a strong incentive for the indigenous communities to collaborate in Cuetzalan's fiesta (Coronado 2000:14, 135–146). Nonetheless, it must be added that this reciprocal relation is highly asymmetrical given that indigenous communities are obliged to volunteer for the mestizo business elite in Cuetzalan's fiesta and help maintain Cuetzalan's position as a regional tourist attraction in order to obtain political goodwill that may bring basic social necessities to the surrounding municipal area. To that end, Coronado launches an additional argument to explain indigenous cooperation in a fiesta that by and large benefits the municipal capital; essentially, the two groups construct and celebrate two different fiestas with different aims. While for the mestizos the fiesta is mainly an important economic event, the fiesta is for the indigenous communities above all an important religious celebration (Coronado 2000:14, 127–132, 192–194). Coronado thus segregates the fiesta into a sacred and secular dimension, aligning each aspect with each group.

Although Coronado intends to chart two ways in which indigenous groups are pursuing their own means, rather than responding passively to mestizo domination, her analyses end up producing a split indigenous subject that both collaborates strategically as part of a wider economic and political interaction with mestizo authorities and is inclined to participate in the fiesta to practice its cultural and religious traditions. Coronado thus charts a social order that not only disconnects cultural and religious practice from economic, political, and social structures, but even hierarchizes and opposes them. This order minimizes the significance indigenous citizens attach to the economic and political structures Coronado finds integrated in the fiesta. Almost miraculously, then, indigenous and mestizo interests are fulfilled alike in the fiesta because of the predisposed inclination of indigenous groups piously to regard the fiesta above all as a religious event, which makes their participation in mestizo accumulation of wealth an indirect one (Coronado 2000:14). In this sense, Coronado's analysis indirectly elaborates on the settler version of local history and the related identity configurations that make the mestizo *homo economicus* and the Nahua *homo religiosus*.

Yet there are indications that surrounding Nahua communities have become increasingly dissatisfied with these asymmetries since the time of Coronado's fieldwork. In the case of Tzinacapan, the relation has long been strained. Coronado (2000:192–194) already noted in 1997 how the date of the procession from Tzinacapan to Cuetzalan, in which San Miguel travels to salute San Francisco, had been altered from October 4, the height of Cuetzalan's fiesta, to take place on October 5, when most tourists have left town. Since then, the number of participating dancing troupes has been decreasing, and in 2013 the fiesta reached a state of crisis. The municipal administration arranged a celebration of the 50-year anniversary of the *huipil* ceremony, inviting past *huipil* queens to a commemorative ceremony that honored the queens of the past. Yet few dancing troupes arrived, and, according to Aureliano who organized the *huipil* ceremony in 2014, Tzinacapan only dispatched two dancing troupes. Subsequently, in 2015, Tzinacapan refused to send a participant for the *huipil* ceremony.

Aureliano traces the conflict to the early 1970s when the PRADE project was launched in Tzinacapan and started spreading the idea that:

> **Aureliano (September 2014):** The people of Cuetzalan are taking advantage of the indigenous people; they are robbing them. And they begin to give the indigenous people the idea that we, from [Cuetzalan], are bad, that we have treated them badly, that we are enemies, and they begin to say to them, "Well, why would you dance in Cuetzalan if they take advantage of you? They are just calling you so that you dance in front of the governor or in front of the [municipal] president. You will no longer dance for San Francisco, now you are dancing for them." [. . .] And now, in these events, we can muster up the presence of all the auxiliary councils, except for San Miguel. [. . .] When [the archangel] San Miguel comes to visit San Francisco, then a group of *quetzales* and a group of *negritos* arrive accompanying the saint. They pass by where the fiesta is, they turn around, they find an entrance [to the church], they enter the temple, they do their salutation ritual – or whatever they want – dance, they withdraw, exit, and leave [. . .] but they do not pass by to dance in the town setting.

Interethnic relations have been marked by conflict and tension not since the 1970s, but since the 1850s, when incoming settlers began to displace Nahuas from Cuetzalan and rearranged the economic and political system to their advantage. Before the 1970s, the conflict revolved around land issues and an unfair local trading system (Bartra, Cobo, and Paz Paredes 2004:11 ff.), and this conflict has been re-actualized since the 1970s by a surging identity political dimension. The PRADE cultural revitalization project and the influx of social scientists to Tzinacapan coincide with a post-indigenist call in Mexico for recognizing indigenous cultural traditions and an incipient tourism to Cuetzalan configured around the indigenous experience (cf. Orellana 1972; Merlo 1979). Since then, a tourist sector has been emerging in Cuetzalan, as tourists have gone there to experience an indigenous fiesta, an indigenous market, and an indigenous town.

In the 1850s, when the settlers began to arrive in substantial numbers, Cuetzalan was already the most important town in the area after Zacapoaxtla

(Thomson 1991:214). In 1895, the settlers took hold of the municipal presidency and the prominent position Cuetzalan already enjoyed in the regional market system. As the coffee trade grew, so did the difference in wealth between people in central Cuetzalan, where coffee was processed, and the surrounding towns that supplied land and labor for cultivation. These historical processes matter today because they paved the way for how tourism has come to materialize. Early tourism was attracted to Cuetzalan due to its small-town life and Sunday market with incoming Nahua buyers and vendors. Tourists were also attracted by the fiesta, which gathered large numbers of indigenous dancing troupes and spectators, and by the *huipil* ceremony, which showcased Nahua women in traditional clothing. All these attractions that mestizo Cuetzalan could present to the visitor stemmed from having overtaken the town's preexisting regionally superior position. The fiesta in Cuetzalan is the regional fiesta because Cuetzalan is the regional commercial and political center.

The tragic ironies of a growing tourism to Cuetzalan nurtured by the growing interest in local Nahua culture were (and are) felt most intensely by people in nearby Tzinacapan, where social scientists went to learn about and revitalize their cultural traditions and language (Lupo 1998), and from where they could observe incoming tourists going to Cuetzalan to experience an 'indigenous' town. Being confirmed in their authenticity by visiting researchers, yet witnessing how profit from tourism organized around indigenous heritage has been following the usual path into central, mestizo Cuetzalan, it is not hard to understand why people in Tzinacapan have become frustrated and wish to rearrange such an asymmetrical labor system. In the early days of tourism, Cuetzalan's position in this translocal network could potentially be shifted or attenuated by withholding dancing troupes from the fiesta and strengthening one's own fiesta.[8] Or, by collaborating more reluctantly, the key resource to the fiesta could be made scarce and provide indigenous communities with leverage in additional political negotiations with the municipal capital.

Yet today, Cuetzalan participates in the Magical Villages Program, which unambiguously favors the municipal capital by directing focus and funding to the town center, and hence Cuetzalan's status as the regional center of tourism – and as *indigenous* town – has congealed. With this consolidation of regional tourism, getting a piece of the tourism economy from outside of Cuetzalan is near impossible without massive funds. In 2012, there were 38 official lodgings in and within walking distance of Cuetzalan, and 12 in the surrounding area, of which at least nine are ecotourism or luxury cabins and resorts located on large plots (BUAP 2013:30–35). Of the total 50 lodgings, a handful or less appear not to be owned by mestizos. Indicatively, three of these are owned by cooperatives rather than being family-run businesses, as are most mestizo-owned hotels.

To suggest, as Aureliano did in the interview, that people from Tzinacapan are discriminating against people in Cuetzalan by not contributing to their fiesta may seem absurd, but it is to be taken quite seriously nonetheless. Tourism is replacing coffee as the prime commercial arena and industrial utopia in Cuetzalan, and everyone is trying to get into the tourism business. Therefore, the fiesta will only gain in importance just as new occasions for displaying indigenous heritage will be created. The centralized tourism economy may then increasingly come to depend on the goodwill of auxiliary councils, but auxiliary councils may also see a need for working to redirect tourism from Cuetzalan and to events in their own towns. To do so may involve gradually debilitating Cuetzalan's fiesta and creating more vivid fiestas in the surrounding communities.

The key resource fought over presently in local tourism is thus indigenous identity and intangible heritage. Acquiring indigenous material culture through which to project indigeneity and around which to construct attractions is not difficult for tourism agents in Cuetzalan. Intangible resources are much more difficult to control and can be done so only indirectly. Local political struggles therefore currently revolve around intangible culture. Since boycotting Cuetzalan's fiesta may lead to political sanctions, other ways of debilitating the fiesta are sought. Ambiguous, frame-breaking performances – rupturing the peaceful atmosphere constructed for the *huipil* ceremony, producing unsolicited political speech, pointing out that Cuetzalan is a mestizo town, contributing a meager number of dancing troupes, or making a spectacular but brief public appearance before disappearing into the church – express a struggle over the translocal order the Magical Villages Program has reinstated by consolidating Cuetzalan as the regional indigenous town. As Cuetzalan is taking on an indigenous identity in front of an external audience, the Magical Villages Program may prompt Nahua citizens to delve further into divisive identity politics that distinguish the indigeneity of Cuetzalan from the indigeneity of the surrounding communities.

The fiesta and the *huipil* ceremony contribute to enforce a translocal order that is disadvantageous to the surrounding communities, who are forced to participate culturally in a political event that celebrates post-discriminatory mestizo Mexico through public recognition of indigenous culture. The ceremony thus gives life to the widespread idea that cultural recognition of indigeneity itself has terminated ethnic discrimination, even as the ceremony is based on a discriminatory Othering that hampers indigenous economic and political participation. As has been shown, the production format of the *huipil* ceremony renews this idea by engaging indigenous agents in autoethnographic self-culturalization and self-localization before a recognizing mestizo audience; indigenous agents are drawn in as embedded sources to legitimize a majoritarian culturalization and localization of indigeneity, which denies indigenous citizens economic and political subjectivity in contemporary Mexico.

Notes

1 The candidates wear long, wide skirts, *huipil* blouses, *quechquemitl* neck-pieces, and *maxtahual* headdresses. The headdress consists of primarily purple wool cords, which are twisted together and tied into the hair. The neck-piece consists of a rectangular piece of cloth with a neck opening and is worn on top of the *huipil* blouse and with the points in the front and on the back. Another neck-piece adorns the headdress.

2 Moreover, San Francisco was removed from the toponym, distinguishing Cuetzalan furthermore from nearby indigenous towns that retain the names of their patron saints

as part of the toponym, once again reinforcing the mestizo (economy)/indigenous (religion) characters.

3 Documents from 1807 show that indigenous Cuetzalan was involved in specialized agriculture, commerce, and production of unrefined whole cane sugar, and purchased maize from mestizo subsistence farmers from Xocoyolo (Thomson 1991:212).

4 In a news broadcast following the ceremony in 2011 (SBC Noticias Zacapoaxtla 2011), the then municipal president lamented Xocoyolo's unusual decision not to participate. Xocoyolo has not been absent since.

5 Note that she said *bailar*, which tends to imply secular dancing, in contrast to *danzar*, which indicates ritual dancing.

6 The phrase derives from the *Cantares Mexicanos* manuscript (fol. 9v–12r), which contains Classical Nahuatl songs collected in central Mexico from the 1550s to the 1580s (Bierhorst 1985:7–9), and is widely known as 'ancient' Aztec poetry. During the fiesta in 1997, a representative from SECTUR used the same bit in a speech to evoke the beauty of Cuetzalan, and, as Coronado notes (Coronado 2000:128), the same verse opens the book *The Magic Sierra* (Merlo 1995:11), which describes towns in the Northern Sierra of Puebla.

7 The mass kidnapping by police (later confirmed to have led to the mass killing) of students during a protest in Iguala in neighboring state Guerrero had happened just eight days earlier, and the comment reflects the crisis of legitimacy that national government confronted in the wake of a scandalous and tragic abuse of power by authorities. Against the backdrop of the rolling political crisis, the candidate thus alluded to Nahua democratic values as an alternative to a defective national political system.

8 "Potentially," of course, since such a strategy may lead to political consequences in other areas.

References

Almeida, Eduardo, and María Eugenia Sánchez. 1989. "Theory and Practice at Tzinacapan (Mexico)." *Psychology and Developing Societies* 1(2):239–250.

Bartra, Armando, Rosario Cobo, and Lorena Paz Paredes. 2004. *Tosepan Titataniske: Abriendo Horizontes – 27 Años de Historia.* Cuetzalan: Sociedad Cooperativa Agropecuaria Regional Tosepan Titataniske.

Bierhorst, John. 1985. *Cantares Mexicanos: Songs of the Aztecs – Translated from the Nahuatl, with an Introduction and Commentary.* Stanford, CA: Stanford University Press.

Brown, Betty Ann. 1988. "All Around the Xocotl Pole: Reexamination of an Aztec Sacrificial Ceremony." Pp. 173–189 in *Smoke and Mist: Mesoamerican Studies in Memory of Thelma D. Sullivan*, vol. 402(1). Oxford: BAR International Series.

Brown, Wendy. 2006. *Regulating Aversion: Tolerance in the Age of Identity and Empire.* Princeton, NJ: Princeton University Press.

BUAP. 2013. *Agenda de Competitividad de los Destinos Turísticos de México: Estudio de Competitividad Turística de Cuetzalan Pueblo Mágico.* Puebla: BUAP.

Carrasco, Davíd. 1995. "Give Me Some Skin: The Charisma of the Aztec Warrior." *History of Religions* 35(1):1–26.

Castells, Manuel. 2010. *The Power of Identity: The Information Age – Economy, Society, and Culture.* Hoboken, NJ: Wiley-Blackwell.

CEPEC. 1994. *Tejuan Tikintenkakiliayaj in Toueyitatajuan: Les Oíamos Contar a Nuestros Abuelos – Etnohistoria de San Miguel Tzinacapan.* Mexico City: INAH.

Coronado, Gabriela. 2000. *Silenced Voices of Mexican Culture: Identity, Resistance and Creativity in the Interethnic Dialogue.* PhD dissertation, University of Western Sydney.

Edgerton, Samuel. 2001. *Theaters of Conversion: Religious Architecture and Indian Artisans in Colonial Mexico*. Albuquerque, NM: University of New Mexico Press.

Foucault, Michel. 1977. *Discipline and Punish: The Birth of the Prison*. London: Allen Lane.

Furniss, Elizabeth. 1999. *The Burden of History: Colonialism and the Frontier Myth in a Rural Canadian Community*. Vancouver: UBC Press.

Furniss, Elizabeth. 2005. "Imagining the Frontier: Comparative Perspectives from Canada and Australia." Pp. 23–46 in *Dislocating the Frontier: Essaying the Mystique of the Outback*, edited by D. B. Rose and R. H. Davis. Canberra: ANUE Press.

Garibay Kintana, Ángel María. 1953. *Historia de la Literatura Nahuatl, Primera Parte*. Mexico City: Porrúa.

Hale, Charles. 2002. "Does Multiculturalism Menace? Governance, Cultural Rights, and the Politics of Identity in Guatemala." *Journal of Latin American Studies* 34(3):485–524.

Hodge, Mary G. 2001. "Market Systems." Pp. 412–414 in *Archaeology of Ancient Mexico and Central America: An Encyclopedia*, edited by S. T. Evans and D. Webster. New York: Garland.

Hutson, Scott R. 2000. "Carnival and Contestation in the Aztec Marketplace." *Dialectical Anthropology* 25(2):123–149.

Knab, Timothy J. 1995. *A War of Witches: A Journey into the Underworld of the Contemporary Aztecs*. San Francisco, CA: Harper San Francisco.

Lupo, Alessandro. 1998. "Los Cuentos de los Abuelos: Un Ejemplo de la Construcción de la Memoria entre los Nahuas de la Sierra Norte de Puebla, México." *Anales de la Fundación Joaquín Costa* 15:263–284.

McAllister, Carlota. 1996. "Authenticity and Guatemala's Maya Queen." Pp. 105–145 in *Beauty Queens on the Global Stage: Gender, Contests, and Power*, edited by C. B. Cohen, B. Stoeltje, and R. Wilk. New York: Routledge.

Merlo Juárez, Eduardo. 1979. "El indígena y el turismo en la Sierra Norte de Puebla." Pp. 35–45 in *Tercera Mesa Redonda sobre Problemas Antropológicos de la Sierra Norte del Estado de Puebla*. Cuetzalan: Centro de Estudios Históricos de la Sierra Norte del Estado de Puebla.

Merlo Juárez, Eduardo. 1995. *La Sierra Mágica (The Magic Sierra)*. Puebla: SECTUR, Gobierno del Estado de Puebla.

Morales Espinosa, María del Coral. 2012. "Tetsijtsilin: 30 Años de Abriendo Brecha." Pp. 35–38 in *Piedras Que Suenan: Tetsijtsilin, 30 Aniversario*, edited by O. G. González and M. del Coral Morales Espinosa. Mexico City: SEP.

Muehlmann, Shaylih. 2007. "Defending Diversity: Staking out a Common Global Interest?" Pp. 14–34 in *Discourses of Endangerment: Ideology and Interest in the Defence of Languages*, edited by A. Duchêne and M. Heller. London: Continuum.

Orellana, Margarita de, ed. 1972. *Artes de México*, vol. 155, *La Sierra de Puebla*. Mexico City: Comercial Nadrosa.

Pratt, Mary Louise. 2008. *Imperial Eyes: Travel Writing and Transculturation*. New York: Routledge.

Reader, Ian. 2013. *Pilgrimage in the Marketplace*. New York: Routledge.

Rogers, Mark. 1998. "Spectacular Bodies: Folklorization and the Politics of Identity in Ecuadorian Beauty Pageants." *Journal of Latin American Anthropology* 3(2):54–85.

SBC Noticias Zacapoaxtla. 2011. *Entrevistas: Evento de Coronación, Reina del Huipil, Feria de Cuetzalan*. October 4. Television broadcast. Retrieved March 19, 2015 (www.youtube.com/watch?v=od_NySt9BKA).

Scher, Philip W. 2014. "The Right to Remain Cultural: Is Culture a Right in the Neoliberal Caribbean?" Pp. 87–110 in *Cultural Heritage in Transit: Intangible Rights as Human Rights*, edited by D. Kapchan. Philadelphia, PA: University of Pennsylvania Press.

Stack, Trevor. 2003. "Citizens of Towns, Citizens of Nations: The Knowing of History in Mexico." *Critique of Anthropology* 23(2):193–208.

Thomson, Guy P. C. 1991. "Agrarian Conflict in the Municipality of Cuetzalan (Sierra de Puebla): The Rise and Fall of 'Pala' Agustin Dieguillo, 1861–1894." *The Hispanic American Historical Review* 71(2):205–258.

Wolfe, Patrick. 1999. *Settler Colonialism and the Transformation of Anthropology: The Politics and Poetics of an Ethnographic Event*. London: Cassell.

Yuval-Davis, Nira. 1997. *Gender and Nation*. London: Sage.

Epilogue

Beyond debate, indigenous Latin Americans are dealing with threats more pressing than the issues with which this book has been concerned. In the *Sierra de Puebla*, indigenous (and mestizo) activists and organizations are struggling to keep out fracking and mining companies and hydroelectric plants. From this perspective, indigenous groups in the vicinity of Cuetzalan may appear to be less concerned about how the past, the Nahuas, and their combination are represented through a national tourism program and made to catalyze a local tourism centered on mestizo Cuetzalan. Shortly before the follow-up fieldwork, the key Nahua activist Antonio Cruz was assassinated by gunshots in front of his house in the municipality, illustrating with chilling precision one reason why activists have labeled their struggle against extractivist projects in the *sierra* as one against *projects of death*.

Finding, somewhat ironically, that indigenous communities were largely absent from the whole business of Magical Villages, I began to wonder how someone pretending to be involved in indigenous issues would justify having spent so much time and energy on what appeared to be almost exclusively a mestizo project, while neglecting to engage with themes of more acute concern to Nahua citizens in Puebla. Having chosen the Magical Villages Program and Cuetzalan as empirical vantage points, I had been deceived by the frame of multicultourism that encapsulates both, and suddenly my research appeared to be at odds with what I had set out to do.

As my research on this topic is coming to an end, I now have another take on this issue. Getting there nonetheless required discarding the frames through which the Magical Villages Program has been asserting itself into the national public realm in contemporary Mexico and to posit alternative frames that provide a distinct view on the activities encompassed by the tourism program. In Latin America, the concept of multiculturalism is deeply tied to an origin myth of achievement according to which transnational and national indigenous movements rallied against governments in the struggle for cultural rights and social equality. Thus, the multiculturalist and pluralist modifications of most national constitutions in Latin America that occurred between the late 1980s and the 1990s are taken to signal a radical break with colonial legacy and former unjust policies, and this notion of a new world order is symbolically reified each time multicultural policies are launched. Interjecting the term multicultourism into the debate, as this book does, constitutes an attempt to dismiss the frame governmentality that operates through the concept of multiculturalism, which in Latin America has the inevitable connotation of mestizo concession versus indigenous achievement. Multiculturalist initiatives are generally thought of as advancements, whether great or small, in indigenous democratic participation and rights issues, as they are taken to celebrate a national and constitutional post-discriminatory age. This tacit assumption needs to be discarded. As this book has pointed out, the connective between multiculturalism and the indigenous rights struggle has created a situation in which the discursive framework of multiculturalism has facilitated the carrying forth of policies and practices that are not particularly sympathetic to indigenous causes.

During a research seminar at the beginning of my research, I was fortunate to meet with an indigenous Mexican activist who has been active in the UN Working Group on Indigenous Issues. During lunch, I optimistically pitched my research ideas to her, starting with a few critical remarks about the Magical Villages Program and the use of intangible indigenous heritage as an economic resource. Still stuck in the starting blocks, she interrupted the pitch with a stern look and posed the rhetorical shutdown question, "Why *is* it indigenous people are never allowed to have their own economy?" Hopefully, with this book, I have managed both to deflect that critical remark and demonstrated precisely why her question is such a crucial one.

One reason why the program has gained a respectable renown in Mexico and wider Latin America is that when inspected from a distance, or through 36-hour stays in a Magical Village such as Cuetzalan, all that protrudes is the mediating frame that casts the program as an emancipatory cultural recognition of marginalized rural, often indigenous, citizens. Thus, through the multicultourism espoused by the Magical Villages Program, urban middle-class mestizos are seen to contribute to indigenous emancipation and their travel is configured as a commitment to post-discriminatory Mexico. Urban middle-class citizens thus simultaneously embrace and reconnect with 'their' indigenous past and engage in a translocal identity project that effectively charts ethnic discrimination as a phenomenon of the past, thus dutifully constituting themselves as compassionate citizens of a post-discriminatory Mexico. To this end, the Magical Villages Program becomes in part a state-sponsored civilizing mission of "neo-Indianism" (cf. Galinier and Molinié 2013) in which the recognition of indigenous citizens consists of mestizos embracing indigenous culture as part of their own identities. In this emerging configuration of citizenship, mestizo identity demonstrates its astonishing flexibility and ability to encompass the totality (cf. Rogers 1998). So, while earlier indigenist policies sought to blur the lines between mestizo and indigenous groups through planned acculturation set to erase indigenous culture, the new project of *mestizaje* is blurring the lines between the two groups through strategic and symbolic indigenization of majority mestizo citizens. In this sense, the identity-based political arena of negotiation that opened for indigenous minorities in Latin America beginning in the 1990s is being closed by the parallel surge in neo-Indian identity politics. Contemporary mestizo approximation of indigenous identity thus amounts to a project of elimination, given that mestizo indigenization tends to opportunistically gear itself to a metropolitan nationalism. It is therefore a paradox that the multicultourism of the Magical Villages Program is fueled by founding ideas about multiculturalism, funded by a growing popular empathy toward indigenous identity, and conceived as an ostensibly benevolent cultural recognition, while nonetheless pushing indigenous citizens out of their prime political arena and upholding their role as vicarious democratic citizens.

The encroachment on indigenous cultural identity following its increasing configuration as a national economic and political resource demonstrates Patrick Wolfe's crucial point about settler colonialism, "Invasion is a structure, not an event" (Wolfe 1999:2 ff.). In this ongoing settler-colonial project, the overall concern is to discursively situate colonizer and colonized in discontinuous spaces that camouflage intergroup conflicts of interest of an economic and political kind. As Wolfe argues, a shared economic interest in land is at the base of the colonizers' tendency to construct indigenous subjects as situated "in an apparently self-sufficient ritual space" that does not interfere with the settler-colonial project (Wolfe 1999:178–180). As illustrated, the invasive settler-colonial project is renewed in Cuetzalan through a multicultourism that configures indigenous identity as the new economic (and political) resource in the context of a fading local coffee industry. Whereas formerly indigenous lands were being split by incoming settlers, notions of indigeneity itself are now being segmented between colonizer and colonized. As Chapter 8 showed, majority mestizo society constructs a sense of indigeneity that is purified of economic and political motives, rendering unproblematic a division of labor in which indigenous subjects are granted the right to publicly display their culture and harvest cultural recognition in the municipal capital, while mestizo elites arrange a local industry around the public culturalization of indigeneity that inserts their businesses in a recognition economy. Such divisions are carved into social structures, as was discussed for the fiesta, which bases itself on the popular conception that mestizo and indigenous citizens engage in two different events, an economic mestizo fair and a cultural and religious indigenous fiesta. In this sense, indigenous subjects are recognized for 'preserving' a pious and traditional way of life that is celebrated precisely for (ostensibly) not operating according to a wider economic and political context. Indigenous agents thus face a "repressive authenticity" (Wolfe 1999:163–214) that grants them a societal role as cultural objects, thus obstructing their social participation as economic and political subjects. In the context of increasingly individualized competition, marketization, and mobility, urban middle-class mestizos celebrate indigenous citizens for preserving subsistence living and not succumbing to modernization. Thus, purified indigeneity becomes a means of salvation for urban middle-class citizens who perform a symbolic 'return' to values that are seen as standing outside of economic and political relations. In this process, indigenous groups are not just configured as vicarious participants in democratic society, but also become vicarious participants to indigenous identity construction.

Preserving traditions: indigenous dispossession in Cuetzalan

Differences and similarities can be noted in struggles over tangible resources such as land and intangible resources such as indigenous cultural heritage and identity. Although settler colonialism revolves around access to and control of land and the struggle over such tangible resources may take on an ethnic dimension when outsiders make incursions into territories occupied by other ethnic groups, the struggle over land is not necessarily deemed to pan out across ethnic divides.[1] This can be seen in the current political campaign against extractivist projects in the Sierra, which is leading to joint indigenous and mestizo cooperation to protect their common resources against external agents. The common threat posed by incoming fracking and mining companies and hydroelectric plants unifies mestizo and indigenous groups in a joint political mission.

In contrast, privatized competition over intangible indigenous cultural heritage and identity is likely to lead to dissension. Ethnicity is configured relative to other ethnicities. Therefore, ethnic identity and boundary marking are necessarily an interethnic affair (Eriksen 2002:11 ff.), and the shared cultural history between Nahuas and mestizos complicates a clear division as to whom belongs the right to claim which cultural tradition as their heritage. As in Cuetzalan's fiesta and the *huipil* ceremony, one cultural tradition laminates another, just as local history-writing is laminated with the grand nationalized Aztec narrative.

Within such shared history, symbolic mestizo appropriation of indigenous material culture is a straightforward matter that basically involves selection, acquisition, and strategic display of indigenous cultural objects. This interlacing of identities is an ongoing process that takes place on many levels in Cuetzalan. The ethnographic museum at the cultural center, which displays indigenous material culture alongside mestizo versions of history, is an emblematic example, but many hotels and restaurants also display a *cuezali* headdress and other signifiers of indigenous identity (Coronado 2000:132). Now, as part of being a Magical Village, indigenous cultural objects are increasingly being included not just as atmosphere-creating decorations in hotels and restaurants, but as the key attractions around which experience economies are created. In 2015, a private *huipil* museum opened, displaying and selling these garments. Moreover, as part of the Magical Villages Program, a *voladores* museum is planned. In such cases, indigenous cultural objects are not just adding to, but are constitutive of, tourists' experiences, thereby potentially producing extra and direct revenue as an independently consumable product. Such formats are different from, say, the *voladores* pole in the town center, which helps attract tourists but does not produce revenue of its own. The revenues of business owners are fixed to the *voladores* pole in an indirect sense, for instance through promotional work emphasizing the popular ritual or by setting up cafés and hotels that provide a good view of the *voladores* as they swing down.

While intangible skills are involved in constructing the material objects on display, mestizos acquire the material results of the intangible skills in such transactions. A labor division thus emerges in which indigenous Nahuas craft the products pro bono or at a low price, and mestizos of Cuetzalan refine and commercialize these products at a better price, precisely as it happened in the coffee industry, before the emergence of the large regional cooperative *Tosepan Titataniske* in 1977 (Bartra, Cobo, and Paz Paredes 2004:19–23). Since intangible cultural expressions involve skills acquired through embodied experience and learning, mestizos find themselves unable to exercise a similar direct control over the performance of intangible indigenous culture and identity. In the fiesta, mestizo authorities and business owners – two distinct terms for the same group of citizens – rely on embodied intangible skills such as ritual dancing and language competencies, and therefore depend on indigenous agents and auxiliary councils to provide live demonstrations of these admired skills. Within this order, indigenous communities employ their sought-for cultural competencies as a lever in a wider political negotiation with municipal authorities to acquire basic necessities such as health clinics, adequate classrooms, paved streets, or sewage disposal.

Nonetheless, as privatized competition over indigenous cultural heritage is intensified, indigenous communities are seeking ways to avoid providing or limiting this resource. As in the case of San Miguel Tzinacapan, Nahua authorities elsewhere are beginning to wonder why exactly they should actively assist the mestizo elite in Cuetzalan in their attempts to gain on tourism through indigenous performances and solidify Cuetzalan as the regional commercial and political center. This is partly why the consciousness-raising campaign surged to convince people that tourism, in its current form, is of benefit to the community, that is, the municipality as a whole, because money ostensibly trickles down from hotels and restaurants to the benefit of all. As the teacher stated, people should "accept that [Cuetzalan] is a Magical Village and accept the development that this entails." This statement virtually means to accept the social order and labor division that has persisted since the late nineteenth century when settlers took possession of central Cuetzalan and made the area 'progress.' As reflected in the production format and participation framework of the fiesta, mestizo authorities have for some decades been engaged in inserting intangible indigenous culture into a labor system that rewards business owners based in the municipal capital. Nonetheless, while direct control over land through the use of economic or political force is possible, direct control over intangible skills is less easily achieved. So far, mestizo elites have managed to acquire an indirect control by inserting indigenous performance into a wider asymmetrical political and social structure that makes a biopolitical governmentality feasible.

Yet as intangible indigenous culture is becoming an economic resource within a growing local tourism industry concentrated in Cuetzalan, indigenous communities are increasingly turning bitter at seeing the mestizo elite profiting from it. Mestizos in Cuetzalan see this reflected in a dwindling commitment to their fiesta and feel they are being 'discriminated' against by Nahua communities that cannot let 'past' injustices stay in the past. Feeling, as they do, that some Nahua communities are trying to put an end to 'their' cultural heritage by limiting their contribution to Cuetzalan's fiesta, embittered mestizo authorities will not tolerate being 'discriminated' against for long. Cultural performance is the duty of indigenous citizens and the right of mestizos, and with the multicultourism of the Magical Villages Program as principal, the first steps toward direct mestizo control over indigenous intangible skills are currently being taken.

In an interview, Enrique, a former official in the municipal government, lamented the dwindling participation of San Miguel Tzinacapan and other communities within Cuetzalan's fiesta. As he explained, the fiesta was fading away, while the fiestas in the surrounding towns continued more or less unrestrictedly. Once up to 20 or 30 dancing troupes would participate in Cuetzalan's fiesta, but in 2012 there had been only around six. Enrique stressed the problem as a political one, since dancing troupes stay away if they are not getting along with the municipal president in office. Now Enrique was seeing how Tzinacapan was becoming the town in the region with a fiesta that hosted the superior number of dancing troupes. As Enrique acknowledged, people in Tzinacapan have been organizing themselves well for decades, and the dances thrive there. Unfortunately, Enrique explained, the people of Tzinacapan are "so politicized" that they want to keep their dances to themselves:

> **Enrique (February 2013):** [People from Cuetzalan] criticize that [dancing troupes from the communities] don't come. But unfortunately, no one from Cuetzalan takes the initiative to say, "Alright, well, if the dancers from the communities *don't* come, we need to set up our own dance." Nobody does it, because they don't really feel the dance. They are embarrassed. Or, we are too embarrassed to dance like *them*. They do it out of devotion. They do it because they *feel* it, because it is their culture. Not us, and we now have a [certain] mode of thinking and we are criticizing that they no longer come and we want to put pressure on them for them to show up, but none of us dares to say, "Alright, let's arrange a dance ourselves." [. . .] The moment will come when – if people want to have dances in the fair – the municipal government will have to set up a school of traditions and through the schools create dancing troupes. [. . .] So that in the fair all the schools that received funds and were supported in terms of costumes are called upon. Well, if they no longer want to come here from the communities, at least you [visitors] and the people will see [the dances] in order to know our roots and what our culture is about. Because if not, I tell you, the day will come when the fair is going to consist of peanut stalls and clothing stalls. But dances?

It is quite the paradox that the moment in which a shift in the power balance between the mestizo elite in Cuetzalan and neighboring Nahuat San Miguel Tzinacapan may be glimpsed in the horizon is also the very moment in which the Magical Villages Program, which ostensibly works in favor of the marginalized, begins to subsidize the tourism industry in mestizo Cuetzalan and help consolidate it as the regional commercial center by consecrating it as the regional indigenous town. But that is not all. Enrique's idea that a school of tradition needs to be installed to preserve the traditional dances so they may be enjoyed in the fiesta did not come out of thin air. At the time, Cuetzalan was exactly preparing to apply for program funding, MXN

15,000,000, for a school set to teach the traditional dances in the cultural center in Cuetzalan (SECTUR 2014). Since then, a *volador* course has been offered at a preschool and primary school in Cuetzalan (Téllez 2015).

A paradoxical take on indigeneity emerges from Enrique's account. Adult mestizos in Cuetzalan are not prepared to engage in dancing activities associated with indigenous culture. Indigenous people perform the dances "out of devotion. They do it because they *feel* it, because it is their culture," although if they are too "politicized" they will stay away. Nonetheless, Enrique still maintains that the dances reflect the mestizo "roots and what our culture is about." Losing the dances within the fiesta is equal to losing Cuetzalan's traditional fiesta, which must be preserved at all costs. With the emergence of these schools of tradition, mestizo authorities initiate a process of embodying the intangible skills of the surrounding Nahua communities in coming generations of mestizos so as not to see their fiesta turning into a fair consisting purely of "peanut stalls." Cuetzalan's fiesta and the *huipil* fair are two of the intangible expressions of local heritage that justify the town's status as a Magical Village. If the fiesta and the *huipil* fair are not preserved, this would jeopardize not only Cuetzalan's participation within the Magical Villages Program, but also Cuetzalan's aspirations of becoming a World Heritage Site, since the fiesta and the *huipil* fair are also key reasons for Cuetzalan's inscription on Mexico's tentative list of UNESCO World Heritage. The Magical Villages Program is thus showing people that they are quite within their rights to preserve their fiesta by any means necessary; because Cuetzalan's fiesta has traditionally included indigenous dances, these dances are now inscribed into mestizo heritage.

Although the traditional schools are not likely to discriminate as to who can sign up, their placement in central Cuetzalan, where the necessity of setting up such schools appears to be most urgent, tells a story of its own. One biopolitical governmentality appears to be substituting another. Whereas nowadays mestizos are putting "pressure" on indigenous communities to perform their identity in the fiesta through dances and the *huipil* ceremony, Enrique is envisioning a more direct access to the sought-for resource by making mestizo children adopt, embody, feel, and perform strategic elements of Nahua culture from preschool age and onwards. Through these means, Enrique and his peers hope that, with the next generation, Cuetzalan will see the number of dancing troupes in their fiesta increase in a way not unlike what has been done in San Miguel Tzinacapan through revitalization programs.

What mestizo authorities in Cuetzalan are gradually discovering through participation in the Magical Villages Program is that indigenous communities are in fact dispensable in the framework of multicultourism, and that Cuetzalan needs no longer depend on them to provide the needed spectacle in their fiesta and other important events. Cuetzalan is therefore able to re-engage with the settler-colonial project of indigenous annihilation through subordination, and regain total control of political negotiations by dispossessing the Nahuas of their newfound identity-based resource and overtaking their spot in the national identity political arena. Worst of all, when inspected through the lens of the unitary community and without a sensibility to local politics, this mestizo strategy of dispossession appears as an altruistic and caring gesture toward the indigenous population; the indigenous population is articulated as the *principal* of what is effectively their disempowerment by mestizo elites, subsidized by the Magical Villages Program and supported by the pervasive cultural recognition that inheres in multicultourism. Moreover, as the news of these traditional schools spreads, it becomes in itself a story of cultural recognition that is set to attract urban middle-class mestizo tourists to Cuetzalan. Whether or not Nahuas outside the municipal capital will come to be engaged in the traditional schools is thus not the point. The point is that the schools facilitate strategic mestizo appropriation of Nahua culture, which in turn solidifies the asymmetrical municipal power grid inherited from a troubled interethnic history. What is therefore arguably preserved in the Magical Village Cuetzalan is a political structure introduced with the arrival of settlers in the nineteenth century and the tradition of dispossessing indigenous communities of whatever resources they may possess. Just as the settlers arrived and "fell in love with the region," their descendants have now fallen in love with indigenous heritage.

Note

1 As historian Guy Thomson notes, agrarian conflict in nineteenth-century Cuetzalan was not just configured across ethnic divides. The conflict also led to factionalism and violence among the incoming land-grabbing settlers (Thomson 1991:247–248).

References

Bartra, Armando, Rosario Cobo, and Lorena Paz Paredes. 2004. *Tosepan Titataniske: Abriendo Horizontes – 27 Años de Historia*. Cuetzalan: Sociedad Cooperativa Agropecuaria Regional Tosepan Titataniske.

Coronado, Gabriela. 2000. *Silenced Voices of Mexican Culture: Identity, Resistance and Creativity in the Interethnic Dialogue*. PhD dissertation, University of Western Sydney.

Eriksen, Thomas Hylland. 2002. *Ethnicity and Nationalism: Anthropological Perspectives*. London: Pluto Press.

Galinier, Jacques, and Antoinette Molinié. 2013. *The Neo-Indians: A Religion for the Third Millennium*. Boulder, CO: University Press of Colorado.

Rogers, Mark. 1998. "Spectacular Bodies: Folklorization and the Politics of Identity in Ecuadorian Beauty Pageants." *Journal of Latin American Anthropology* 3(2):54–85.

SECTUR. 2014. *Portafolio Cuetzalan Puebla*. Mexico City: SECTUR. Retrieved October 29, 2014. (www.sectur.gob.mx/wp-content/uploads/2015/02/CUETZALAN-DEL-PROGRESO.zip).

Téllez, Alfredo. 2015. "Tiene Cuetzalan Primera Escuela de Voladores." *Reto Diario*, September 24. Retrieved February 2, 2016. (www.retodiario.com/noticia/MUNICIPIOS/Tiene-Cuetzalan-Primera-Escuela-de-Voladores/79762.html).

Thomson, Guy P. C. 1991. "Agrarian Conflict in the Municipality of Cuetzalan (Sierra de Puebla): The Rise and Fall of 'Pala' Agustin Dieguillo, 1861–1894." *The Hispanic American Historical Review* 71(2):205–258.

Wolfe, Patrick. 1999. *Settler Colonialism and the Transformation of Anthropology: The Politics and Poetics of an Ethnographic Event*. London: Cassell.

Index

Printed and bound by CPI Group (UK) Ltd, Croydon, CR0 4YY
01/05/2025
01858430-0002